SOMEBODY HAD TO DO IT

a woman's journey in a man's world

By

Freda R. Stumpf

ISBN: 1-4140-1022-2 (e-book)
ISBN: 1-4140-1021-4 (Paperback)

This book is printed on acid free paper.

1stBooks – rev. 11/19/03

ACKNOWLEDGEMENTS

I'd like to thank my daughter, Audrey Loughridge for her help during the sixteen years it took to write this book; and especially for her instructions on writing, when she said,

"INSTEAD OF OPINIONS, GIVE FACTS, AND DON'T ACCUSE."

My thanks also to my son, Wolf Stumpf for giving me my first computer with floppy discs, and instructions, so that I could put my book on a computer; to my daughter, Marlene Hitchcock, for her support; to my grandson, Jeff Stumpf, who replaced that first computer with a newer model, and more instructions; especially when I wanted to throw the computer out the window, he said: "PATIENCE IS A VIRTUE;" to my granddaughter, Kathleen Malcolmson for continuing instructions on computer use, and urging me to get my book published.

My sincere appreciation to my friend, Teresa Hood, for a larger monitor and further computer help, and to my friends Arnold and Audrey Vollmers for a new computer printer.

I extend my thanks to my seven siblings, and the many friends and relatives who supported me and encouraged my efforts.

And finally I want to thank my good friend Susan Marshall for editing the finished work.

HOW & WHY I WROTE THIS BOOK

In the 1940's, I saw and felt discrimination. I went to my Bible and read Galatians 3, verse 28: "There is neither Jew nor Greek. There is neither slave nor free. There is neither male nor female, for you are all one in Jesus Christ."

I became a 'woman libber.' (Now they call us 'feminists.') I didn't really stop at EQUAL RIGHTS FOR WOMEN, I included EQUAL RIGHTS FOR THE POPULACE. Now that I'm older, I am working for EQUAL RIGHTS FOR THE AGED. After all, SOMEBODY HAS TO DO IT.

To recall events in the book, I used old photographs, old letters, papers in my box of memiors, talks with my family, (especially Audrey,) siblings, friends and relations, and best of all was the 'round robin' letters that my mother started in the 1950's. I had saved all my returned letters. This round robin is still making its rounds.

Many people I know, asked me to write a book. I had such a diverse childhood, (as we know it today,) I turned my book into an autobiography. I've been writing this book for at least 16 years. My son, Wolf, said that I'd never finish it, because something is always happening. But here it is.

The book moves fast. Every chapter is a story in itself, sometimes with little stories. ENJOY!

TABLE OF CONTENTS

PART III
A CAREER

PART IV
NEW LIFE

PART V
RETIREMENT

PROLOGUE

"The dishes are six inches deep in that sink, I can see them from here," said the man behind the cash register. I was in a restaurant up high in the mountains west of Denver, Colorado, and the usually immaculate kitchen was clearly visible from the dining area.

Every weekend I would travel up a canyon to this restaurant. I was trying to get over the traumatic effects of a divorce. This man was always sitting on a stool behind the cash register and a woman, whom I assumed to be his wife, was the cook and sometimes waitress. I had missed seeing her for quite some time. The waitress to whom he was directing himself was very busy and replied, "I realize it, and will get to them soon.

I then noticed a woman get up from her chair. It was the woman who used to work in the kitchen. I hadn't recognized her; it was obvious that she had been very ill, for she was white and frail. As she rose from her chair she said, "Well I guess I can do that much," then walked into the kitchen.

The man just kept sitting on his perch behind the cash register. Then the waitress came over to him and whispered, I think sir, I must tell you that she isn't ready for that, why don't you stop her?" He got off his stool and went into the kitchen. The woman came out and sat behind the cash register.

A friend came in ... "Why Mary, you are here already," said the friend. "Yes but I can't do much, my husband won't let me. Why just now he sent me out of the kitchen."

She was giving her husband credit for something he didn't deserve. I quietly finished my homemade pie, drank my coffee, paid my bill and went out.

I stood outside of the little restaurant for a long time viewing the fantastic scenery, but my thoughts were on a woman whom I had previously observed carry out a good part of the workload in the place. She made excellent meals, baked the homemade pie and still served the customers. Now she was ill and given very little consideration. I reflected back on my own life and saw myself in her role as a woman without personhood. I made the decision at that moment to write this book.

PART I

CHAPTER I

LIFE ON A TRUCK FARM

I don't know how young I was, maybe five or seven or some age between. The family was smaller then, maybe five of us girls, no boys yet, and Mom and Pop. It was a summer I will always remember because Pop bought a blue iris with a lovely scent from Buskirk's Nursery. It's odor and blossom were beautiful and delicate, and it was so special that he planted it at the head of the fishpond. I am in my eighties now, and through the years and over several thousand miles, I have carried its roots and planted them wherever I have planted my life.

It was during the time of World War I that my father built the beautiful fishpond in our side yard. It seems that he used the upper part of an old cistern that was no longer in use, and stocked it with beautiful gold fish and water lilies. About once a year we would go to the near by Ohio Canal and gather a beautiful little plant that grew on top of the water. We would transfer some of it to our pond. Gradually he and Mom landscaped around the pool with special plants that others had given them. My love for flowers was born in this beautiful spot.

I never knew when my father wasn't a truck gardener or planted things that grew. One of those things that grew was myself. And like the blue iris, I'm different.

In the summer Pop raised radishes, beets, asparagus and lots of celery. During the winter season his crops of tomatoes and cucumbers were grown in his two-acre greenhouse.

The best part of the greenhouse was the sand. Wonderful, glorious sand! We played in this sand winter and summer, between crops and where space was available. It was in these greenhouses that I started to build houses, wonderful houses out of celery boxes. My father's main crop was celery and I remember the little model T Ford truck loaded down with these boxes that were full of celery. The little truck bumped along on its solid rubber tires to the bunching shed where the celery was prepared for market. The little Model T Ford was only used for farm work, but my father also had a big truck, that had been used by the military in World War I, to haul our produce to market. As I remember, it had no doors. Everything was open to the elements except the roof. On the windshield was a wiper operated by hand and it was equipped with acetylene lamps for headlights.

Sometimes my twin Louise and I would get up at 2 o'clock in the morning. We went along with father to the Cleveland Market where he parked along the curb to sell his vegetables. As soon as it was light, Pop gave Louise and me each 10 cents for our 'work.' Then we ambled off to the near by restaurant to buy our breakfast. I felt very grown-up when I sat on the high stool. I put my little hands that were clutching a dime on the long marble counter and ordered a big luscious doughnut and a cup of coffee.

We lived in Brooklyn Heights Village on the first high ridge above the City of Cleveland, Ohio. The village was known for its greenhouses, acres

4

and acres of greenhouses! This ridge was the shore of Lake Erie zillions of years ago and the greenhouses were located on the lake bottom sand.

The roads down to these greenhouses made a perfect hill for sledding in the winter. It was a long ride to the bottom of the hill, which was usually close to the boiler shed of one of the greenhouses. In the winter a fireman was always on duty tending the coal-fed boiler. It made a good place for me to rest before pulling the sled up the quarter mile long hill. The firemen welcomed little visitors, for we broke up the lonesome monotony that came along with their work.

Uncle Charlie, a cousin of mine, but called 'uncle' out of respect for his age, played his violin while tending the boiler in his greenhouse. When I heard the violin as I entered his boiler shed, I quietly took a seat on the blanket-covered bench above the boilers. I loved to listen to him while he played. I didn't know at the time, or cared I guess, that his violin was a Stradivarius.

Father gardened on a seven-acre farm. By heavy fertilizing and constant watering, he could make a living for his family by rotating three crops on the same soil in one season. He fertilized the land with horse manure thanks to our two workhorses, Frank and George. The manure was hauled with a low-sided manure wagon with large wooden wheels drawn by the same horses.

HALLOWEEN

Father delighted in telling us about his life in the late 1880's. One Halloween his gang unloaded manure from a neighbor's wagon, took the wagon apart and reassembled it on the farmer's barn roof. Then hauled the manure up to the top of the roof and filled the wagon. In my day we knocked over outhouses and put lawn swings in trees. The lawn swings were made of wood and had two seats facing each other. The swings were enjoyed by one to four adults, but if you were a kid, maybe seven or eight of us hanging all over it.

My friends and I made a mistake one Halloween. As was the custom, we would rap on the door and receive a doughnut. This particular night we went to the town marshal's house and put his swing in the tree before we rapped on the door. Instead of a doughnut we received a deluge of water pouring on our heads from an upstairs window.

Shh quiet! I was sneaking up to the living room window where Pop was sitting in his big leather chair and listening to the Grand Ole Opry. I had made a little 'ticker,' and I was quietly fastening it to the window frame. I had put a pin through the hole of a button and attached one end of a string to the pin. At the other end of the string I had tied knots about one inch apart. I kept the string taut as I ran my finger nails along the knots. The button was hitting the window: tick, tick, tick. I knew Pop could hear the noise, but he sat in his chair as if nothing was happening. Of course he heard this before, in fact every Halloween it was my favorite trick, and I knew he would act as if nothing was happening!

The night before Halloween we celebrated 'cabbage night.' On this night we took celery scraps, cabbage leaves and whatever else we could find in the harvested fields and threw then on the neighbor's porches. The next morning Mom made us clean up our own porch, but we calculated that we threw more scraps on the other neighbor's porches than we received.

GOOD BYE HORSES

To get back to my story; a small tractor replaced the horses when I was about eleven years old. I remember when Pop drove the tractor for the first time. Very few farmers had tractors, so he proudly drove it around the back yard, then thought he would try the reverse gear. He promptly backed it into the cherry tree. The tree was my favorite climbing tree. Pop came out of the accident without any injury, but I was concerned about the tree because it had a slanted groove in its bark.

With the invention of the farm tractor, the use of horse manure was lost. The gardens were then fertilized with cooked garbage that was hauled from the 'garbage-works' down by the Ohio Canal. My father hauled it with the same World War I truck equipped with solid rubber tires. It was thoroughly cleaned after each use, because we had 'running' water.

Garbage was collected from Cleveland homes, then cooked to a fine granular substance. The cooked garbage had its rewards for in it we found sterling silver spoons. When a neighbor found a gold ring with diamonds still intact, we scanned the fertilizer extra careful. My mother had about thirty or so beautiful teaspoons and gave me two of them for my 'hope chest.'

After the tractor replaced the horses, the barn behind the house had no live-in occupants, but a few skunks underneath it. One of the occupants was an old daddy skunk who had no teeth and was too old to make a stink. My father felt sorry for him so fed him hamburg every evening. The skunk was getting too accustomed to my father and he didn't realize that anyone else in the neighborhood was as friendly as our family. One day he wandered out

7

too far from the barn in the daylight. A neighbor saw him, and went home and came back with his shotgun, and that is the end of my skunk story.

THE 4H CLUB

On the plot next to the barn was an area where the horse manure had been tossed out when the stalls were cleaned. My father knew it was too rich to raise celery, so he told me that I could raise anything I wanted on the plot. I was a member of the 4H club and always wished I had something to enter in the Cuyahoga County Fair like the other members. I spent many winter evenings with my father's seed catalogs going from one beautiful colored picture to another. I finally picked out my flowers and my father sent for thirteen seed packets. I planted my seeds in a corner of the greenhouse in early spring. My seeds sprouted just like I knew they would. Then when the danger of frost was over, I planted the little seedlings on the plot that had been used for a manure pile. Pop never had much to say, but I think he knew what would happen to my flower garden.

I carefully watered the garden and hoed out the weeds. The plants grew to enormous heights, and the blooms were large and healthy. I kept telling the County Extension Agent who came to our 4H club meetings to please come to see my garden like he visited other members, but he never came. I only supposed it was because my father was not active in the Grange. The Cuyahoga County Fair was coming soon. At a 4H meeting they handed out entry blanks for the fair exhibits. I was a small child and extremely shy, so quietly asked for thirteen entry blanks. Everyone at the meeting snickered and laughed at me, for they thought I was kidding. No one had come to see my garden, so had no idea what I was growing. I entered blooms from the thirteen varieties of flowers in my garden. I entered them, because all the blooms were much larger than the seed catalog said they should be.

When I went to the fair after the judging I was astonished! Every one of my entries had a blue ribbon on it. I received thirteen blue ribbons! This was more blue ribbons than anyone else in the club. So the club's first prize, which was a beautiful set of garden tools, was given to me. The most surprised person was the extension agent as he handed me the prize. I don't think my father was surprised, I think he expected the outcome of my efforts. The next year, the plot went into celery. But that was OK with me, for I started a rock garden next to the fishpond in our yard.

HOUSEWORK

Our house was located on Schaaf Road, which was a dirt road on a high ridge. I remember the mail delivery every day by a horse-drawn mail wagon.

In the house it was busy for on Mondays my mother washed clothes. I recall my mother's large wooden tub that was mechanized! On one side of the tub was a long wooden handle. It was the children's duty to push and pull this handle back and forth to activate the round piece of wood with three wooden pegs in it, much like an upside down milking stool. While we were doing this, Mom was boiling sheets and white linens in a big copper wash boiler. She picked up the hot linens out of the boiling water with a long wooden stick and put them in the rinse water. My, what wonderful smells came from them as they boiled away! Mom also had a modern wringer with a handle on the side to manually turn the rollers round and round to squeeze out the water as the clothes were inserted between them.

After all this work, she hauled them up a flight of stairs, opened the back door and down six or seven steps to hang them in the back yard. When dry, they were sprinkled in preparation for Tuesday, which was the day she ironed.

When I was very young, Mom used a sadiron with a removable handle. She clamped this handle to the iron as it heated on a gas burner on top of the stove. Before ironing the clothes she ran the iron over a cloth with bees wax inserted in it. Everything was ironed; 'Sunday' clothes, work clothes, play clothes, sheets, underwear, handkerchiefs and even socks. No wonder she finally hired a housekeeper.

Wednesday was the day for odd jobs like cleaning the cupboards from top to bottom, including washing all the dishes in the cabinet. Our house was spotless!

MY TWIN AND I GET INTO TROUBLE

Thursday was the day for shopping in the department stores. On rare occasions we drove to downtown Cleveland to shop at the Fries and Scheule Dry Goods Store, or the May Company because they gave double green stamps on Thursday.

It was on such a day as this when my twin sister and I got into trouble. The big open touring car was parked in the driveway which, was on a steep hill. As was the custom in those days, the car had been washed inside and out for the downtown trip. The pressure in the tires was checked, the radiator was filled with water and the gasoline tank was filled from the hand-pump, which was located alongside the garage. (A gasoline truck came now and then to fill our underground gasoline tank.) Everything was in order just waiting for my mother and older sisters to appear.

Louise and I were sitting in the front seat of the car, patiently waiting. We were five year-old twins dressed up in our Sunday clothes for this exciting trip, but waiting can be a worrisome thing. We decided that we would do the driving that day.

Louise — "I will do the driving because I am bigger than you. I can reach the steering wheel better than you, see?" Well of course she could for she was 2" taller than I.

Freda — "So if you do the driving, what do I do?"

We looked at the thing sticking out of the floorboards with a handle on it. That was the handle that the driver pushed on before the car started to go. My job was to squeeze the handle.

The car was parked on a steep hill, and it was the emergency brake we were referring to. When I squeezed and pushed the handle I released the brakes. We forgot one thing, and that was how to stop the car. Even if Louise was bigger than I was she couldn't reach the brake pedal on the floor. But who cared? Wasn't it our plan to drive to Cleveland?

Down the hill we went; ... backwards ... beautiful ... we were on our way downtown! But the lean-to shed next to the barn got in the way. It was totaled and the big touring car stopped right in the middle of the mess. If it wasn't for that shed we could have gone far; down a hill, through the asparagus patch, smash through the glass in the greenhouses, travel through the bunching shed, then across the celery field and down another steep hill towards the Cuyahoga River and into the Ohio Canal. (If indeed we could have gone that far.) But it would have been a great short cut to Cleveland for it bordered the canal and river.

CHRISTMAS 1917

I was five years old, World War One had taken its toll, money was scarce, the winter was especially cold and the snow was very deep. Mom managed to feed her brood out of the well-stocked storage cellar with home-canned food and very little meat. No money could be spared for Christmas (if indeed there was any.) Our next door neighbor came to the back door with a Christmas tree. He said he cut it from his woods. The next summer we scanned his woods to find the stump of the tree, of course we couldn't find it.

THE BIRDS AND THE BEES

The spring of 1918 finally began to show its colors when I found a dead bird. As usual I showed my precious find to the neighbor kids. "Let's have a funeral for the bird," said Cupie the next door kid. "I'll lead the procession because I thought of it."

"Where will we go with the procession?" quipped another kid.

"Why not through the greenhouses?" said another.

So we gathered all the kids in the neighborhood, for the dead bird's funeral. It was my bird, but the other kids were bigger than I, so I was last in line.

In our greenhouse my father kept a beehive. The bees pollinated the blossoms of the cucumbers growing there. My twin sister was ahead of me in the line. The procession went through Foote's apple orchard, through the opened doors of the greenhouse and past the beehive. Everything went fine until Louise passed the beehive. Like kids do, she gave the hive a whack with the stick she was carrying, and the bees came out as I passed by. They attacked me instead of her and put me in such a state of shock I couldn't scream, but Louise did and was hysterical. The hired man came to the rescue, scooped up Louise in his arms and ran up to the house with her ... and me, I followed on foot. When I arrived at the house, Mom put me in a bathtub she had filled with cold water and rubbed my stings with brown soap. I sure was in misery for a few days. I don't remember who buried the dead bird.

THREE BIRTHDAYS ON APRIL 2, 1918

On April 2, our sixth birthday, Louise and I received a three-wheel cycle. It came equipped with a buggy seat and a long rod to steer it. It was unlike any bike in today's world. But besides the interesting bike, we had another surprise when we got home. A new baby brother was born at home while we were gone. Now we have three birthdays on one day. My three sisters are older than we are, and he is the first boy in the family. He was named Arden, but we soon nicknamed him 'Skinny.' The dear lady who lived down the street came on that day, and gave Louise and I each a flat box with a handkerchief in it. This was nice for we each had our very own birthday present, in our very own box. It overwhelmed me to have a new brother, a new cycle and a new handkerchief all on one day!

Everyone who knew her, loved the dear lady who lived down the street. She was genetically deformed with a large face, hands and feet, which gave her an elephantine appearance, but I do not recall any child in our neighborhood that was conscious of her enormous features. She was so kind that she was liked by all who knew her.

Louise and I entered the first grade in September 1918 and it was late that year when the flu bug hit us, the whole family came down with it except my father and the baby. Pop went to the city to get my Aunt Tillie, Mom's sister, to help him care for us, but then she caught the flu. We had good care for we experienced none of the disastrous effects of the disease that was so prevalent throughout the whole country. Old Doc Webster came to call on the family and gave Louise and I cough syrup. One was red, the other green. It was probably the same stuff, but he was playing it smart by making individuals out of us. Bless him, I was now my own person.

CHILDHOOD ENTERTAINMENT

One of the joys of childhood in my time was that you created your own entertainment. It was in Cupie's apple orchard that we dug World War One trenches. This was wonderful lake bottom sand, and just right for digging. We made secret rooms by covering the trenches with celery boards. Celery boards were used in those days to bleach celery a solid white.

Some gardeners in the area grew acres and acres of asparagus and after the crops were harvested, the field was allowed to go to seed. The result was a field of plants with high foliage much like a very dense forest. It was higher that the tops of our heads. This was the age of cowboy and Indian silent movies and this field was perfect for Indian Wars with shrill whoops coming from the children.

WE WORK ON THE FARM

My sisters Gertrude, Elenora and Marceda had their turns with helping on the farm and now it was the time for Louise and me to do our part. We thinned beets, planted celery and weeded rows and rows of radishes. I thought these 100 foot rows were at least a mile long. It seemed like an endless job. In the winter our job was to pick hothouse tomatoes in the greenhouse. No one in our neighborhood grew tomatoes outside; I never knew anything but a hothouse tomato. After picking them we sorted them to size and wrapped the best ones in green tissue paper and packed them in a basket just so.

Father bought a new fandangle-bunching machine to bunch celery hearts. Celery hearts were celery that didn't make it to full growth. We bunched them three to a bunch while my father manually tied 12 large statlks into a square bundle. The machine that bunched the hearts had an arm with a string looped through it and when you pressed the pedal with your foot, this arm would come out in a flash towards your face, go back, and wrap the string around the celery and tie a knot. It was Louise' job to run the machine and my job to hand her the celery in groups of three. Father would not let me run the machine and never told me, why. One day after much pleading, I took my place behind the machine. I soon found out that father knows best, for my arms were much shorter than my twin sister's and I tried again and again only to be smacked in the forehead with the arm that had the string running through it. That was the first and last time I ran that machine!

The back part of the farm was a dense woods that sloped down to the Cuyahoga River. Near the top of the hill was a spring that was used by the Indians many years ago, and Pop found many arrowheads and other artifacts near-by. The spring fed a pond where a gasoline pump was located to pump water to irrigate the fields. One could hear that pump for a quarter mile, bahROOOOOOOM-pah-pah, bahROOOOOOM-pah- pah. Someone had disposed of an old touring car near this pump and it was a favorite place to play. The car had leather button upholstery. I wonder if it is still there.

AND NOW WE ARE EIGHT

In April 1920 another baby boy was born into the family. Donald was the first to be born in a hospital. He was born in Fairview Park Hospital, which was founded by my grandfather. I don't remember how he got his nickname 'Diddle' but it stuck with him until he served in the Navy in World War Two. He asked that we address our letters to 'Don' because too many guys looked over his shoulder as he was reading our letters, and he got a lot of kidding. So from then on he was 'Don.'

In February 1922 another baby came along and completed the family of eight children. He was named after my father, 'Frederick,' so he was called 'Junior.' He outgrew this nickname, and then we called him 'Juny', now we call him 'Fred.' He developed Perthes Disease in his hip and always walked with a limp. As I was washing dishes one evening little Junior came in the kitchen and was looking out the window at the full moon. He turned to me and said, "Look Freda, Jesus has his flashlight out."

CHAPTER 2
SCHOOL DAYS

Uncle Gustave was always a welcome visitor. I was about 6 years old when he brought Louise and me a large art set on one of his visits. This was surprising for as I remember him, he didn't usually bring presents. In it was everything an artist needed: art pencils with square leads, stencils, watercolor paints and an art gum eraser. I had never owned an art gum eraser, so this was a wonderful present! At first the pretty stencils were my big interest, but then I was soon creating my own pictures without them, using the pencils and watercolor paints.

Uncle Gustave was father's brother, and taught history in the Cleveland Public Schools. I remember he visited when my parents were canning corn in our enormous pressure cooker. He put on an apron, cut corn from the cob, and helped with the whole process. My father would bring home burlap bags full of cabbage, and Uncle Gustave helped make sauerkraut and pack it in large crocks. It was during World War I when I remember Uncle Gus and Pop talking in our old attic while hiding heirlooms or anything that showed our German ancestry. They talked about German marks and their value, but I didn't know what they were. Then the conversation changed to

17

concern about our hired man. He was from Germany, but would be drafted into the United States Army, and would have to kill his own brother. I was sitting on the attic steps watching and listening. I remember how horrified I was to think our hired man would have to kill his own brother!

Uncle Gus and Pop were afraid, because houses were being searched by the government for any German connections. This was during World War I and I wonder if some of the things I have were some of those items. I have Grandpa's scrap book, a book on the German language that he authored, and a few other things from grandpa, who was Herman Julius Ruetenik. He was a German preacher and founded twelve Reformed Churches, mostly in the Cleveland area. He taught the German language at Heidelberg College in Tiffin, Ohio, and founded German Hospital, which is now known as Fairview Park Hospital in Cleveland, Ohio.

About 150 years ago Grandpa's first ministry was in Perrysburg, Ohio. The most prominent man in the church was the rich saloonkeeper. Grandpa needed living quarters, so the saloonkeeper gave him the rooms over the saloon. It wasn't too long before Grandpa was down in the saloon converting the drunks. It made him unpopular because the congregation needed the monetary donations of the saloonkeeper.

His life in Perrysburg is a little hazy to me, for I was only two years old when he died in 1914. As was the custom in those days, women were not important enough to be recorded as significant human beings, so I know little about his wife, my grandmother Emilie Martin. She was the daughter of Christian Martin, the founder of the Martin Guitar Company. I know very little about their marriage, but I do know that they lived in Perrysburg when their first child was born.

SCHOOL DAYS

The school I attended had approximately 300 students enrolled in 12 grades. I had been in school only a few months when the Armistice ending World War I was signed on November 11, 1918. I was among the 300 students who gathered around the American Flag on the front lawn of the school at 11 o'clock in the morning on that day.

The pupils observed the signing of the Armistice by two minutes of silence as we saluted the flag with our right hand above the right eye. (This is the way the flag was saluted at that time). No one needed to tell us when the two minutes were up, for the bells and horns in the city made a deafening noise, and the train passing through on the Beltline Railroad was blasting its horn as loud and long as it could blast! The noise was something I will never forget. It instilled a lasting love and respect for my country, the United States of America!

When I started first grade, the school principal was in France serving in the United States Army. He returned after the signing of the Armistice. The students of all grades were in the assembly room to greet him on his return. I sat in the front row because I was a first grader. I was young and impressionable and it was a very emotional homecoming. His wife was hanging onto him and crying. He finally broke away from her so he could make a speech about his experiences in the war.

Maybe it was the principal's service in the Army that prompted the marching we did in my early years in school. As the closing bell rang we lined up at the door, then in orderly fashion we marched out of the room to the stirring tune of Sousa's "Stars and Stripes Forever." The privileged senior class in the high school section of the school operated the wind-up phonograph, which was set up in the center of the main hall. The phonograph was equipped with a very large horn with scallops on the edge and painted on the inside of each scallop was a beautiful red rose. Starting with the first grade the students walked by this music-making machine down the front steps and out the front door. The high school students were making fun of the music machine, so the marching stopped. I felt sorry about that because as a first grader it made me feel important to have the privilege of doing that marching.

As I grew older my art ability began to show. When I was in the fourth grade I drew the cover for the school paper, The Brooklyn Heights X-ray. This was quite an honor for a fourth grader to draw the cover. It was also in the fourth grade that I decided I'd be a hat designer. I found an old straw hat, and made what I thought was the most beautiful hat in the world. I put lots of ribbons and flowers on it that only a fourth grader could fashion. I put it on and stood in front of the mirror so long that I was late for school. Maybe I was late on purpose so I would be noticed with my beautiful hat. I proudly walked in the room expecting a lot of oohs and aahs, but all I got was laughs. I was very upset, because no one in the room knew what beauty really was, or so I thought. Nevertheless I put it in the cloakroom, and wore it home just as proudly as I did when I came into the room late.

me with beautiful hat on, 4th grade

I'm up in the seventh grade now, and very proud to be sitting in the Junior High room. This was the first year that we traveled to different rooms for different subjects. We still lined up at the door when the closing bell rang, but without the marching. I was the first kid out the door because we were lined up according to height. The drawback to that was I had to duck quickly or be run over by the mob. It should have been the other way around don't you think? Or maybe the marching should have continued.

The school district required all students to be tested for their athletic ability. A big circle was drawn on the far wall in the gymnasium. We were to stand back of the line that was drawn on the floor and throw a baseball at the circle and try to hit the center. The school principal was standing on the sidelines with another man who was taking notes. I suppose he was looking for future athletes to compete in the athletic programs. When I came into the gymnasium I was relieved to see that the circle was so big! This was going to be a piece of cake! It was my turn. Someone handed me the baseball. I grabbed it, and with determination I aimed for the center of the circle and threw it. The ball not only missed the circle it hit the principal! He looked at me in awe as if to say, "No one could be that bad, could they?"

My friend Helene lived two miles from school and because the district had no school buses, she had to walk it. She met me at our house and we would walk the last half-mile together. Helene's legs were so well formed by all this walking, that she easily won all the race competitions, high jump, broad jump etc., but me ... I was always the last one chosen for a baseball team. I wasn't so hot in athletics, but I felt inferior and insignificant to always be chosen last. I was a shy and withdrawn child and this rejection caused me to go into my own little corner. However Helene who was quite the athlete, accepted me for what I was. I don't ever recall that she bragged about her athletic ability to me. We were good friends.

Can you imagine this? Our playground behind the school was smack in between Cook's greenhouse on one side and Keyes' greenhouse on the other. There were zillions of greenhouses in Brooklyn Heights and zillions of fertile gardens. We were lucky to have a playground, but a playground surrounded by glass? The wire fences were high, but not high enough for sometimes a ball went astray. The kid, who was responsible, paid for the glass. Because I was a bad ball player, I never hit the ball high enough to pay for the glass, if indeed I could have hit the ball in the first place.

The school was located in a rich tax district because of numerous greenhouses and possibly a steel mill. The school board put the money to good use for they hired many special teachers, including music and art. Only four students enrolled in many of the high school classes. We almost had a one-on-one education. An excellent library was located in the school, and it was common to see the local residents of the village in the library during school hours for it was the only library in the village. The upper grades were offered excellent courses in science, industrial arts and cooking in well-equipped rooms, even though the high school enrollment was only 45 students. The only requirement for graduation available to us was for college entry. Of the fourteen students in my graduating class, at least ten of them went on to higher learning.

Mr. Sharp was the music teacher for all grades one through twelve. He played the violin and if you sang a wrong note or misbehaved, you received a sharp tap on your head with his violin bow. He taught us to read music in the first grade, but I often wondered how many violin bows he ruined. He always seemed to have a few extras in his case.

Once a year a Music Memory contest was held. If I remember right it consisted of all high schools in Cuyahoga County. Cleveland is located in this county, and our little school always came out pretty close to the top. We had classical music playing during lunch hour in the cafeteria, in the typing room and other places with the students loving it, and yelling out the title and the composer. The contest was held in Severance Hall with the Cleveland Orchestra performing. Why don't they still do a contest like that? Not every locality could have such a famous orchestra play for them, but there are some local orchestras that are not too shabby.

I am now in high school. It was in high school that I acquired the nickname "Fritz." It happened when three girls in the same classroom were named Freda. It was too much for my friend, Gladys, so she gave me my nickname and called me Fritz.

When I was a Freshman I was given the title of "school artist" and designed and drew the covers for the school paper. The Brooklyn Heights X-ray not only published school news, but news of the people who lived in the village. I was in high school when my married sister was sick in bed. No one told me what she had, I only knew she was very sick. When my family read it, they pounced all over me for putting it in the paper. What my sister had was a miscarriage, things no one talked about!

I flunked ancient history in high school. My mother called the school to talk with the teacher, who told her that I was always drawing pictures in my history book instead of listening to him. He was partially right I was drawing pictures in my history book. It was full of pictures that included some excellent portraits of the teacher. After all, he was a good subject for he lectured in one spot so long that he made a good model, but best of all, he had the baldest head I had ever seen! It was so bald that someone gave him a comb with missing teeth for Christmas. AND IT WASN'T ME! I don't recall that my parents reprimanded me for my artwork because I was always drawing pictures of my father. He was a good subject too, for he had a lot of personality in his face. One evening I did what I thought was a good drawing of him. The next morning I wanted to show it to my Mom and it was gone. Pop had seen it when he got up and put it in his pocket and took it with him to the Cleveland Market to show it off. But evidently my history teacher didn't take to drawings like Pop, for I flunked his ancient history class.

I was sent to summer school in the Cleveland school system to make up the history credit. My twin sister flunked French that year, so we went together to West High School. She ended up speaking French fluently, and I ended up taking an American History class. This was the best thing that could have happened to me for I made lemonade out of a lemon. I went into the ancient history class, and the first thing the teacher gave us was a test in Ancient History. OH, NO, not another ancient history test! I dreaded it, but then we were told if we passed the test we could skip it and go on to another history class. The teacher came up to me and asked me if I was sure I flunked Ancient History and said it would be a waste of time for me to repeat the course so she sent me to an American History class. I reflected back on the drawings I did in my history book. I really was listening, wasn't I? Many people doodle while they listen, don't they? Look at the phone books.

I went across the hall and entered the American History class that was taught by Lois Beman. She was calling the roll, and stopped dead when she came to my name. A startled look came over her face. "Freda Ruetenik, are you any relation to Gustave Ruetenik?" Of course I was, so I answered "He is my uncle." "Mr. Ruetenik was my history teacher in high school, he was my favorite teacher. She taught me the same history that Uncle Gus taught her. This started a friendship that lasted for many years. She traveled extensively, and sent me a present from wherever her travels took her. One of the presents was rose-shaped beads scented with rose perfume. I will never forget them

The Brooklyn Heights School Board gave the students an opportunity of attending summer school in Cleveland by paying our tuition, whether we needed to make up a credit or not. The next summer I attended West Technical High School. It was difficult to get to the summer classes in Cleveland for I lived two miles from the streetcar line. This was called the 'Dinky Line.' It's run was only five miles long and the oldest streetcars in the transit system serviced it. After the long walk to the line, it was a comfort to sit on the straw-covered seats that lined each side of the streetcar.

I transferred to the West 25th Street line and again transferred to the Loraine Avenue line. When I alit, I still had two blocks to go to the high school. It took over an hour to get to school. I used a school pass to travel by streetcar. My mother gave me 25 cents each day to buy a ham sandwich and a glass of milk in a small restaurant on the corner of West 25th Street and Loraine Avenue. I liked the sandwich because a long sliver of a delicious pickle came with it.

Summer classes in the Cleveland School system were held in a different school each year. When I went to West Technical High School I had no credits to make up, but I took advantage of the free tuition to attend an art class under Paul Ulan who was well known for his paintings hanging in the Cleveland Art Museum. Mr. Ulan asked me why I chose commercial art instead of fine art. I answered: "I want to make money from my art while I'm living. Fine artists don't make money on their art until they're dead." This satisfied him.

Mr. Ulan was an excellent teacher, and liked one of my paintings so much he had it hanging on the wall behind his desk for two years. I would visit him now and then, and he would say, "Ah, my little Bohemian!"

It was Paul Ulan who recommended me into John Huntington Polytechnic Institute. This was an endowed school, and the tuition was $15, which was returned to you if you attended 85% of the classes. I would have made the effort to attend this night school even though I must walk two miles to the Dinky Line, transfer to the West 25th Street line to the Public Square and transfer to the Euclid Avenue line. I had no support from my family or my boy friend, who was very much against it, because he said that he was afraid that I might meet someone else I would like better than him.

I graduated from Brooklyn Heights High school in 1930. The principal would not recognize the art credits I received from West Technical High

School towards graduation. This was the first time I showed my spunk! He thought art was a subject not worthy of credits, and surely my ancient history teacher carried the same thoughts. My feelings in the matter was that if the Cleveland Public Schools thought the courses worthy of the credits they gave me, Brooklyn Heights High school should also honor them. Then to top it all off I asked for art credits from both schools. The principal said my request was ridiculous for I didn't need all those credits to graduate. But it was extremely important to me to use those credits for graduation, for didn't I take an art course under a famous artist, Mr. Paul Ulan?

My case was approved by the school board. I must have presented it in good form, for I graduated from Brooklyn Heights High school with art credits from both schools.

CHAPTER 3

HOME LIFE IN THE 1920s

It is now 1919. My father bought a new appliance for my mother, the very latest model washing machine, and gone was pulling the handle back and forth on the washing machine, and gone was the handle to turn the wringer rollers. The tub on the washing machine was wooden, but an electric motor with many pulleys rotated the activator in the washer and also turned the rollers in the wringer. No mechanism was enclosed and we were told not to go near the pulleys, especially the wringer! DO NOT TOUCH IT! But early on I was inquisitive about machinery, so alone in the basement I thought I would try the wringer, and promptly ran my arm through it along with some clothes. I screamed to the top of my lungs, and the family came on the run to rescue me. Someone released the wringer, then I looked at my arm, it didn't hurt, but it was so flat that I wondered if I would always live with a flat arm, forever and forever! But that didn't happen.

Mother also had a new American Beauty electric iron. It was not automatic like the irons of today, for she pulled the electric plug out of the socket when the iron heated up too much. Mom still used the cloth with the beeswax between the folds to smooth the bottom of the iron before she ran it over the clothes.

While Mom worked she often sang a little song that she remembered from her childhood back in the 1880's. I found this song in my mother's scrapbook after she died. It is the song she sang.

I DON'T WANT TO PLAY IN YOUR YARD

Once there lived side by side, two little maids,
Used to dress just alike, hair down in braids,
Blue gingham pinafore, stockings of red.
Little Sunbonnets tied on each pretty head,
When school was over, secrets they'd tell,
Whispering, arm in arm down by the well,
One day a quarrel came; hot tears were shed,
"You can't play in our yard!" but the other said:

CHORUS
I don't want to play in your yard.
I don't like you any more:
You'll be sorry when you see me
Sliding down our cellar door.
You can't holler down our rain barrel,
You can't climb our apple tree,
I don't want to play in your yard.
If you can't be good to me.

Next day the two little maids each other did miss.

Quarrels are soon made up, sealed with a kiss,

Then hand in hand again, happy as they go,

Friends all through life be, they love each other so.

Soon school days pass away, sorrows and bliss,

But love remembers yet, quarrel and kiss,

In sweet childhood dreams we hear the cry:

"You can't play in our yard." And the old reply

Mom had a housekeeper, Emma. About the only thing I remember about Emma is the swat on my bucket when I was in her way. It didn't hurt anything but my feelings, but it did keep me away from her when she had a broom in her hand. Emma was born in Tennessee and was the sister of our hired man, Jake, who by this time had returned to his home in the Tennessee Mountains.

MUSIC, MUSIC, MUSIC

One day Pop brought home a wonderful invention, a crystal radio set! It was put in the middle of the dining room table, and we all took our turn listening to it by passing the earphones around the table. I was impatiently waiting for my turn when I had a bright idea. I was remembering the popular megaphones that entertainers and band leaders were using on stage, so I fashioned my own megaphones out of paper and we put one in each ear piece. It worked out just fine, so now we heard the popular song, "Yes, We Have No Bananas" as it came over the airwaves from the KDKA radio station in Pittsburgh, Pennsylvania.

The radio added to the music we played on the Edison phonograph, which was wound manually for each thick record. Father bought many classical records for our Edison record player, the popular marching songs played by Philip Sousa's Band, Hawaiian songs, some cute songs like "Little Cupids in the Briny" and many German recordings.

To add to our musical background was a player piano. This instrument had bellows that were pumped with our feet. So we had our exercise while we played our music; for with our arms we wound the Edison, with our feet we pumped the piano and some kid was always doing a dance or special pantomime along with the music, and sang little ditties:

Oh, Mr. Johnny Furbeck
How could you be so mean?
I told you you'd be sorry for
Inventing that machine.
Now all the neighbor's cats and dogs
Will never more be seen.
They'll all be ground to sausages
In Johnny Furbeck's machine.

The house we lived in had a very large basement with a furnace equipped with a large boiler on the top to heat the water for the radiators. The radiator I liked was the one in the bathroom. I would put my towel on it, for it was too hot to sit on with a bare bottom. Here I sat while putting on my clothes. It was too cold in my bedroom to put on my clothes, because I slept in the attic. First I put on the long-legged underwear, which was just fine when it was new, but lost its elasticity, then it was folded neatly in the back of the legs, or else it looked like we had deformed legs under the long black stockings. Garters attached to a pantywaist secured the stockings. Next came the bloomers, which covered the ugly long-legged underwear so it wouldn't show when I did cartwheels. When I was a little older, my mother made bloomers to match the dresses she made for us. Mother always dressed Louise and me alike, but we were fraternal twins and had no resemblance to each other.

The gas hot plate in the basement had another use besides heating water for boiling clothes, for this is where the large pressure cooker was placed to process canned food. Mother's well-stocked fruit cellar showed her canning efforts. Beside the many shelves of canned food, a crock of sauerkraut and another of dill pickles graced the floor. My father made a special treat for us; homemade root beer, which cured for three very long weeks before we were allowed to drink it. By the stairs, was a keg of vinegar, and 100-pound bags of potatoes and onions. But in the corner was a special bag. It contained 100 pounds of black walnuts. I spent many hours in this corner cracking the hard shells with a hammer, and picking the tasty nuts out of them. On special occasions, father brought home a stem of bananas and now and then a very large bag of freshly roasted peanuts from the peanut roasting plant in Cleveland.

The large extension table in the kitchen was folded every evening after the dishes were done, and then the younger children were put to bed. In the evening Mom played a card game called Flinch with the older kids. It was a long time before Mom accepted playing cards. "They are for gambling," Mom would say, "they are devil cards."

Another large extension table was in the dining room. It was a nice Queen Anne piece of furniture and was extended only for Thanksgiving, Christmas, special company and weddings. I was sitting at this table one evening sewing a hem in a dress I wanted to wear to church the next day. It was storming outside and the electric lights went out, so I lit a candle to finish the hem. I dropped my needle and used the candle to find it and promptly set the curtains on fire. Mom quickly extinguished the flames with kettles of water, but the room was a mess! Mom was the heroine of the event, but I never did *that* again.

· At the back of the house was a long closed-in porch. Facing the back door was a long vacant wall with zillions of coat hooks. No kid ever had an excuse to throw a coat on a chair, and no one ever did.

Three bedrooms were upstairs and one bathroom was at the head of the stairs. It was not unusual to see three or four kids lined up on the stairs waiting their turn in the bathroom. It never occurred to us that we needed another bathroom for it was rare in those days that we even had a bathroom. As the family grew, three bedrooms were not enough, and then the front part of the attic was enclosed with 'beaver board.' As the family grew again the back attic was used, but this room had bare walls with the roof rafters showing. The only way to get to these rooms was through the bathroom. The bathroom was busier than just for bathroom purposes.

Louise and I slept in the back attic, even though it was unfinished with wooden rafters, but the window in this room was the best window in the whole house. I could see the City of Cleveland from the West Side to the East Side, pick out the Terminal Tower, City Hospital, and the new telephone building, and beyond all these buildings, Lake Erie. In the lake we could see Cleveland's Five-Mile Water Intake Crib and the cargo ships. In the foreground of this beautiful picture were the large fields of vegetables and the greenhouses.

greenhouse with Lake Erie beyond City of Cleveland

Brooklyn Heights was a good community. Everyone knew each other, and they were all in the same occupation, truck gardening. Each gardener specialized in a different fruit and vegetable. It was not unusual to find a basket of fruit or vegetables on your back steps. The donor never knocked, you just found them, and from the nature of the produce, you knew from whence it came.

My Uncle Martin, father's brother, lived about a half-mile down the road. In summer I liked to go to his greenhouse and watch the large

34

goldfish in his big pond near-by. In the winter, the pond was frozen over and the teenagers could skate on it. I was about ten years old when I broke through the ice and was pulled out of the water and told to go home. The temperature was below freezing. The teenagers did not like us young kids on the pond, and even though many of them had cars parked by the pond, no one offered to take me home. I walked and cried all he way home in my wet clothes which were frozen stiff by the time I arrived. I am surprised that I didn't catch pneumonia.

TRIPS, TRIPS, TRIPS

Father took us on many trips. One of them was to Tennessee to visit Jake who was the hired man when I was a child. We used the "Blue Book" for directions, but after we left the main roads, the Blue Book could not be used. We traveled the local roads to reach Gruetli where he lived. The local road followed the center of a dry creek bed (a most unlikely place for a road) then it veered sharply off to the right, and up a stone ridge of a mountain. I had bad visions of staying in this spot forever, but Pop kept right on going up. It did not look like a road, and we thought Pop had lost his way. We were suddenly surprised to find a grocery store up high on this ridge. We must be on a road! We came to a dirt road that was nothing but two ruts. It wound through thick woods, and eventually we found the house we were looking for in a big clearing. In fact it was a group of homes, which housed members of the same clan or family.

These people had as many kids as we brought along, so it did not take my brothers long to find another bunch of boys to play with them. One of the boys had two thumbs on one hand, and another accidentally chopped off

35

one of his thumbs with an ax. My brothers did not understand why they couldn't take the extra thumb off the one boy's hand and sew it on the other kid's hand. They were probably glad to get rid of us, for my brothers were always hanging on some calf's tail and having a merry time of it. Marceda, Gertrude and Elenora spent their time with a cousin who had a new baby, but I scarcely left the house where I slept, for the mother was always baking biscuits in a big cast iron stove that was heated by putting wood in a side compartment. Lovely big fluffy biscuits, biscuits for every meal. Breakfast included sauerkraut, pancakes, sausage and sorghum molasses among other good things.

A few years later the young mother with the new baby came down with appendicitis. She needed an operation. She had never been in an automobile and was not about to ride in one, so was driven to the train station by horse and buggy, and then waited for the train to take her to the nearest hospital in Sewanee. Her appendix broke and she passed away. Our family was very saddened by this news.

On the next trip, we went to Kentucky. Again we used the Blue Book which told us where to find what road by which store and to turn at what farm and to ask for further directions at what gas station. Our destination, Mammoth Cave was finally reached. I was very impressed with the grandeur of the cave, the underground rivers and the fish without eyes. Then we went to Horse Cave, and then on to the cave where spelunker Floyd Collins lost his life when a boulder came loose and pinned his leg while he was exploring a new section. We saw the hole that was dug from the surface to rescue him, but it was in vain.

On our way back we stopped to see Abraham Lincoln's birthplace and the Lincoln Memorial that enclosed the cabin where he was born. Then on to home, where we lost our way around Columbus, Ohio. It was late in the day and was too dark to find the right road. The Blue Book was of no use for stores that gave us information were closed, and it was too dark to find our landmarks, and too dark to read the Blue Book.

Pop stopped the car on a narrow dirt road and said it was useless to find our way in the dark, we would sleep in our car for the night, but Pop left the car and slept under a tree. It was a dark night to be sure for he didn't realize that he was sleeping on a bed of poison ivy. In the morning his face was already starting to swell, and he was the only one who knew how to drive the car. He begged my mother to drive, he would show her what to do, but she refused to have any part in it. Pop drove home in misery with his face dripping and his eyes were almost swollen shut, but we did make it home that day.

ONE SIBLING LEAVES THE NEST

I was about thirteen years old when my sister Elenora married her neighborhood sweetheart, Les Thompson. We thought Les was a neat guy for he had a superheterodyne radio in his mother's pantry, and a Ford Model T coupe. Elenora and Les were married in the living room. The dining room table was opened out for the wedding and the linen tablecloth from Germany was used for the reception. It was a fine affair and Mom served chicken-ala-king in store-bought pastry shells. To me, this dish was far more important than the wedding cake.

ANOTHER TRIED TO FLEE THE NEST

Mom was a homebody who firmly believed that a woman's place was in the home. The only places she went, other than shopping was to church and the Ladies Aid Society.

One day Pop came home with two tickets for a clambake. He and Mom had never had a night out together as long as I could remember. The only member of the family who was not delighted with the tickets was Mom. She would be with people she knew but she worried about leaving the kids home alone. My twin and I were fifteen, Marceda and Gertrude were older than that, but she worried. We tried to tell her that we could do the job, but the last thing Mom said before she left the house was," I'll never forgive myself if something happens while I'm gone."

Of course this was the day that my brother Skinny ran away from home. He was nine years old, and at eight o'clock that evening he still was not home for supper. My sisters called friends. One of the boys told us that he had a girl friend. "Maybe he confided in her," said one of my sisters, so she phoned her. The girl friend said that Skinny and his gang decided to run away and live in the shack behind the railroad tracks. She did not know where the shack was located. We knew of this shack, and the boys were there often, but no one knew where it was. I told my sisters that I heard there were railroad detectives who walked the tracks. Maybe they would know, so I called the Beltline Railroad Company. Yes, they had a detective, and they would send him out to find the boys. The detective found the boys in the shack and sent them home.

Skinny arrived home just before Mom and Pop came in from the clambake. Mom was all excited when we told her what happened, "I knew I shouldn't have gone to the clambake and leave you kids home alone," she

38

said, "I knew it, I knew it, I knew it." We thought we handled the situation very well, (probably better than Mom for she was prone to get too excited in a crisis) and I know Pop thought we did the right thing, but Mom ... she never went out again.

I LEARN TO DRIVE THE CAR

I was about seventeen years old when my father phoned from the garage where he had taken his big World War I truck for repairs. He wanted me to come and pick him up. I had been learning to drive the car, but had not driven alone. I told him I would call somebody else to drive over to the garage. "No, YOU come and get me," he said. I did. I drove the eight miles to the garage that led down a steep hill to the Cuyahoga River, then up another steep hill to the garage. At this time in my life I thought this was quite an accomplishment. I was glad to arrive without incident, for I expected Pop to drive home. WRONG, he made me do the driving. I made a wrong left hand turn at the bottom of the steep hill, and a policeman stopped me.

While he was writing up the ticket, I was sobbing as if my heart would break. I guess I broke the policeman's heart too, for he asked Pop if he knew Charlie Howe, the Brooklyn Heights Marshall. Pop told him we were close friends, so the policeman tore up the ticket. I begged Pop to drive the rest of the way, but he just sat in his seat and said, "No, you drive!" I did.

. After that incident I did a lot of driving. One day I had reason to drive in the city. Now this was the days of electric streetcars, and they went down the middle of a brick street. The street was barely wide enough for a car to pass between the moving streetcar and the parked cars. It was a well known

39

fact among the teenagers that to be a good driver, you must be able to pass a moving streetcar when cars were parked at the curb. So what the heck, I was alone in the car and thought I would try it. I was traveling down West 25th Street in Cleveland; I caught up with a moving streetcar. Cars were parked at the curb. I made a run for it … this is great! I passed one parked car and then another and another, but if it hadn't been for the car with lots of stuff that was tied to the running board, I would have had a perfect record. I didn't hit the streetcar, nor the car parked at the curb, I hit all the stuff that was tied to the running board of the car. The street was a mess.

My brother Junior, had been complaining about a pain in his leg for at least a year. It was very apparent that something was wrong, for he had quite a limp. Mom would rub the leg every night before he went to sleep, but the pain persisted and was getting worse. I drove Mom and Junior to the doctor who diagnosed the ailment as Perthes Disease. The top of his hipbone was flat and rough which caused the pain. Our cousin, Doctor Julius Ruetenik who was on the staff at Fairview Park Hospital referred us to a specialist at the hospital who wanted to experiment with a new treatment. Junior would get the treatments without cost. Consultations with the specialist at the hospital confirmed the diagnosis and my brother was put in a cast for seven weeks, then wore the cast on and off for over a year. It was impossible for him to attend school, so Mom asked me to make arrangements at the school with his teacher so we could teach him at home. With close contact with his teacher, I taught him the third grade at home. He passed into the fourth grade. This was my first teaching job. I can't take credit for it for I had a lot of cooperation from his teacher.

Part of Brooklyn Heights was annexed into the City of Cleveland. This was a political move by a few men. We lost a school. It was now in the Cleveland School system and they boarded it up. The grade school children were sent to Benjamin Franklin School in Cleveland. This was two miles farther from home, and even though Junior was well enough to attend, he couldn't walk to get there. The district did not provide school bus transportation, so Diddle pulled Junior to school every day in a coaster wagon. The treatment did help Junior, but he would always walk with a limp because one foot is shorter than the other is. The case was written up in the American Medical Association Journal.

The Ruetenik clan held a reunion every year at Heidleberg Beach, located on the shores of Lake Erie just west of Vermillion, Ohio. We went there often, for many of my relatives owned property in this resort. My Cousin Miriam's parents owned a lot, and it was on this lot that Miriam, Louise and I, along with a few friends pitched a tent. Our next door neighbor from Brooklyn Heights owned a cottage here and so we were able to chum with Janet Walter while we were camping. On a day when Lake Erie was especially rough and high waves were breaking on the shore, I ventured out too far and an undertow took me out beyond the pier. I couldn't swim. My twin sister Louise and Janet who were on the pier, jumped in to help me. They took turns holding my head above water, and I was fighting them. Louise hit me on the head, and the last thing I remembered was when a man on the beach came out to help and dragged me onto the shore. If it hadn't been for Louise and Janet, I wouldn't be here today. I am forever grateful to them.

The next winter, I went to the YWCA in Cleveland and learned to swim in their large pool. After I could swim the length of the pool and back, I quit because all I wanted to do was learn to swim; I didn't like it enough to be an expert in the field.

CHAPTER 4

A TRIP TO COLORADO

In 1927 Pop took us on a trip to Colorado to visit his sister in Granby. Aunt Lottie wrote the most interesting letters about her life in the high country of Colorado. She was a former journalist and her talents came out in her letters. She wrote the 'Advice to the Lovelorn' column in the Cleveland Plain Dealer and was known as Dorothy Dix. She said she must not have been very good at the advice because she divorced her husband. Of course this was not true because he was a drunkard and they had two little boys. In fact I think it gave her good experience. But this was in the early 1900's and divorce was looked upon as being evil.

Eventually she took another job as housekeeper for a widower who decided that because she was his housekeeper people would talk. He thought the talk was already going around, so he married her and took her to Colorado to get away from the gossip. Uncle Ernie was a self-righteous man who never failed to say, "There was never a divorce in MY family in 200 years!" I never understood the point.

Pop and Mom made elaborate plans for the trip. The 1919 Studebaker sedan seated nine people and looked like a long box car, but it was even longer when a big metal box was installed on the back of the car for food, campstove and luggage. We carried two tents, one for the boys and one for the girls, which were lashed to the running boards. The tents were Army tents and were big enough to house the whole bunch in one tent, but Mom and Pop thought it indecent to house boys and girls together. We had several extra tires, and I try to recall, but I think the front fenders came with indents for tire storage. The interior of the car was equipped with pull-up seats between the front and back seats. A board was laid on these seats and covered with our blankets. We traveled very well with nine in the car. Missing was my oldest sister who was now married. Thus we began our long trip to Colorado.

The road between Cleveland and St. Louis Missouri was paved with brick, and in many places the road was bricked on one side only, as was common in those days. Driving was a little hairy at times, but very few cars were on the road and their fastest speed was only 35 MPH.

Once we were over the Mississippi River and into St. Louis, so few roads existed that the directions we were receiving from the gas stations were easier to follow. So it was due west to Kansas City, Kansas. From Kansas City the road west through Kansas and Colorado was gravel. It followed a railroad track, which it crossed many times as we traveled through the flat, yellow prairie. The driver had to be alert because we met more trains than cars on the road. No gasoline stations existed on this long stretch of road, so we stopped at a ranch where the rancher sold us gasoline from his pump. The gasoline was measured out into five-gallon cans until you had enough to fill the tank. The cost was figured and once again, due west.

Travelers' checks and credit cards did not exist, the traveler had to carry cash. Pop gave each of us some paper money to put in our shoes. Even though no one tried to rob us, it showed how much Pop trusted his children.

Across Kansas and into Colorado we went, and soon saw what we thought were clouds in the distance down on the horizon. We didn't think they were mountains because we were on flat ground. When we traveled through the Appalachian Mountains in the East we experienced many rolling hills before we came to the mountains. We watched the clouds all day and they never moved around, then what a thrill when we realized that the clouds were mountains! I had not expected to see them rise so high!

We arrived in Greeley, the first town for hundreds of miles, and soon were going through the Big Thompson River Canyon. A winding gravel road took us to Estes Park, which wasn't much of a town, but a new resort hotel, The Stanley, was on the north side of the road. Across the river were many log cabins type buildings and a few horse stables.

Up the Fall River Road we went, and we rose to a height of 12,000 feet above sea level. For a bunch of flat-landers, this was very remarkable. The narrow dirt road was no wider than one car width. If we met a car coming down the mountain, we had to back up into a place that could accommodate two car widths. With all the tents and other stuff on the running boards, the car passing us had very little room to be sure. This clumsy boxcar surely was not built for mountain driving! When it was maneuvered around a hairpin curve, my father went forward and back many times with a 1000-foot drop and no guardrails. Where the road went around the outside of the mountain, a sign warned us to stop and blow our horn before proceeding. The narrow road with the high drop was too much for Mom to bear. "Fritz, Fritz, Fritz be careful," she would scream at my father. Finally Pop stopped the car and told her that my sister Gertrude could drive. "No, no, no you drive," she said, and that quieted her for the rest of the trip. Many times on this high road we had to stop because the engine was overheating. We passed a ranger station near the top of the pass. (This stone building is still there after all these years.) Near this station we saw a snowfield. We had never seen snow in August so stopped to have a snowball fight. Being a bunch of flat-landers who were used to a 600 feet altitude, our legs were wobbly and our snowballs fell disgustingly short of our target.

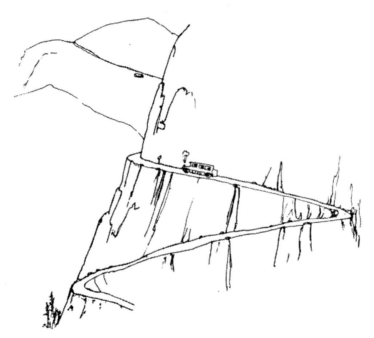

Milner Pass, Colorado

Over Milner Pass we went, then down past Grand Lake and into the town of Granby. After inquiry, we were told how to find Aunt Lottie's house. We were surprised to see the house because it was a little mountain shack with a wood stove in the kitchen for cooking and heating. In the backyard was an outhouse, which was the only "plumbing." It was a hard life for Aunt Lottie, for besides the lack of conveniences, she still had a full time job working in the lettuce packing plant. I cannot remember what kind of work Uncle Ernie did, for they didn't live on a ranch. Aunt Lottie had not lost her witty remarks and was cheerful in spite of her hardships. Her two sons took us over the territory and led us through a big sheltered place between some mammoth rock walls. This was an old Indian hunting ground. We were able to find a few arrowheads and an old buffalo horn so were satisfied that THIS was the WEST! Mom thinking the buffalo horn was a piece of wood threw it in the wood stove. The smell told us for sure, we found a buffalo horn. On Saturday night we attended the weekly movie in the Granby Town Hall with all the residents of the village. We sat on backless benches instead of the seats we were accustomed to in the Cleveland movie houses.

Windows! I love windows! Aunt Lottie pointed out Mount Holy Cross from her window when we first arrived. One morning she was all excited, "Look at Mount Holy Cross," she said, "it is snowing up there!" A snowstorm in the first week of September, and it was time we return to Ohio. We took the road over Berthoud Pass on the return trip. It was a gravel road, but two lanes wide and seemed tame to Fall River Road, which we climbed to get to Granby.

Down to Denver we went, and then on to Golden where we went up Lariat Drive to visit Buffalo Bill's grave on Lookout Mountain. Driving up this road we once again experienced the same hairpin curves as on Fall River Road. The Studebaker was just too long to maneuver those scary back ups with ease. The Buffalo Bill Museum was the same as it is today, but the large room where we dined on a large table next to a fireplace is

46

gone, and in its place is a modern snack bar. I do not know what happened to the beautiful fireplace.

Our next venture was to drive to Colorado Springs to see Pikes Peak. Of course Pop wanted to drive to the top, but Mom would hear nothing of THAT! She would not let Pop go up either. I always felt bad about that for father never got to the top of Pikes Peak.

CHAPTER 5

THE ROARING TWENTIES

I was a teenager in the Roaring Twenties. When I was a very young teenager I was invited to a party. I think this was the first boy/girl party I was invited to. They had a wind-up phonograph and lots of up-to-date records. Most every party in those days had a contest of some sort. This night it was a Charleston dance contest. I entered and won the booby prize.

Wolfram had a Ford Model T roadster with a rumble seat. My mother insisted that we take my twin sister along on our dates because my twin didn't have a boy friend. Wolfram taught her how to drive the Ford, then he and I got in the rumble seat and she drove us all over town. She was happy to do the driving and we were happy to be alone.

This was the time of the big dance bands. They came to the popular dance halls in Cleveland and the amusement parks in the surrounding area. I believe it was in Geauga Lake Park where we danced to the music of Guy Lombardo. My friend and I danced to their beautiful music the whole evening.

It was also the age of those famous vaudeville acts that were performed on stage in the big theater during intermission time of the silent movies.

Our favorite place was the Palace Theater in Cleveland. It was in this theater that we saw Fannie Brice, and heard her sing 'My Man.' Fred Waring and his band also performed on the stage during intermission. I think I enjoyed these performances more than I did the movies. What a pity, for now the intermission time is advertising time for the silver screen.

With talking pictures, the vaudeville acts slowly faded from the scene. The first talking picture that I remember was 'Sonny Boy' with Al Jolson playing the lead. I am not ashamed to say that I cried all through that wonderful movie.

I was a young lady now, so I didn't attend the kid shows in the movie houses on Saturday afternoons. I said good bye to Pearl White in her Saturday afternoon serials 'Perils of Pauline.' Comical Harold Lloyd never seemed to die from the scene, but Mary Pickford movies fell by the wayside, and my heartthrob, Rudolph Valentino, who played in the movie 'The Shiek of Araby,' passed away.

A whole new set of movie stars came along, and my new heart throb, Rudy Vallee. His beautiful voice vibrating through his megaphone sent the shivers up my spine, and he was handsome to boot! I had a passionate teenage one-sided loved affair with him.

The Twenties was a fast moving age. Prohibition had been in effect since 1920 and the Speak Easys were in every block in the city with their illegal 'booze.' (Well, almost every block.) Traffic on Lake Erie was heavy because boats were bringing booze from Canada.

Radio finally came into its own about 1920. I heard President Warren G. Harding give his Inaugural Address when it came over the airwaves. Someone had brought a superheterodyne radio to school and set it up in the high school room. This was not like the modern boom boxes of today.

When one of these radios was moved, it meant that six large storage batteries came with it. Evidently the invention of plugging the radio into an electric wall socket had not been invented. All the students in junior and senior high school met in this room to hear this important speech.

Eventually my father bought a superheterodyne radio with many tuning dials. Six storage batteries were on the floor underneath the radio. After all this equipment, a long aerial was attached to it. Pop strung an aerial from the barn to the house to catch the airwaves, but it attracted as much lightning as radio stations. The aerial was disconnected during a rainstorm. This radio was a far cry from our portable radios of today, but Pop did receive the radio waves from station WSM in Tennessee.

Charles Lindbergh soloed his airplane across the Atlantic Ocean. When he flew The Spirit of St. Louis to the Cleveland Airport, I stood in our front yard to catch a glimpse of his plane as it flew over our house. It was easy to spot him; it was the only plane in the sky.

I fell in love with Wolfram, the young man who worked for my father on the truck farm. He plowed and fitted the land to make it ready for planting the crops. He also was in charge of the workers when my father was away from the farm. When he plowed and fitted the land, he used a farmer's 'boat' to smooth the ground. He needed some weights, so I stood on the boat behind him. Of course he could have used some stones, but there wouldn't be much fun in that! It gave me an excuse to put my arm around him for support. I had to hold onto something!

Then the stock market crashed! I graduated from high school in 1930 and went right into the Depression! Jobs were hard to find after I left high school. It was now late fall in 1930. Louise and I decided we could find a job if we looked hard enough. We didn't have much encouragement from home, for this was the age when a lady looked for a husband, not a job!

Nevertheless, we went to the only place we knew in Cleveland, The Fries and Schuele Department Store. We both landed a job, and the folks at home were very surprised, especially my father. Louise worked in the stock room and I behind the candy counter. When I came home after working on my first day I was all-exuberant about my wonderful job. I was selling pistachio nuts! I hardly knew what they were. I did not have the candy clerk job too long before I was given a job as an elevator operator with a UNIFORM!

In those days, elevators were temperamental. It was not a matter of pushing buttons to operate it; the operator turned a handle. The doors were operated by sliding them open and shut manually. The door must be closed tight or the elevator would stop between floors. I had a temperamental elevator.

One day I had a load of Christmas shoppers on the elevator and as I was going up, the elevator stopped between the third and fourth floors. I had no way to signal the head operator on the first floor that I had a problem for the elevators had no emergency signals.

The head operator was on duty on the first floor. She always had her eyes on the dial above the doors. She sensed something was wrong when the arrow to my elevator stopped between floors, and stayed at that spot. She sent someone to each floor to inspect the door for proper closure. They were all closed in the right manner, so there was only one thing to do, remove the people out of my elevator. They opened the third floor door, and removed the people by using a ladder. I think I was more upset than the passengers were, but I could not let them know how I felt. I calmed them down, even though I had been an elevator operator for only a week.

An elevator operator was expected to call out all the items that were sold on each floor. You did this as you closed the door of one floor and until you opened the door on the next floor. This store consisted of five floors, and it was hard for me to remember all those products. I tried, but never finished before it was time to open the door on the next floor.

One day the store's Vice President rode up on my elevator and chewed me out for failing to call out all the items before it was time to open the door on the next floor. On the next run up, the store's President, Karl Schuele, rode with me. Now I was really nervous, for he rode the five floors to his office on the fifth floor. I did the worst job I ever did!! When he went out of the elevator, he patted me on the back and told me I was doing a fine job, and not to worry so much about it. Then he handed me an envelope and said "Here is a Christmas present for you. Don't tell the other employees about it." In the envelope was $10.00, an enormous sum in those days, for my salary was only $15.00 if I could work the full week.

After Christmas I was kept on the elevator job, but things were getting rougher as the Depression progressed. I was put down to a few days a week, so I changed jobs to work closer to home, doing housework and baby sitting for Bea Stieglemeier. Bea was five foot eleven in her stocking feet, and I was five foot two inches tall. She cleaned the upper cupboards and I the lower ones, so we worked together very well. We formed a lasting friendship.

In 1930, my sister Marceda married Jerry Keyse, and in 1931 my sister Gertrude married Theodore Wagner. Both of them were married in the living room of our home. The dining room table was again opened out to its full size, and the German tablecloth was used for the fine receptions.

It's now Thanksgiving 1932 and I invited Wolfram to dinner. Even before we were married, my future husband should have known what I was like. I should have known him, too. He had good beagle hounds, and he tried to interest me in hunting. I never hunted, and the only thing I ever did in the woods was to pick flowers and gather blackberries. "On Thanksgiving, you hunt," so said Wolfram.

He took me into the woods in the back of our farm with his good beagle hound. He was going to show me how to hunt. We found a woodpile. My friend said that rabbits are usually found underneath it. He gave me his 10 gauge shot gun, and told me to stand there and wait for the rabbit while he jumped up and down on the wood pile to scare it out, and when I saw the rabbit I was to shoot it. I had never held or shot a gun in my life, but there I was aiming his big shot gun and trying to keep it as steady as I could. The dog's tail was wiggling, wiggling. "There's a rabbit in there for sure," said Wolfram as he climbed to the top of the woodpile and started to jump on it.

I was aiming, shaky of course, and determined that I would shoot that gun. While I was aiming, the cutest, sweetest and most darling little rabbit ran out of the woodpile. His little tail went bobbing along as he hopped and hopped and hopped. After I was sure that he was out of sight, I called out to Wolfram. "Oh, you can stop jumping now, the rabbit went that way."

"Why didn't you shoot it?"

"I couldn't shoot a cute little thing like that!"

My friend was furious with me. I thought our marriage plans were over. Then he said, "I think you should get some practice with that gun." I had no idea how powerful this big 10 gauge shot gun was, nor was I told.

"Okay, what do I shoot?"

"Shoot that tree over there."

So I aimed for that tree and pulled the trigger. The repercussion promptly threw me to the ground. I don't remember if I even came close to hitting the tree, but I NEVER TRIED THAT AGAIN!

Our marriage plans were set for June 1933. Wolfram had left my father and his farm, and now he was renting a farm in Creston, Ohio. He was on his own. He had asked for, and I gave him all the money I had in savings to build a place to house his dogs on the farm. It was only $9.00, but that was a lot of money in those days, for I only made 75 cents a day, and it took me a long time to accumulate that much in the bank account. He said that raising pups would add to our income after we married.

One Saturday I packed a picnic lunch and went down to Creston to see Wolfram. I was driving his car. Coming down West 25th Street the steering rod broke and I almost hit a streetcar head on. A garage mechanic put in a new steering rod. I paid him and then was on my way. I was four hours late getting to the farm.

When I arrived, Wolfram wasn't concerned in the least about the problem I had with his car, nor that I was four hours late. He didn't even miss me.

All of these things bothered me. Unbeknownst to anyone but myself until now, I almost called off the wedding. The evening before the wedding, I took a four-mile walk to the dinky line and back. I had a lot of thinking to do for I had a deep feeling that I did not want to go through with this marriage, but felt obligated to go through with it, because of all the wedding presents, my mother's preparations for the wedding and the house in Creston was rented, scrubbed and furnished just waiting for us. I was wishing for more time to do some profound thinking about my future with this man.

PART II

CHAPTER 6
NEWLYWEDS IN CRESTON

Wolfram and I were married in the evening of June 17, 1933. It was a simple ceremony performed in the living room of our home. I was dressed in a gray suit that I had made. My mother planned a nice reception, and the dining table was extended to its full length and the German tablecloth was used.

I don't remember what was served at our reception. It's probably filed in that dusty little corner of my mind. I do remember after all the formalities were over, we left for our home in Creston, Ohio. Wolfram's new wedding suit that cost $9.00 was bought on credit. The flowers were bought on credit. I don't know about the wedding ring, but it was a pretty white gold ring with ten small diamonds that cost $15.00. The furniture was also bought on credit. We were in debt from day one of our marriage.

We started life together on a shoestring. I knew it, but I didn't realize that the shoestring would be so short, for the depression is in full swing.

The next morning as we were eating our breakfast, we had a visitor. It was a young boy who did weeding for my husband on the farm. He presented us with a wedding present nicely wrapped in brown paper. Inside was a pretty pink platter. Underneath was a price tag that said 15 cents. I know he had worked about 2 hours to pay for the platter. This is now what is called Depression Glass. I treasured that platter and cried bitterly a few years later when I broke it. I cried not only because it was so pretty, but I also liked the young boy and his thoughtfulness.

Our little home was only a few years old and was a nice place to live. My mother gave me a root of the blue iris that grew at the head of the fishpond. I planted it in the front yard by the steps. It was the only decorative plant, so it stood alone in its entire splendor.

In the backyard was a long concrete walk leading to a new outhouse. This was the first time in my life that I lived in a house without inside plumbing. I had to get accustomed to a whole new way of living. We used galvanized wash tubs in the kitchen for a Saturday night bath with water that was heated on the stove in metal buckets.

In a corner of the basement was a large cistern that caught the rainwater from the roof. Nearby was a gas stove to heat the laundry water. The kitchen sink was situated over the cistern, so we had a good set-up for 'running' water by using a hand pump. The neighbors, Vic and Agnes Bricker, offered us drinking water from their deep well. I can still hear the squeak from the handle of that pump as I filled a galvanized pail. I was very happy in this house, which had been repossessed by a bank that rented it to us for $10.00 a month.

Wolfram worked a truck farm and had been renting it for two years since leaving my father's farm. The soil was black muck, which is peat moss common to the area and was excellent fertile soil to raise vegetables. The muck was really an old swamp area that was endlessly flat. A very large drainage ditch surrounded it. Wolfram was doing very well with this muck land, but the nature of the soil sometimes burned the crops, or a heavy rain flooded it. He walked two miles through cow pastures and farms to get to the farm. A family, I would visit on occasion, occupied the farmhouse. It was papered with newspapers and magazines to stop the wind from whistling through the cracks. My recollection of it was that it was very old and small with a loose fitting door and a porch that had seen better days. A large barn, located nearby, housed two workhorses and was in excellent shape, as were barns on most farms, for the barn was more 'important' than the house.

A railroad track ran through the farm in such a way that when a train was switching, one would have to wait until the tracks cleared before going from one barn to another. Those who worked on the farm had to do a lot of waiting for there were three tracks. Before we were married Wolfram bached it in a small building that probably was the office for this large farm. At one time the farm must have been very productive, just by observing the many buildings that occupied the area, but the house told you that it was a long time ago.

Wolfram raised Irish setters and Beagle hounds. I didn't realize until after we were married that raising dogs could be very expensive. They had to be fed, which is the main concern. The dog raising business was supposed to add to our income, so Wolfram told me many times, but it only seemed to dig into it. Puppies did not sell well during the Depression except maybe Beagle hounds, which this farming community used to hunt rabbits for food. The first Irish setter litter had thirteen male pups, and it seemed everyone wanted bitches, so we had lots of pups to feed.

I helped by cooking dog food of cracked wheat, lard cracklings and cow lungs that came from the slaughterhouse. I did the cooking in the basement, but the foul odor permeated throughout the house. The dogs were an

59

expensive investment and the cost of it took most of our income. We were starting to argue about it.

I had a little Chihauhau dog that Wolfram gave me before we married, and now he bred her. Maybe these pups would sell! But the dog died in childbirth and though I tried to save the puppies by feeding them from a baby bottle, they also died. I never forgot the look of helplessness in my dog's eyes as she looked up at me just before she died. I realized that raising dogs is not my cup of tea.

As the summer progressed into fall during our first year of marriage, the hot sun on the black muck baked the new plants until they burned, the winds came and blew off the tops of the seedlings, and the rains came and rotted the roots. The Depression was not our only problem. We never seemed to win. I soon learned that when things got so bad that it seemed you couldn't take it any longer, they got worse.

The first summer did start out well, and we had lots of company. Among them were my mother-in-law and her second husband, Jake who was a dress designer. She was working as a seamstress in a dress manufacturing company when she met him. He was a pretty nice guy, I liked him, and the feeling was mutual. A few years after they were married, Jake was taken ill with tuberculosis. He bought a cow for fresh milk, because he thought this would be good for his failing health.

Jake raised canaries and gave me several birds so I could start a breeding program. He drove down from Cleveland every few weeks to instruct me and help me with the birds. He gave me a rare Cinnamon canary with a beautiful voice. I loved this little bird and we became close friends. I knew how to make him sing along with me when I inflected my voice in a certain way. By doing this I trained him to sing our favorite song, "Listen to the mocking bird" for by inflecting my voice he would warble when I paused. It was a joy for me to have this bird.

The last dress Jake designed before he died was a maternity dress for me. He gave my mother-in-law expensive blue material for the dress with a pattern so she could sew it. She told me that Jake designed the front of the dress too large, so she made a dress for herself with the extra material. My dress was too skimpy to wear after the seventh month of pregnancy.

After Jake died, my mother-in-law 'borrowed' one bird after another for her breeding programs until I had only the Cinnamon canary left. Then she told my husband she needed the Cinnamon. I protested in vain, but Wolfram gave it to her, and I never saw it again.

Agnes and Vic were good friends. Agnes worked in the grocery store and Vic worked in the basket factory. It was Agnes who told me that my morning sickness meant that a baby was on the way. Then she revealed her own pregnancy. She came over every morning with a cup of coffee and an orange for me. We took long walks together, either to Vic's mother's farm or another farm to buy eggs, or just for the walking.

It was Agnes who taught me how to can tomatoes. I learned very little from my mother for my work was helping my father on the truck farm.

Vic and Agnes owned a large two-story house with four bedrooms on the second floor. They bought it for $12,000 before the depression hit, but the real estate market had devaluated so much that their house was worth less than the remaining balance on the loan. The bank holding the mortgage knocked $3000 off the principle so they could hold the good people living there.

About the time this happened to Vic and Agnes, the bank that owned the nice house we rented from them offered it to us for $2000. It was a new house and would have been an excellent buy, but we were a year behind in our rent. The wisest thing to do was for me to get a job and take them up on their offer, but I was pregnant and not in the best shape to get a job, if indeed there was a job to be had.

Summer went and with the fall season came friends and brothers of my husband to hunt. Walter was a welcome friend, for he owned a meat market and brought us steaks, roasts and always lamb chops, just for me. Walter did not know, or maybe he did, that this was the only meat we had to eat. Our fall crops did not bring in enough money to support us.

Winter was upon us and the long walk that my husband made to the farm in the deep snow was difficult. He brought his half-grown dogs home and put them in the garage. Wolfram started to go to dog shows. We could not afford this, but his excuse was that he needed to go to dog shows in order to sell his puppies. The expense of raising dogs, especially the Irish setters, was more than we could afford, and the costs were rising. I still helped by cooking dog food, but our bills were mounting and the rent was defaulting more every month.

The neighbors were complaining about the noise the dogs made in the garage. Our arguments about them were increasing and I was beginning to feel that he thought the dogs were more important than I, with a baby on the way.

I discovered a trait about my husband that I did not know. He got so angry when I tried to talk about the cost of the dogs that he lay on the floor and kicked his feet and banged his arms down on the floor just like a child in a tantrum.

Divorce really swept through my mind, but I thought I would be more secure staying with him because of the baby. I must have been too young to know the real meaning of security; or else I was stupid. But where would I go? I didn't feel right about going home to my parents because I had a feeling when I married that my folks didn't like the idea, and to go back to them seemed to be the wrong thing to do. Or maybe I didn't want to own up to the fact that I was wrong to marry, and here I was, pregnant to boot.

It was the start of our first winter in Creston. The house we lived in had an excellent furnace, but we had no money to buy coal. When the tracks of the three railroads that ran through town were repaired, the rejected ties were thrown alongside the tracks. Wolfram hauled these home, and we both grabbed a handle on a crosscut saw and cut them to size for the furnace. Finally it was hard to find ties, for we were not the only ones in town who needed fuel for their furnace.

To keep warm, we used the oven in the gas range to heat the house even though we were several months behind in our gas bill, the company did not turn off the gas, nor did the electric company. Today this would not happen, the service would have been turned off and we would have frozen to death. The utility companies were kinder to their customers, but I am surprised that we didn't die of carbon monoxide poisoning. The oven did not suffice when the temperature went down to zero. I hung blankets in the arch between the dining room and the living room. It grew colder and the temperature went down to 20 degrees below zero.

I closed the kitchen door and we lived in the tiny kitchen to keep warm. We slept in a cold bedroom with one inch of ice on the window.

The turnips and carrots from the farm kept us from starving to death. We were out of staples such as flour and sugar. We supplemented the carrot and turnip diet with the tomatoes I had canned. This was our diet for three meals a day.

Wolfram set a few muskrat traps in the ditch on the farm. One day he came home with a muskrat and received $1.35 for the pelt. We had money once again. That muskrat saved us from starvation. The first thing we bought was a loaf of bread, which we hadn't had for a very long time.

My mother-in-law didn't know what to do with the cow Jake owned, so she lent her to us. The cow ate the same turnips and carrots we ate, but gave us rich milk. With the money from the muskrat we bought flour, sugar and eggs, so again I made cream pie for Sunday night supper. After the eggs and the money were gone, the pie left something to be desired.

Wolfram called it 'crappy pie,' so I stopped making it. Forever after that, he vowed I didn't know how to make cream pie.

Agnes and Vic brought over their ice-cream freezer, some eggs, sugar and ice, so, with our milk we made ice-cream suppers. These were good times with our friends. Agnes did just fine working me into Creston life that was so different from the life I knew in the village south of Cleveland. Her baby was born six weeks before mine and I spent many hours watching her bathe and care for her little boy. A few weeks before my baby was due, I went to Cleveland to spend the last few weeks with my sister Gertrude and her husband, who were very gracious to me.

Our baby was born in Fairview Park Hospital in Cleveland on April 5, 1934. She was a sweet, tiny girl we named Marlene Louise. Wolfram came to the hospital while I was giving birth to the baby, but neglected to make arrangements for the care of his half-grown Irish setters. They made such a noise that Vic broke into the garage so he could feed and water them.

I stayed in the hospital twelve days because of complications. One day the doctor came in and said to me, "I don't think you want to go home, do you?" He was right, I didn't want to go home, but I did go to my mother's house. I stayed there for a few weeks and then back to Creston. That dreadful winter had come to an end. It seemed so nice to be fed good food at the hospital, Gertrude's house and my mother's house for the last three or four weeks of winter.

Agnes and I continued our long walks, only this time we each pushed a buggy with a baby in it. This summer went much better than the summer before. Then winter came again.

Winter always made our life miserable because we had no money to buy coal for the furnace. When my husband could find work, it was only 9 cents and hour. This is 1934 and in 1933 he paid his help 12 cents an hour so the Depression is getting worse. In spite of the low pay it would have eased our finances, if only we didn't have to feed the dogs. He made less than $3.00 a week and the dog feed took most of that. He sold more dogs than in the previous year, but never enough to make a profit on them in the long run. Now he was striking up friendships with other dog fanciers he met at dog shows.

The man who owned the farm hired Wolfram to take his produce to market in Cleveland. One night, after one of these trips, he didn't come home. The baby and I were alone without heat except for the oven again. That night was a nightmare for me. My husband often fell asleep at the wheel of any vehicle he was driving. Many times I had to grab the wheel, and this worried me.

It was midnight and he wasn't home. I started to cry and sobbed and sobbed all night. Morning came and no husband. My sobbing continued until I was hysterical, and not knowing what to do for we had no phone, nor did anyone else in the neighborhood.

Wolfram came home in the afternoon, all happy with little regard for my anxiety. "You should have known I was at my mother's house. She had friends over and we had a wonderful time." This happened the whole winter, so never again did I worry for his safety. My love for him was fading because I realized that he was more interested in himself and his dogs than in his family.

We went home for Christmas that year. It just seemed that home was the place to spend Christmas. We had only enough money for one bus fare, and the baby could ride free if I held her on my lap. It was arranged that I should ride the bus and Wolfram would hitchhike. His shoes were worn through at the bottom. It was winter and he had no boots, so we fashioned lots of cardboard to fit his shoes. We walked down to the bus station and he started out before the bus came. The bus passed him about a mile out of town. He had not found a ride yet. I waved to him and then cried the whole forty miles into Cleveland. I don't understand why we didn't stay home in Creston. It was such an effort to go to Cleveland, and we had no money to take such a trip or to buy presents.

Spring came and with it, Marlene's first birthday. She had been walking since she was nine months old. Despite some of the hardships we experienced, times had not been as bad as the first winter. We were a year behind in our rent. We never seemed to catch up on our gas bills, let alone the bills for the furniture, the wedding suit and flowers. Very little money, (if any at all) had been paid on these bills and they were now two years old.

Our house was in the city and the neighbors on all sides were complaining about the noise that the dogs made. Instead of taking them back to the farm where he had a building for them, Wolfram built a fence in the backyard of our house. The Irish setter puppies are nearly full-grown and we hadn't had any sales and we had a hard time keeping them in the fence. I say "we" because it was my job to keep them in the fence when Wolfram was gone.

My husband rented another farm with a house on it for $15.00 a month. We were a year behind in our rent for $10.00 a month, but he had high hopes that more land would be the answer to our problems. The farm had many acres of the same muck land, and the barn could be used for the cow and dogs.

So we moved out of that nice house into a big old farmhouse on the edge of town. We never did pay the rent we owed the bank, but I did remember to take the blue iris.

CHAPTER 7
THE OLD FARM HOUSE

The new place was on the edge of town, but still in the country. The house was very large with four bedrooms on the second floor. The first floor had two large living rooms, a mammoth dining room and a very small kitchen. Our furniture did not begin to fill it up. So one living room had nothing in it. Our little kitchen table and chairs were the only furniture in the dining room. The kitchen was tiny and cramped with no plumbing. It always amazes me to see a house this large with a kitchen so small that four of them could fit in the dining room. The house lacked a furnace or a space heater. We were lucky it was summer. A big porch surrounded the house on two sides. Alongside of this porch is where I planted the blue iris.

An excellent fruit orchard was near the house. Wolfram pruned all the trees. The result was we had enormous and delicious fruit.

The building that he built for the dogs was moved from the farm to the front of the house alongside the CCC Highway. I sold produce from this stand and it worked out very well. I felt good about being able to help with our income. We had a good variety of produce raised by my husband and the neighbors. I was so busy with this stand I couldn't leave to visit Agnes, so she came with her baby in the buggy once in a while. Our friendship never ended

A nice family with lots of children lived across the street. The children came over so often that it made a very interesting summer for me.

Wolfram bought a Springer spaniel hoping these pups would sell better. I liked this dog, and because she was our house dog, she got to know the family very well, especially Marlene. They were constant companions. The dog kept Marlene from going in the street by taking her dress in his teeth and pulling her back to safety. That dog was smart!

Both farms were doing well. It was easier for Wolfram to milk the cow, because the barn was close to our home. The neighbors were buying milk, which gave us a little more money, and we did not live so near to them that the noise bothered them.

A big storm hit with a bang one evening. Lightning was playing all around us and it was frightening. The neighbor's house was struck by the lightning, and in quick succession a bolt hit our house, knocked off all the light fixtures and burned out the sump pump in the basement. A ball of fire swept through the house and little Marlene went screaming around the darkened rooms. We were finally able to catch her, but it was a few years before this horror left her mind. Every time a storm would hit, I took her in my arms, cuddled her and watched the lightening play around outside. After a while she was able to enjoy the storm with me.

This storm had other effects on our life. The rain came down in sheets and just wouldn't stop. We began to realize that we had a cloud burst on our hands! It rained all night and in the early morning we saw that the whole farm was flooded. The water was just fifteen feet from the house. The farm was one enormous lake! All the crops we depended on were underneath one foot of water. The other farm was the same, and it took two weeks for the ditches to drain the farms and all the crops rotted.

And I was pregnant again!

Wolfram went to the wholesale market in Cleveland and bought produce to sell on the stand. On one of his trips to Cleveland Wolfram found a job driving truck for a man who had a contract with the WPA projects in Cleveland. He lived with his mother, and came home once a week with produce. I bought what I could from the neighbors.

I was alone with Marlene most of the time now. One evening I noticed a 'Peeping Tom' looking at me through the window. It frightened me, especially since I was keeping the stand open until nine in the evening. I closed the vegetable stand early. The 'Peeping Tom' was making regular visits by the window. There were three outside doors, and every one of them could be opened with a skeleton key. When Wolfram came home for the weekend, he put a bolt on the stair well door leading to the bedrooms, and then he gave me a shotgun to protect myself. I wouldn't hear of shooting a man, so he removed the pellets from the bullets. I was fortunate I never had to use the gun.

Fall had come; it was beginning to get nippy outside. We had no way to heat the house or the produce stand. Wolfram found an apartment in Brooklyn Village near Cleveland and we left Creston, never to return. In our hurry to move out, we forgot to take the blue iris.

BROOKLYN VILLAGE

We moved into a first floor apartment of a house in Brooklyn Village. The cow and dogs were housed in the garage. The landlady lived on the second floor with her husband and four children. She liked the arrangement with the cow, because she had fresh milk for the children. For the first time since we married, we had a bathroom!

The landlady came down and visited me too often, because the father was beating up on her and the children. It was upsetting to have all those children sitting in my living room all the time they were home from school. The father was complaining about all of our animals and conditions were always in an uproar. Even though we had lived in this place only a month, we moved again. This time it was back home to Brooklyn Heights Village.

BROOKLYN HEIGHTS VILLAGE

In the fall of 1935 we moved back to my hometown of Brooklyn Heights, Ohio. So much has happened to me that it seemed more like ten years instead of two and a half years since I married and left home.

We moved into a hundred-year-old house that had been converted into a side-by-side double house. It was comfortable, and we did have a bathroom! The house had a coal furnace and we had enough money to buy coal! Behind the house was a large barn where the dogs and cow were housed, and a wonderful back yard for Marlene to play in. The neighbors had a little girl a few months older than Marlene, so she had a nice playmate.

We lived only a short walk from my mother's house. One day, Marlene and I walked down to her house to ask for another root of the blue iris. She graciously gave us a few roots and we planted them in a special place in the front yard of our home.

The cow paid off again, for my cousins and neighbors were regular customers for milk and butter. And Wolfram had a job! It was difficult for my husband, for he milked the cow before he went to work, and again 13 hours later when he came home.

The WPA projects that he worked on were started by President Franklin D. Roosevelt to give work to the jobless during the Depression. Because he worked for a contractor, he made enough money for us to live comfortably for a while. Then the contractor lost his contract with the government and he was without a job again.

Winter always had a habit of showing up and making my life miserable. The Brooklyn Heights neighborhood again did the same thing I remembered from my childhood. We found fruits and vegetables on our doorstep. From the nature of the produce we knew from whence it came. The large hothouse tomatoes came from Uncle Frank's greenhouses, which were located just across the street and down the hill from where we were living. He owned these greenhouses with Uncle Charlie, who was the man who played the violin in his boiler shed when I was a child. The money from milk sales and produce carried us through a very rough time.

Wolfram was now doing odd jobs for the village. One job was manning the snowplow. We lived about three miles from his mother who insisted that since Wolfram was not working, he should take her to the store every Wednesday. It snowed hard on a Tuesday night in January, and on Wednesday morning the snow was very deep. Wolfram had to man the snowplow for the village, so he asked me to take his mother to the store.

It was very cold and the streets were snow packed. The car's floor had rusted out so much you could see the street as you drove along, which didn't do much to keep the heat in the car. I was seven months pregnant, and went into labor that evening, but a visit to the doctor averted a miscarriage. The stupidity of it all!

My mother-in-law had two grown sons at home, each with a car that could take her to the store. Why did I have to do it, and why did I agree to do it?

Wolfram had recently thrown a chair at me in his anger; was I trying to avoid another incident like that? I don't think he was really mad at me, I think he was mad at himself for not being able to support the children, the dogs and me. Our second baby was nearly due and he had not paid the doctor anything for delivering the first baby.

Divorce again crossed my mind, for it seemed to me that Wolfram should give up his expensive hobby so we wouldn't be so poor. I probably nagged him about it, but it seemed to me that I was the only one who worried about the bills.

We were living closer to Cleveland now, where Wolfram could enter his dogs in more dog shows, and he always found the money to do it. He entered the dogs in the Cleveland Show. It was so close to the due date of our second baby, that he took me to my mother's for the day.

That evening my Mom went to church and left Marlene and me alone with Pop. Marlene was upstairs in bed and Pop and I were alone. I was sitting in his large chair not budging an inch all evening. He said, "You are going to have your baby tomorrow." "Now how do you know that?" I asked. "Because you have been sitting in that chair for hours, you better leave Marlene here tonight."

I should have known that father knows best, but I took Marlene home with me, only to bring her back at seven o'clock the next morning on our way to the hospital.

Our new baby arrived at eleven o'clock the same morning on March 16, 1936 in Fairview Park Hospital. She was a chubby and pretty little baby who smiled all the time. We named her Audrey Alida.

Wolfram's Aunt Polly, who was my mother-in-law's sister, and her husband Ben were wealthy and lived in a fine house. They wanted to adopt Audrey because they thought we were too poor to raise her properly. We refused right off! They asked for her again and again, but we still refused. Aunt Polly wanted her because we were poor, but didn't do anything to help us in any way, either.

We visited Aunt Polly and Uncle Ben one Sunday afternoon. Just before we left our home, Marlene who was all dressed up for the visit, went into the basement to watch her father fire up the furnace, and sat on the coal dust covered steps. I was too busy getting Audrey ready to check her over again, and she had coal dust on her panties.

When we arrived at Aunt Polly's house we found another visitor, Ben's German aunt. She and Aunt Polly spoke fluent English, but chose to remove me from the conversation by speaking German. They probably thought I didn't understand them, for they were talking about me. They were blaming me for not keeping Marlene clean. "Just look at her pants." I suppose Aunt Polly was justifying her desire to adopt Audrey.

We had gone there to talk to Uncle Ben about the new driveway they wanted put in from the street to the house. I assumed that they were trying to give my husband some work in our time of need.

The driveway was over 100 feet long. And Wolfram did a beautiful job. Instead of paying him for his work, they gave him a jacket, when we needed money, especially for the gas he used in the car to drive the 15 miles to their home. I think the jacket was one that Uncle Ben had discarded. It wasn't a new one.

They took advantage of my husband. Why did Wolfram let them do this to him? We were right for not giving up Audrey for adoption to these people.

Selling milk from our cow kept us going more than our customers realized. (Or maybe they did.) Wolfram sold his dog litters before they got too expensive to keep. He did eke out a living for us somehow. At least we were able to buy coal for the furnace, and food too.

My mother-in-law was a self-regarded atheist who could not understand why I took my girls to Sunday school. "When are you going to quit this foolishness?" she would say. The day Audrey was baptized, she insisted on putting on a big dinner for the relation on her side.

Audrey was six weeks old, when I had a doctor's appointment for her check-up. I bathed and dressed her and Marlene, then got in the car with them. We were just in time to make it for the 7 o'clock appointment. We were sitting in the car waiting for my husband when a car pulled in the yard.

It was a friend of his who came to see the dogs. The conversation was long and I was getting nervous about meeting the appointment. I blew the car horn and called him to tell him we were getting late. He and his friend just kept on talking. Finally the friend left, and we were already too late, for it was past 7 o'clock. We still had a 30-minute drive to the doctor.

Then I got a barrage of words about chasing the man away when he could have sold him a dog. I never seemed to win with this man. The children and I did not matter; neither did the doctor who gave us the appointment. I ask him why he didn't tell the man we had an appointment. He said, "You just don't do that to a friend."

While we lived in this house, my friend Gladys, who gave me the name 'Fritz', called on me and brought Helene, the girl who had walked with me to school. All three of us pushed baby buggies. My cousins visited me and I went to their house. This was a nice summer for me.

The dogs were not my cup of tea, so I never had much to do with them. I was afraid of the cow, which was just as well, for then I didn't have to learn how to milk her. I did my part by taking care of the milk. When the milk accumulated I made butter.

In the meanwhile, Wolfram had been scanning the help wanted ads in the Cleveland Plain Dealer. He found an ad for a handyman. We would be moving to a large estate in Mentor, Ohio if he was chosen for the job. Out of 176 applicants, he was selected. He was well qualified for the handyman job; he could do almost anything.

I do not remember what happened to the cow when we moved to the estate, but we did take some Irish setters. I remembered to dig up a root of the blue iris.

I asked Wolfram to get some boxes for packing. He was always too busy to get them, so I didn't have anything packed for the move. One day Wolfram came with a borrowed truck and threw everything in it, whether it was packed or not, and off we headed for Mentor, Ohio.

CHAPTER 8

MENTOR, OHIO

In 1937 we moved into a small cottage on an estate that is nestled in the woods on Little Mountain just four miles south of Mentor, Ohio. I planted the blue iris in a nice spot in front of the house.

Audrey was one year old and Marlene was three. The nice backyard was at the edge of the woods, so the girls shared their playground with a host of animals, including chipmunks and rabbits.

The estate owners are multimillionaires. Wolfram's salary was $90.00 a month plus a cottage situated near the entrance to the estate. This was more money than we had seen since our marriage in 1933.

The cottage was pleasant, but had a foul odor. An inspection showed that the outside of the house had been banked up with manure to keep the floors warm. This was job #1 for me. I used a pitchfork, put the manure in a wheelbarrow and transferred it to the garden plot. While removing the manure, I uncovered a nest full of newborn rats. The sight was nauseating. I killed all the baby rats with the pitchfork and was sick to my stomach the rest of the day.

There was a good potbelly stove in the living room to heat that room and the two bedrooms. In the kitchen was a kerosene hot water heater. They both did a very good job of heating the entire house. A closed stairway off the living room took you up to a pretty little bedroom on the second floor. I spent many hours in this room for the walls were lined with my book collection. I sat on the floor by the window and reread all those books. My ancient history book gave me the giggles for all the drawings of the history teacher were still there. My geometry book was my favorite. I didn't realize at the time, but geometry would be a big part of my life in the future.

The woods surrounding the house were endless, and the girls didn't wander into them. We took walks among the trees, which satisfied them. The woods came right up to the house on two sides, which was enclosed by a chestnut log fence. This fence was the chipmunk's playground. My girls had a very interesting place to play. The outhouse was on the edge of these woods. I was in it one day when I heard a blood-curdling squeal! I ran out just in time to see a weasel dragging a rabbit into the woods.

The cottage had running water with a bathtub and sink in the bathroom, but no toilet. So again we had the outhouse. The estate owners bought a toilet and septic tank and Wolfram installed them on his own time. It was hard work for the ground was very stony, but eventually we had a good bathroom.

We had an excellent garden that year, and it was very productive. The manure was doing a better job in the garden than around the house, though most of the vegetables were shared with the rabbits and other wild animals.

We lived among the other estate employees. The butler lived across the street and the cook, the upstairs maid and the housekeeper a little farther up the road. Across the street and closer to the entrance lived the estate superintendent. The nursemaid lived in the big house so she could be closer to the children.

The millionaire's son, who was a little older than Marlene, visited us quite often to play with her.

Marlene — "We are going to Mentor-on-the-lake for a picnic tonight. Have you ever been there?"

"I don't think so, is it a public place?"

"Mom, is Mentor-on-the-lake a public place?"

"Yes it is. It's for the people living in the area to enjoy."

"My Mom said it is a public place."

'It sounds like so much fun, but I can't go to public places." This is what I call a poor little rich boy.

The fall of the year has come and Wolfram's knowledge of dogs pays off. The estate owner sent him on a scouting trip with his dogs to find a good place to hunt. He found a place near the Ohio/Pennsylvania state line.

The estate owner and his friends picked Wolfram up without prior notice one morning before breakfast. If I had known that they were coming, I would have prepared for it. I told Wolfram I would make him a sandwich, but he refused; he was too anxious to get going. They found the quail and easily caught their limit. Being millionaires, they did not stop to eat, because they didn't go into pubic places. A very hungry husband came home that evening! He should have let me make him a sandwich.

Winter in this cottage was the most pleasant one we ever had all the time we were married, for we were warm and had good food to eat.

We bought a new Hot Point range. A home demonstrator, who worked for Hot Point, called on me often and taught me how to bake bread. She came one day when I was rolling out cookie dough with the girls 'helping' me. I remarked that I liked to see her come so often. She said, "I like coming to your house because you are always involving your children."

There was a time during this period that I wasn't involving my children. I was starting to paint pictures again. I had a nice little business making Christmas cards for my relations and friends. I wanted peace and quiet!

I had forgotten how being quiet can be a worrisome thing for a child. I finally came to my senses and heard no sound coming from anywhere in the house. I was frightened and mad at myself for not being attentive to the children. I ran into the living room.

"Hi, Mommy, isn't this beautiful?" said Audrey. Audrey is a perfectionist, and she had spread soap flakes in an even layer on the tables and sofa. What a perfect job!

Then I went into the kitchen. "Hi, Mommy, isn't this the most prettiest room you ever saw?" said Marlene. She had the flour sifter in her hand and had completely covered the large kitchen floor with a fine layer of flour! And me without a vacuum cleaner.

Well, why should I get angry with them? They were being quiet… RIGHT … They weren't bothering me while I was painting… RIGHT … And what they were doing was very pretty… RIGHT!!!… So without further ado I cleaned it up. I was thankful that they didn't wander out into the woods.

The estate superintendent was from Scotland. He was a good artist and I admired his beautiful paintings, but so many of them looked familiar. One evening he brought his latest painting to our house for us to see. It was an Eastern American scene and beautiful.

The next day we were shopping in Mentor, and as I was glancing through the magazine rack, one of them caught my eye. On the front cover of the Saturday Evening Post was a painting of that beautiful autumn scene.

I thought the superintendent was really a famous artist. Then I had second thoughts. If he painted it for the magazine, why did he have the newly painted original? I wrote to the magazine and they gave me the artist's name and address. It was not the superintendent. The superintendent was an imposter, or was he?

It was pleasant living here, and we had many visitors from Cleveland. My mother-in-law came with a couple who drove her. It was not long before only the husband of the couple drove her to our house. I could see what happened and it saddened me, for his wife was a nice lady.

Wolfram had only two Irish setters while we lived here. He was now attending many dog shows, and added an Irish Water Spaniel to his kennel. The dog was funny looking with a rat tail and very curly like a poodle, but was a great retriever. The whole family enjoyed playing with this dog.

One day Wolfram drove us to Cleveland so he could enter his dogs in the Cleveland Dog Show. The enrollment office was in a large downtown hotel. I stayed in the car with my sleeping girls when he went into the hotel. I had been waiting several hours for him in the car. Both children had fallen asleep and Audrey was in my arms.

A drunk came up to me. He wanted to drive the car. The locks on the car were broken, and he kept opening the door on the driver's side. I had a hard time trying to get rid of him. I was screaming for people to help me, but when they came to the car he would tell them I was his wife. They believed him and not me!!

I begged them to phone the police, but no one wanted anything to do with a family fight. I put Audrey down in my seat and went behind the wheel. I started the motor and went forward and backward until he fell off the car. When the drunk got too much of my actions he would leave, but always came back again.

An hour later Wolfram came back to find me screaming and hysterical. I told him about the drunk and said he probably would come back again, for he left a package in the doorway of a store. Wolfram waited in the doorway and when the man came back I gave him a nod. I never saw a guy get such a hard beating! The strangest part is that no one paid any attention to what was going on.

The estate superintendent was giving Wolfram very dangerous work to do. I surmised that he was a homosexual when my husband had to meet with him in the evenings because he was using him for a 'model' for his artwork. Wolfram brought the artwork to show me and I saw that I was right about the superintendent. Wolfram refused to be a 'model' any more. We had a suspicion that he was giving him this dangerous work because of his refusals.

Things grew worse. One night as I was turning off the lamp which was alongside the bedroom window, I saw someone looking at me from the woods. His face was not more than five feet from mine. My fingers froze on the light button. I couldn't turn it off! I stiffly crawled into bed and whispered to Wolfram, "Someone is looking in the window and I am sure it is the superintendent." "You stay right where you are," he answered, "I'll go upstairs and look down from the window that is right over this one."

He took the stairs to the upper bedroom and looked down, and the man was still there. It WAS the superintendent. Wolfram came back down into the bedroom and turned off the light, and then we both watched as the form slowly moved away into the woods. We spent the whole night talking and wondering what to do.

Wolfram went to the estate owner the next day. He did not believe the spying incident. "The superintendent was imported from Scotland and he is under contract," he said.

Things were getting worse. We never left the children out of our sight. Either their father or I was with them constantly.

The superintendent sent Wolfram up on the high barn roof with a roll of tarpaper to reroof the barn. It was extremely windy and the tarpaper was ripping around my husband, causing him to loose his balance time and time again. He came down and refused to go up again.

We felt that his life was in danger, my life, and also the lives of our children. We were both frightened, maybe unduly frightened, but I don't think so after the roofing incident. It had been so nice living here until this situation came up. The only thing we could do about it was to move again. So I dug up the blue iris, and we moved to Painesville.

CHAPTER 9

PAINESVILLE AND THOMPSON

In 1938 we moved from the estate in Mentor to a farm in Moody Hollow on the outskirts of Painesville, Ohio. Wolfram and my cousin were going into truck farming on this property. Both men were well qualified as experienced vegetable gardeners. The land needed no clearing and was very fertile.

I don't remember how I renewed my acquaintance with my cousin, for I hadn't seen him in years. He was a smooth talker, but he did have a truck and a horse that was necessary for farm work. The place had a large barn for the horse and plenty of room for the dogs.

The house was a large Western Reserve/Colonial type of structure of the 1800-1830 period so common in those years, and especially in Painesville. The house was so elegant with details and cornices that I have no doubt that it was designed by Jonathon Goldsmith, an architect of this period who was noted for houses with those distinctive features. The center of the house was a large two-story structure with a one-story structure on each side. The owners bought the house for its historic qualities, but it needed extensive repairs. I planted the blue iris in the front of this house.

The house was rented to us 'as is' for it had no electric power coming into the place. No electricity meant that I could not use the new electric range or my washing machine. We bought kerosene lamps and I cooked on kerosene stove. Next to the kitchen was a milkhouse with a hand pump for water. In the backyard was an outhouse.

My cousin tilled the land from six until ten o'clock in the morning and then was through for the day. People thought he was a hard worker because they saw him so early in the morning, but he spent the rest of the day with his cronies in Painesville. Wolfram put in many more hours than my cousin did.

I found out the hard way that what a woman does is not worth much, for whatever work fell upon my shoulders, I was given no credit. Of course my cousin had a horse and a truck, but I didn't think I had to work like a horse to compensate for it. I weeded the pickle patch and picked pickles, did the cooking and dish washing and cleaned the house.

It was also my job to run the produce stand we built in front of the house. My work was never considered. We soon found out that we got the worst of the deal. My cousin accused me of stealing his money when I cleaned his room, so I never cleaned it again. He found the money in a book he was reading, and apologized, but I told him the inequity of our situation was not acceptable. Then he laughed at me. I had lost my personhood.

The lack of inside plumbing was the most worrisome thing for me. I was raised on the outskirts of Cleveland. Before I married I never lived in a house without inside plumbing, city water and electricity. In the 1930's when one lived away from a big city, an inside bathroom was a rarity. The good living in Brooklyn Heights certainly didn't prepare me for outhouses and hauling buckets of water for every little thing that water was used for.

Without electricity and inside plumbing, I had to go back to my grandmother's day and do my laundry with a washboard and a tub. The only difference was that her tub was wood and mine was galvanized metal. The washboard never changed.

The kerosene stove in the kitchen was too flimsy and risky to heat water for the laundry, so Wolfram built a bonfire to heat the laundry water. Hauling water from the milkhouse filled the tub. I washed clothes in the back yard by scrubbing them by hand on a wash board, wrung them out by hand, and then rinsed them in cold water and wrung them out again by hand. The hardest clothes to wash were Wolfram's heavy work clothes and the sheets.

I recalled what I left behind when I married. When I was very young, my mother had a wooden tub with a handle on the side that we pushed and pulled to activate the water, and a hand wringer. How I longed for that stuff now.

Marlene and Audrey were about four and two years old and I was doing some very nice sketches of them. The pencil drawings were good, but I felt that I needed more training. My thoughts returned to Paul Ulan, the art teacher I had when I attended West Technical High School in Cleveland. He had recommended me into John Huntington Polytechnic Institute for further art studies. I was having a feeling of deep remorse about the decision not to attend that school, but that was ten years ago. I wondered if that recommendation was still open. My feelings persisted, so I drove to Cleveland to see if it was possible to take up the recommendation. It WAS possible and I was accepted without standing in the two block long line of 600 students waiting to enter the school.

I drove to Cleveland twice a week to take an art course under Paul Travis, a well known artist who had paintings hanging in the Cleveland

Museum of Art. I attended John Huntington Polytechnic Institute for the first time.

Despite the hardships, the house in Moody Hollow was a pleasant place to live and raise children. Big green frogs lived in a small rill that ran near the house and Marlene was very adept at catching them. The only problem was that she brought them into the house, so I had to get used to big frogs hopping all over the place.

Across the road in front of the house was a large creek. It had a dual purpose, for the girls and I would don our bathing suits, grab a bar of soap and take a bath while enjoying ourselves in the water. We took long walks in the woods.

Unbeknown to me, the woods were also used by the neighbors for a cow pasture. One day we met a heifer. Although we had a cow at one time, I was afraid of all cattle. I supposed that the heifer was a ferocious bull and spent an hour protecting my children on a steep hill. The heifer just stood in front of me and gave me a dumb look. This has been a laughable memory for the girls. They always wondered why I made them sit with me on the hill. They KNEW the heifer wasn't a bull. Now that I think of it, the heifer probably could have climbed that hill better than I could.

This house must hold many pleasant memories of picnics for those who lived here in the last hundred years. If only we had electricity, but the landlord made it very plain when we moved here, that he was working on getting electric power to the farm, and when he was successful, he would move in with his family.

Wolfram bought a utility trailer to haul produce to the stores. My cousin didn't want him to use his truck, but no matter, it was a flatbed and unsuitable for the purpose. Wolfram was working up a good business with the stores and restaurants in the area. Fall had come and the lack of produce from the farm was hurting the business. He went to The Northern Ohio Food Terminal in Cleveland to buy shipped in produce and continued to supply his customers, and the business grew.

The car, trailer and operating costs were ours. Wolfram was going to Cleveland every morning to buy produce and doing all the delivery work. I'm doing the housework and cooking for all of us. There is nothing for my cousin to do, but he thinks he should get half of the profit. To make matters worse, Wolfram blamed me for our predicament because a cousin of mine caused it.

Wolfram wanted to move us to Thompson, Ohio, which was twenty miles farther out into the country, and sixty miles from Cleveland. I tried to reason with him that his new business was in Painesville; why move farther away from it? It was too far for me to continue with college and too far from our families, but I protested unto deaf ears.

I did talk him into looking at a few places in Painesville, but he always found fault with them. It seemed a farm was the only place for the dogs. Our arguments over the dogs were still persisting and getting worse. It seemed to me that the children and I were never considered, the dogs came first. My life is going backwards instead of forwards. Once again divorce crossed my mind.

Wolfram won out, so we left my cousin, his horse and truck and moved to a desolate farm in Thompson on a lonely, narrow dirt road with ruts in it to guide your car.

THOMPSON, OHIO

Wolfram always had a dream: raising dogs, selling the puppies for great profit and winning in dog shows and field trials. Now it is the fall of 1938, and the only part of his dream he had realized so far was raising pups and trying to get rid of them before they became too expensive. My husband probably could have realized his dream if he didn't have a wife and children to support, but he still had a dream.

When we left Moody Hollow, it was so stressful that I forgot the blue iris. When we got to the farm, I discovered that a hired man came along with the rent. Wolfram seemed to know all about this, and told me that the hired man could take care of the dogs.

A few days after we were nicely settled, Wolfram told me that he was going to live with his mother in Cleveland, because it was too far for him to drive into Cleveland every day for produce, then to deliver to the stores and then another 20 miles to Thompson. The very thing I was protesting about before the move. He said he would come home every weekend.

He left his daughters and me alone in a house with a man who was a total stranger. I did have a lock on my bedroom door, and the girls slept in a loft with a ladder coming from my bedroom. The hired man occupied the other bedroom

The hired man, who emigrated from Hungary, could speak no English. The landlord also came from Hungary. The hired man lived on the farm to take care of the landlord's cow, chickens and rabbits, but he spent most of his time with some Hungarian neighbors who lived down the road. These people could speak a little English and I would visit with them. They were very clean, which is something I could not say about the hired man.

89

The hired man did teach me how to cook on the kitchen wood stove, and was very helpful, especially when both the living room potbelly stove and the kitchen wood stove needed more wood to keep the fires going. Because of the language problem, we had very little to say to each other.

I do not recall much about the farm except that the house was very dreary, dark and dirty. The living room was gloomy with smoke-covered walls and only one small window. The kitchen was pleasant with a large corner window and a big cast iron cooking stove. I spent most of my time in this pleasant room. When it was too cold outside to play, the girls spent their time in the loft.

Not everything was dreadful. Marlene and Audrey thoroughly enjoyed the chickens and rabbits. They had a nice yard to play in when the weather permitted.

The Strava chicken farm was about a mile down the road. This was a pleasant walk for the girls and a good place to buy fresh eggs. Of course there were chickens on the farm where we lived, but they belonged to the landlord and the eggs were collected just for them. The Stravas were good people to talk to, and on occasion I met their son and daughter, who were attending college.

One day the hired man left the feed bin cover open and the cow got into it and ate too much corn. This was a serious problem for she bloated. The hired man came into the house and took me out to the barn to see what happened. I wanted to walk to the neighbors to use their phone to call a veterinarian, but the hired man wouldn't let me. He said he knew what to do, but I doubt if the vet could have saved the cow's life. The two of us spent the entire day with the sick cow. I finally left the hired man with his problem. The last I saw of that cow was when the hired man had his whole arm up the cow's rectum trying to get the corn out.

The landlord came the next weekend. Instead of being angry with the hired man for not closing the feed bin, he got angry with me. He said I should have known how to take care of a cow. Heck, the one thing I didn't know was how to take care of a cow! I thought that was what the hired man was for, but the blame was put on me.

The hired man's work now consisted of feeding the dogs, the chickens and rabbits, so the landlord asked us to GET OUT!

So because of a dead cow, we must move again!

CHAPTER 10

BACK TO CLEVELAND

Wolfram and I were having heated arguments over our future. The Depression of course was partly to blame, but did my husband believe in himself enough to face his responsibility toward our children and me? He demanded that he take us to Cleveland to live with his father. I was determined that we could make it on our own if only he would get us a place closer to his business in Painesville. I was positive that the business would succeed if we lived in the town where he established it.

Wolfram had his way again, borrowed a truck and drove the girls and me along with our furniture and household goods to Cleveland. Wolfram and I fought and argued the sixty miles to Cleveland. He hit me so hard that I was black and blue on the whole side of my body that was seated next to him. Divorce again crossed my mind. Why couldn't we talk? He always did the opposite of what I had in mind, and made me feel so stupid. So we moved in with his father. The dogs came along.

My father-in-law and mother-in-law had been divorced, and Wolfram's father remarried. His second wife had left him to live with her daughter in Wisconsin, because he drank too much. So now I had the problem.

Despite the drinking problem I liked my father-in-law, but he was hard to live with and all of a sudden I had to care for him. His clothes were in a sad state of repair. He wore white shirts when he ran his business at the West Side Market, and it was my job to wash and iron them, but if a button was missing, or I overlooked a little tear, he threw the shirt on the floor and stepped on it. I had to wash and iron it all over again. We had long talks with each other, and one day he told me that he really didn't want us there. I told him that I didn't want to be at his house either, then revealed the heated arguments I had with Wolfram, and the fight on the way to Cleveland. I told him I tried to tell his son that we should move in the Painesville area and take hold of our own responsibilities, but he demanded that we move in with him. Neither my father-in-law nor I could solve the problem.

Wolfram was his son, he should talk with him, but the confusion was put on my shoulders. Right then I had a suspicion that Wolfram moved us in with his father without asking him, or telling him, that we were coming to live with him.

Christmas had come while we were at his house. I just faintly remember a small tree in the living room, and nothing more. I don't remember trimming it, what ornaments I used, or if it was really I who did it. I just can't remember that Christmas. Maybe it is something I don't want to remember and shoved it off into that dusty little corner of my mind.

My father-in-law migrated to Cleveland from Germany. He spoke fluent German, which he used with his customers in his German sausage stand. He had two sons, Rob and Carl, who helped him make sausages in a small building behind the house. These brothers came twice a week to work in the building, and if they minded my presence in the house they never showed it, and were very gracious to me. I do remember they brought me my favorite sausage and fresh bakery bread for our lunch when they came to work.

The next door neighbors were Hungarians. Audrey and Marlene spent most of their time with these good people who spoke no English. My daughters had a good exposure to Hungarian people by now, and soon Marlene was speaking 'Hungarish.' She was very good at this language of hers, and it sounded so foreign to me that I assumed she knew the language, especially when Audrey started the 'Hungarish.' The girls were constantly talking in their language with perfect understanding.

My father-in-law was drunk most of the time, and I was constantly cleaning up the bathroom. One day he decided to go bowling with some of his buddies. The next day he complained about a pain in his arm. I thought he was coming down with a stroke. His sons told me that this was the first time he ever bowled, but he wasn't feeling well. His condition worsened and he took to his bed. He then admitted to me that he was spitting up blood. After a talk with his sons, we decided he needed a doctor. The doctor sent him right to the hospital with a bad case of pneumonia. His body had taken so much abuse from his drinking that he died within a few days.

His wife in Wisconsin was notified. She came back to Cleveland, claimed ownership of the house and asked us to move.

BACK TO PAINESVILLE, OHIO

It was early in the year 1939 that we moved back to Painesville, where Wolfram's business was located; but he really didn't have much choice in the matter. Where else could we go? When Wolfram's father died his wife also asked his brothers to get out of the building where they were making sausages. Our little family wasn't the only ones to be put in this predicament. I was satisfied that we had to move. We shouldn't have been in his father's house, and the move to the desolate farm in Thompson was unbelievable. We should have moved to Painesville in the first place.

We had been married about six years, and this was the ninth time we moved. The produce business continued to improve, but we still didn't have much money and Wolfram continued to make his produce deliveries from a trailer pulled behind the car.

We moved to a large house on Bank Street. The house was in the city, but there was a large barn just right to store crates and boxes. A smaller building was just right for the dogs. Long ago the place must have been a farm, or the people who built it might have had at least two or three horses in the days of that kind of transportation.

The house was so large that we shut off the upstairs and still had five rooms and a bath on the first floor. No furnace was installed, so again a potbelly stove in the dining room. As usual in these kind of houses the kitchen was TINY! But we did have a BATHROOM! For the first few weeks I used the potbelly stove for cooking by putting the kettle right on the hot coals, until we had $15 to have the gas turned on and then I used a two-burner hot plate. The house was not wired for an electric range.

After a few months we were able to install a phone. This was the first phone we had since we were married. The girls thought the phone was a big novelty, and came running every time the phone rang. Our phone number was close to the hospital number, and when these calls came through, little three-year-old Audrey would be so dismayed. "What the, they want the horsepital AGAIN?"

With installation of the phone, the business improved immensely. Now we received the grocery store orders for the next day. I made up the produce list and did the bookkeeping, and Wolfram controlled the inventory.

The business increased so much that the trailer was too small. We needed a truck if we were to increase the business to be more profitable. We didn't have the money for a truck.

I wrote to the people who hired me to do their housework when I was eighteen years old. They lent us $175 to buy a truck. A neighbor and our friend, John Winter from Perry, helped Wolfram build a stake body for the truck and enclosed it with plywood. With this truck, our business increased again.

Our housedog was an Irish setter named Larry. He was a character and very smart. He was a people dog. A neighbor would feed him every afternoon at 5:50. When that time came, Larry put his empty dog dish in his mouth and took it over to her house. He'd wait until she filled it and then brought it home to eat it. Larry rode in the truck with Wolfram so he got acquainted with a grocer who never failed to give him a bone. When Larry made his own rounds, he included this grocer, then brought the bone home to eat it.

On St. Patrick's day I tied a big green ribbon around his neck to show his friends that he was an Irishman. He came home dragging a whole leg of beef bone that the grocer had given him. The green ribbon still graced his neck and the grocer had returned my buffoonery. Despite his wonderful personality Larry was very protective of his family. He would let the milkman come to the door once, but not twice. To protect the milkman I left orders for more milk a day ahead of time.

In the back of the barn we had a large vegetable garden. Marlene spent a lot of time in this garden, and one day I discovered what she was doing.

She was watching the tomato worms. One day she brought a large green tomato worm in the house. It had parasites hanging all over it. "Mommy, isn't this the most beautifulest thing you ever saw?" I almost fainted. Since the day I worked in my father's greenhouse picking tomatoes, I never lost the horror of big green tomato worms.

We had not been here a year when Wolfram decided to raise puppies again. He used the same old excuse! "The sale of puppies would add to our income." He wants to move out in the country again. We could raise puppies where we were, but he reminded me that we had a problem in Creston with the neighbors complaining about the noise. So here goes that same old heated argument!

Life had been moderately pleasant in this house. Why can't we just stay where we are? We are getting on our feet now, why move? As usual Wolfram had his way and we moved for more dogs.

THE HOUSE OUTSIDE OF THE CITY

We moved into a house on Riverside Drive just outside the city limits in Painesville Township. Wolfram always chose the houses. I was not involved. This house was on a small lot about one-third the size of the lot on Bank Street and smack up against a neighbor's house. The house had city water in the kitchen, but NO BATHROOM. Maybe this was his problem, I liked bathrooms. He always seemed to be against me in his choices. All his reasons for this move didn't hold water.

Nevertheless, the house was pleasant with a large building in the back, a chicken coop and a dilapidated outhouse that was too dilapidated to use. I had to have a slop jar in the house!

I appreciated the electric power in this house where I could use my electric range and washing machine. It had been over two years since leaving the little cottage on Little Mountain and the first time since leaving that I could use my new electric range. Again a potbelly stove graced the living room. The house was sunny and cheerful despite the old outhouse.

I had been without the blue iris since leaving Thompson. My mother and father had moved from Brooklyn Heights and now lived in Orwell, Ohio. I wondered if my mother took a root of the blue iris with her. We went down to visit Mom and Pop, and I asked her if she had a root of the blue iris. She did, and shared it with me. I planted it in the front yard of the house on Riverside Drive.

Wolfram thought this was a good place to raise dogs, so he bought a Doberman pinscher. He tied him to the clothesline in the back yard. The dog came with an excellent pedigree to be sure, but he was so mean I couldn't let the children play outside. For the first time since our marriage, I was emphatic about getting rid of THAT DOG! He did.

Since we had that nice chicken coop in the back, I thought it would be a good idea to raise chickens. We bought a carton of 100 chicks from the hatchery, and I started to raise them. I did as the directions said, but I didn't realize that the nature of little chicks is to peck the weakest one to death. What a problem, but I did raise about a dozen chicks to maturity. When Marlene heard the familiar cackle of a hen she would run to the coop and watch the egg come out of the chicken.

Some railroad tracks passed through within a quarter mile of the house. One day a hobo who walked the tracks wandered over to our house. He rapped on the back door. I opened it a tiny bit and asked him what he wanted. Behind the door I had my hand on Larry's collar so he wouldn't dash out of the house.

"I want some food," the hobo said.

"All I have in the house for you is a banana." I said.

"I don't want a banana, I want a meal," he said as he pushed on the door to come in and see for himself. I was alone with the children and frightened. I had my hand on Larry's collar and prayed that he knew what to do about the situation. He did, for just as the hobo stepped in I released Larry and the dog lunged at the man. The hobo was so startled that he tried to run away, but the dog kept nipping at his heels and the man knew if he ran the dog would set his teeth in his leg. He walked out of the yard at a slow pace with the dog right at his heels. Saved by an Irish setter!

The business was still growing and it got to the point of needing another man on the truck. My brother Donald came to live with us so he could help Wolfram.

One day I heard screeching of brakes in the street. I looked out of the window only to see Marlene lying in the street, and a car nearby. She had crossed the street to get the newspaper and was hit by a car. She was unconscious.

While Donald called Dr. Stephens, Wolfram and I took her to the emergency room of Painesville Memorial Hospital. The doctor was waiting for us in the emergency room. He quickly examined her entire body. An X-ray showed no broken bones and he diagnosed her as having a concussion. The doctor surmised that she was not actually hit by the car, but the car hit the newspaper and it threw her to the pavement. She was not hospitalized, but we kept her in bed for a few days because she was very disoriented. I cannot begin to describe how I felt when my own child was involved in a car accident.

Marlene would be six years old in the spring and must start school the next fall. We bought some property on the other side of town to build a house. We wanted to be settled in a house of our own before Marlene started school. The property was on Fairgrounds Road in Painesville Township. We paid $10 down on the lot and started to build a garage. We had intentions of living in this building until we could afford to build the rest of the house. My brother Donald helped with the building, along with our friend John Winter.

By this time Wolfram was attending many dog shows, and besides showing his dogs, he was handling a nice Irish setter that he sold to Dora Winter, who was John's mother. I went along with him and tried to interest myself in his dream, but all I could think of was the cost of his hobby when we needed the money for clothes.

By the time September came around, the garage was showing promise of being livable, so I entered Marlene in Mentor Avenue School where she would be a first grader after we moved. I drove her to school every day across town so she would not have to change schools when we were finally settled in our garage home.

We were packing for the move to our home, when I noticed a large bonfire in the back yard. I went out to see what it was all about. Wolfram was tending the fire. "What are you burning?" I asked. "I'm burning all those books you had, we won't have room for them in our house," he answered. Gone is my geometry book, gone is the history book with pictures of the teacher and all the other sketches. My books are gone.

We moved into our garage home in October 1940 with the chickens, dogs and the blue iris, never to move our family around again

CHAPTER 11

OUR OWN HOME

In October 1940 we moved into our garage home. We started our house on nothing but ambition and scrap lumber that Wolfram picked up at the produce market in Cleveland. The lot was 125 feet wide and 600 feet deep; it had been part of a former hay field and it was overgrown with blackberries, thistles and poison ivy, but it was OURS! (Well, almost.) We bought the property with $10 down; the balance was paid with 50 lb. bags of onions 100 lb. bags of potatoes and other produce. The owner of the lot had a son with many children and he was giving this produce to him.

We moved into this tarpaper-covered garage knowing we would be hauling water, but it's ours! I felt that because of all I had gone through, I surely could endure this problem, so I planted the blue iris alongside of our new home.

My brother, Donald dug a 30-foot deep well, but it yielded only enough water to flush the toilet about three times a day, and barely enough to wash ourselves, but not enough to do our laundry. I sent the laundry out and it was returned wet, to save money. I hung it in our small living quarters during the winter months.

Laundromats did not exist. It was unpleasant to live in a place where laundry was hanging all over the house, but this time it was my fault. I desperately wanted to stay put so our children could attend school without changing from one school to another. We moved around too much, sometimes for uncontrollable reasons and sometimes for ridiculous reasons and building this house was the start of settling down.

Wolfram hauled water for drinking, dishes and cooking, in five gallon bottles. Electricity was available, and once again I could use the electric range

We were living in the garage section of our future house with a flat tarpaper covered roof. It was 24 feet square, so there was not much living space. A coal stove graced the center. It was in the dead of winter when Wolfram decided to make an oil heater out of the coal stove. We practically froze until he had time to change it back to coal. Knowing what I know now, we were lucky it didn't blow up.

We only lived here a few months when Donald joined the Navy because of the United States participation in World War II.

Marlene now rode a school bus to school and I joined the Parent Teachers Club. I became very active in the PTC, but was very self-conscious about my clothes. I had bought only one dress since we were married seven years ago. I wore this dress to every meeting, and it was so faded I dyed it a maroon color with disastrous results. I had no other dress, but no one seemed to notice my clothes, and I was elected secretary of the club.

In the meantime, Wolfram built dog kennels in the back of the lot and was attending every dog show and field trial in the area.

Oh, here I go again, isn't this the reason we bought such a large lot? I thought the best thing for me to do was to join him. I went along with him even though the bitterness I felt about the dogs was so deep. I thought it would be best to get acquainted with other dog breeders.

I remember a woman who raised beautiful Skye terriers. Her dogs were perfectly groomed with their hair tied up in rags before the show. I stooped down to admire them, then looked up at the woman to address a remark to her. She smiled down at me and I noticed that she had very few teeth in her mouth and what she did have looked rotten. I saw the neglect of her own body, and surmised that it was because of her hobby.

We were acquainted with a couple who had a daughter about 3 years old. The pretty little girl could scarcely walk because her shoes were too small, but they had champion Doberman pinschers. It made me wonder if the cost of their hobby caused the neglect of their child. Later one of these Doberman pinschers bit and mauled the little girl so badly her face was covered with stitches. Despite this, the parents wouldn't give up the dog because he was a champion. The court stepped in and ordered the dog destroyed.

I was thankful I made Wolfram get rid of his Doberman pinscher. I saw and felt these things so deeply that it instilled more bitterness about raising dogs. It is not my cup of tea.

A year after we moved into our garage home, Audrey contacted rheumatic fever. We knew we had to move out of the damp garage as soon as possible. Every time it rained, water would seep into the garage home; it seemed it was never really dry.

Wolfram started to build the rooms overhead. He worked hard on the house during this time and still conducted the produce business. I helped him in any way I could. I learned how to use a hammer and installed the siding boards where I could reach. It was slow work for me because he wouldn't let me use his electric saw. I doubt if I could have used it, for it, was too heavy for me to handle. I used a handsaw for my work.

Soon we had framed out two rooms, a bathroom and a large hall. When the roof was on, the exterior covered with tarpaper and the windows installed, we moved into these rooms. We climbed a 13-foot ladder on the outside to get into the house. Wolfram had to haul a 5-gallon jug of water up the ladder. Eventually Wolfram built an outside stairway, and installed a coal furnace in the garage area.

Audrey spent a good part of the next two years in bed. When she entered the first grade, the teacher was instructed to exclude her from all exercises and she was not to lift any thing. Marlene took it upon herself to be a watchdog. She reported to me that she saw Audrey carrying her chair up the stairs with the rest of the class. Marlene ran over to her, took the chair from her and carried it up the steps against the teacher's wishes.

I contacted the doctor who suggested that we pull Audrey out of school unless the teacher cooperated with us. The principal settled the matter with the teacher and Audrey was allowed to stay in school. Eventually she recovered from rheumatic fever without any heart defects.

Up to this time, Wolfram had not made any payments to my friends who lent us the money to buy his truck. They wrote us a letter asking for the $176 that they loaned to us, without interest. Wolfram was mad at me because they were MY friends. He said that friends don't do this even though three years had gone by and owning the truck helped him build a profitable business.

I never understood his reasoning, but I insisted that they were right to ask for their money, so he paid off the truck. Because his business had grown, the truck was too small, so it was replaced with a new Dodge truck.

I entered an art course at Lake Erie College in Painesville for modeling figures from clay. These courses made me do some thinking about John Hunting Polytechnic Institute. How can one make figures out of clay not knowing the muscles and shape of the human body? I needed more classes in drawing from life. Lake Erie College did not have this kind of art course.

I was in an office supply store in Painesville where I was deeply engrossed in buying ledgers, when a woman came up to me and said, "Hello, Mrs. Stumpf, and what have you been doing since leaving the estate? Are you still pursuing your art work?"

I looked up and to my surprise it was the millionaire's wife from the estate where Wolfram had been the handyman. She was very gracious to me, and it surprised me to think she knew me, let alone speak to me. I told her VERY briefly about our life since leaving the estate, and that we were building a house. I also admitted that our knowledge of constructing a house was very limited. She talked with me for a while, and when I mentioned that I was contemplating going back to John Huntington Polytechnic Institute for courses in drawing from life, she looked me square in the eye and said, "Why don't you take a course in architecture?"

She probably never knew what that bit of encouragement did for me, but it was she who started the spark to go back to school and change my course to architecture. I didn't have that kind of support to go to a school of higher learning since my art teacher, Paul Ulan had encouraged me. I give all the credit for changing my life to the millionaire's wife, but she never knew what she did.

Freda R. Stumpf

A COURSE IN ARCHITECTURE

In the fall of 1941 I went back to John Huntington Polytechnic Institute to see if my recommendation from Paul Ulan, my high school art teacher, was still in effect. It was, but my course this time was in architecture. This school was known for a good architectural course, for all the instructors were prominent practicing architects in Cleveland.

Wolfram finally agreed with me about going to school because we were making blunders in the building project. My intention was to only stay in school only long enough to help us with our construction project.

I went into the school to enroll and met the head architect who interviewed me for the class. I was surprised when he told me women were not accepted in the architecture classes, then he said that I should sit down and wait so all the architects could consult on my case.

A board of four architects met over the matter and the decision was: inasmuch as the peacetime draft of 1940-41 had taken so many men, it was difficult to fill the classes so they accepted me, a woman. I didn't realize until that moment that it was a detriment to be a woman in this field.

Walter Smith, a former president of the AIA (American Institute of Architects) was my instructor for the first year. Mr. Smith was not only an excellent teacher, he was a peach of a guy, and he made a very distinguished appearance with pince-nez glasses on his nose. The class was three hours long, twice a week, and soon Mr. Smith recommended I enroll in the art class, 'drawing from life' to get a better feel for architectural design. The additional class was the very course I had planned to attend in the first place, so I doubled my classes and came to school an hour earlier

I had long blonde hair at this time; so long I could sit on it. I braided it in two pinwheels over my ears. I probably appeared to be a German girl with my hair like this, so Mr. Smith stood behind me while reciting Siegfried or some other German poetry, in German. I finally confessed to him that I didn't speak German. I told him that I couldn't understand much of what he was saying, but to please keep it up as it sounded so beautiful. He did.

Soon after I started this class, a tragedy struck my family. My father had a bad accident with his truck. He couldn't get his truck started, so he tried to crank it and forgot he had it in gear. He did get the engine started but it moved forward and pinned him up against the barn. He was taken to Fairview Park Hospital in Cleveland. (This is the hospital his father founded.) He was in serious condition with compound fractures in both legs above the knees. One of the legs had to be amputated above the knee and the other was in bad shape, but the doctors were able to save it.

On the nights I went to school I left my home early in the afternoon to visit my father before class, twice a week. He looked forward to seeing me, and one night I stooped down and kissed him and told him I loved him. He cried and said he thought nobody felt that way about him. I did love my father, but it was difficult to get close to him. I think this was the first time I kissed him since I was a child.

My father was bedridden for a year, and the doctors never expected him to get out of a wheel chair, but eventually he was fitted with a wooden leg and walked with a cane. I still have that cane, and now I use it.

On December 7, 1941 the Japanese bombed Pearl Harbor. This event took more men out of the school and two more women were accepted into my class.

During the last semester of this first year I started on the plans for my own home, the home we started to build. My papers averaged 4.8 out of a possible 5. I had the highest grades in class.

Before the first year was over I discovered I loved architecture. I wanted to continue my studies, and prepared to enter school again for the second year. The first year did help us with the construction of our house, and before the year was up I was drawing plans for local contractors.

The college course did a lot more than train me in architecture. My teacher believed in me, and so did the other architects in the school. I had finally come out of my shell. I was a person! I had personhood!

In the fall of 1942 the country was building up its defenses and the Army needed engineers. My teacher, Mr. Smith, joined the Army Corps of Engineers. Now he was Major Walter Smith.

I entered the second year under a new instructor who was more contemporary in his ideas. Mr. Smith leaned more to a colonial style of architecture. The head architect also interested himself in my work, and put in his ideas which were more elaborate, for he designed many of the large churches in Cleveland and elsewhere. These were all excellent architects, but with different design ideas. I wondered about my house design. My plans did turn out to be a typical American farmhouse type of architecture with rubble stone on the first floor, and white siding above. Maybe the design was too elaborate, but the plans were excellent.

During the second year I continued with my house plans, and the teacher made me his assistant. He called me the framing expert. I helped the other students with framing buildings and cabinetwork.

Word came to me during the Christmas season that Walter Smith had passed away with a heart attack. I was shocked and dismayed. This was a person who believed in me, a person who gave me strength to continue in architecture. For the first time I was doing something productive, and he had a big hand in my transformation. He gave me personhood. I lost a friend. I went to the funeral and met the other architects.

When I came back to class in January, the head architect came into my classroom. He came right up to me, put his arm around my shoulder and said, "We all loved him, Freda." Then he walked out of the room. He didn't have to say anymore.

It was during my second year of architecture that I poured out our water problems to my teacher. A waterline was planned for our street, but the residents had been waiting for over two years for the county sanitary engineer to obtain a priority for water pipe from the War Production Board. This was during World War II, and a priority was needed for a civilian project.

My teacher heard me out. Then he drew a deep breath and told me he would help me with the water project. He said it would entail a lot of work on my part, but he made the stipulation that I never reveal to anyone that I was being helped or by whom.

I went to the Lake County Sanitary Engineer. I was someone new on his list of complainants. I told him how desperately we needed water and we had waited for him to get a priority for the pipe for two years. I added that I would like to take over and see what I could do about it.

"Well, what do you think YOU can do about it?" he said.

"I'd like to try," I said.

"Well, if you think YOU can do a better job than I, go ahead," he said with a sneer. He treated me like I was a dumb woman. Oh, oh here goes my personhood.

The sanitary engineer had no idea I intended to do what I did, for I went to the War Production Board in Cleveland, and talked to Mr. Leisa. I found out some startling things. The sanitary engineer had been able to get a priority on cast iron pipe all along, but it seemed he was favoring a company that manufactured cement asbestos pipe, and had a contract with them that could not be broken.

Hmmm, a contract for pipe he legally couldn't buy! What could a person like myself do about it? I took my tale of woe back to my teacher. He smiled and said he found out about it too, but was letting me find it out all by myself. He offered me the service of his lawyer and said he would personally pay him, but first I should go back to the War Production Board.

I did this and Mr. Leisa told me to keep working on the situation. First I must take a petition back to the people on the street, and get specific water problems for each house, then apply for a cast iron water pipe priority. After a lot of work I accomplished my task. The War Production Board granted us the highest priority available for a civilian project.

The Sanitary Engineer called a meeting of all the residents involved in the waterline project. "Inasmuch as it was so easy to get a priority for cast iron pipe," he said, "we must now ask for a priority for cement asbestos pipe.

I was horrified; that man wasn't going to give up, was he? I knew he would never get it, the War Production Board told me so. He also stated that we were $900 short of the necessary funds.

Then I got up and gave my speech. I directed myself to the Sanitary Engineer when I said, "I don't think we should monkey around anymore." I won the argument.

The Sanity Engineer was furious; he had to do what we demanded. The residents had footed the bill for the line; he was fooling around with our money. Then he gave me only 5 days to come up with the extra money or the deal would be called off. He had that right. I again went around to the residents house to house, and picked up the $900 in three days.

I thought everything was settled until I received a phone call from the cement asbestos pipe company. They were suing me for $3000. Now I was REALLY frightened, so I went back to the War Production Board.

Mr. Leisa heard me out and then told me, "stand your ground, dealing with the United States Government is serious business. They approved cast iron pipe and THAT IS WHAT WILL BE PUT IN THE GROUND! It isn't possible to get a priority for any other pipe." Then he assured me that he would use government lawyers to fight the case. I would have no expense whatsoever. The cement asbestos pipe company would actually be suing the United States Government.

I waited until I received another call from the cement asbestos pipe company. I told him the United States Government will defend the case and they should get in touch with the War Production Board. They dropped the suit.

We had water flowing through our pipes just nine months after I started the fight. And the Sanitary Engineer joined the Navy.

I received more from the architecture course than I had ever dreamed possible. The help I received from my teacher was a lot more than backing me up for what I had to do. He let me do my own thing. What better training could a student get than actual experience? I got more out of that course than obtaining the waterline down our street. I got self-confidence, a feeling of self-worth and personhood.

The waterline is in; the monies had to be compensated for. Some residents put in more than their share. The monies would come from future tap-in fees. They elected me as trustee for this work. It took seven years and all the monies were compensated for. Then we were able to turn the waterline over to the county.

While I was going to college, I was my husband's bookkeeper. I left for school about 4 P.M., then came home on the midnight bus. I wrote out the produce orders for the next day, figured out Wolfram's load and produce needs, did whatever bookkeeping was needed and crawled into bed about one or two o'clock in the morning.

Wolfram rose about 4 A.M., and made his own breakfast. I rose about 7 o'clock and got the girls off to school. I continued to be active in the PTC, and was made president of this organization.

I was in my third year of architecture when I learned I was pregnant. I received a lot of flack from Wolfram about this pregnancy. Because I was going to college, he had an idea that the baby was not his. I finished out the year, and the baby was born in Fairview Park Hospital on July 13, 1944. We called him Wolfram Jon, but shortened it to Wolf. He was a nice baby, had black hair about an inch long, and was the spitting image of his father

I went back to John Huntington Polytechnic Institute for my fourth year in architecture, but the pressure was too great and I had to quit college at half term.

While going to college, I had a feeling that Wolfram was feeling subordinate towards me. Another course in the school on Tuesday night should interest him, which was good for he didn't work on Wednesday. He would not consider it because he was too tired, so he formed a dog club that met on Tuesday nights, and he was made president. Well really, this is HIS DREAM, isn't it?

I turned it around again, and every weekend I went along with him to a dog show or field trial. The girls participated in the children's handling class and I took the baby along. I got interested up to the point of wanting to handle a dog myself, but knew it wouldn't work out. This was the feather in Wolfram's hat. I thought it should stay there. The life I was leading was so different from his, but it was what I wanted to do, the same as the dogs were his life.

Wolfram raised lots of dogs, all good pedigree Irish setters. He was showing them and selling them, putting them in field trials and breeding bitches. At one time he had 45 dogs in the kennels. The dog business was getting more expensive. Our only social times were at dog shows or dog clubs. We frequently entertained dog clubs in our home. Dogs, dogs, dogs.

Then Wolfram bought a horse. He built a horse barn for it and from then on it was horses and dogs.

The girls were entered in the horse show classes. I sewed their outfits for the events. Marlene excelled in these classes as she did in the dog shows. One blue ribbon after another. Audrey was more like her mother, and even though she did get ribbons for her efforts, Marlene got the blue.

This was not what her father desired so it caused more conflict. Our life was horses, dogs, horses, dogs......

CHAPTER 12

PART-TIME DRAFTING JOBS

Our home had not been worked on for three or four years. We were living in two small bedrooms and the hall, which was our kitchen. The girl's bedroom was a combination of dining room, bedroom and office. The addition that was to be built on the side at the level of the garage would be a basement, with fireplace in a recreation room, above it, a living room with fireplace, kitchen and dinette. On the second floor were two more bedrooms and a bath. The hole was dug for the basement, but nothing else.

We tried to get a loan to finish the house, but the banks would not lend it to us because the construction was too slow. This angered me. I agree that the construction was too slow. I thought we would get a loan easier if we hired a contractor or a carpenter to finish the house, but Wolfram wanted to do the work all by himself. He did hire a contractor to do the concrete work and a carpenter to do some of the work, but he did almost all the work by himself. These problems got to me and I came down with a stomach ulcer.

I applied for a job designing prefabricated homes in the fall of 1944. The baby was only three months old, but we needed the money to continue with our building program. I got the job and enjoyed the work. I was my own boss. A good woman took care of the baby and girls on the days I worked. This was my first job away from home since I married eleven years ago. Because of the ulcer, I carried a thermos of milk and a box of crackers to work. I ate strained vegetables and milk soup at home. When Wolf was born we bought our first electric refrigerator, now we needed it for my milk. My final assignment for the prefab company was the artwork for their first catalogue.

I free-lanced architectural drawings for several contractors. As soon as the contractor left with the plans, Wolfram took the check because he was short in his checking account.

I received a phone call from one of the contractors, who was having problems with the foundation plans; he asked me to come to the site. In the basement of the house were two men. I asked them where I could find the contractor. They said that they were the men who phoned, there was no problem, and they just wanted to see if a woman draftsman looked like a man. My personhood was attacked and I didn't like it.

In February 1945, World War II took a turn for the better. Germany was retreating. This was good news, not only for the country, but also for our business. It was difficult running a business with war rationing. Potatoes and onions were hard to get, and gasoline rationing hurt the business so badly Wolfram couldn't expand it. The last few years in college I rode the bus because I was unable to get gas stamps. I had four riders to qualify for stamps for a year, and then nothing.

On April 12, 1945 President Franklin Delano Roosevelt died. I was in a record store when I heard it. I had just purchased a classical record, 'Cavalleria Rusticana,' when the storeowner told me that President

Roosevelt had just passed away and that the record I had bought was his favorite melody. I didn't have to play my new recording, for the radio stations had no scheduled programming, and were playing this tune constantly.

Harry Truman was now our President. Germany surrendered to General Eisenhower in the early part of May; and the atomic bomb was dropped on Hiroshima on August 6, 1945. A few days later another was dropped on Nagasaki and by August 14, 1945 Japan surrendered. September 2, 1945 was the end of World War II.

During the summer of 1945, a warehouse was built to house the truck and a cold storage unit with a large area overhead for future storage. When this building was completed the truck was under cover and we had cold storage for the produce.

Late in February 1946, Wolfram came home from his deliveries with a splitting headache. He lay down on the bed and said he would get up and feed the dogs and horses when he got a little rest. He was irrational, and then slept. It didn't seem like a common headache. I asked him how to feed the dogs and take care of the horses. All he said was "I'll do it."

I called Dr. Stephens, who came to the house and said it looked like spinal meningitis. By this time Wolfram was unconscious. The doctor did a spinal tap. When the fluid came out, he looked at me and said, "It is spinal meningitis." A test to positively identify the illness still had to be done at the hospital, and in the meantime the doctor started him on sulfa diazene, then called an ambulance. I rode along in the ambulance when he was taken to Cleveland General Hospital, where they have a building for communicable diseases. At four o'clock in the morning it was confirmed that Dr. Stephens was correct, and they commended him for his early diagnosis.

My twin sister, Louise, cared for Wolf who was about nineteen months old; my mother came to care for the girls who are ten and twelve years old. A friend of my husband took care of the dogs and horses.

I took over Wolfram's produce business and went to market to do the buying at four o'clock in the morning. My husband's brother Carl was helping on the truck. Carl drove the truck and I followed in the car, so I could do the banking and get home early. Many times I drove back to Cleveland to see Wolfram. He was in the hospital for five weeks before he came home, but he was so deranged from the sulfa medication that he became suicidal. I put him in a private hospital to recover.

While Wolfram was in this hospital, I got a call from my twin sister telling me that Wolf was sick. Her doctor said it was probably meningitis, so he was taken to Cleveland General Hospital, where they diagnosed him with erysipelas because he had a mark on his leg that looked suspicious. The mark was a burn he got a few days earlier, but the doctors wouldn't listen to my sister.

My cousin, who was a doctor in Cleveland, said they would accept him in Fairview Park Hospital as soon as Cleveland General Hospital released him. My sister, Elenora, did the transfer for me and the doctor diagnosed his illness as a severe earache. It had been untreated until my cousin took over the case.

Now I was working my husband's business, going to see him in the private hospital as often as I could, and then going into Cleveland to see Wolf. I'd get orders from the store, do the bookkeeping, and take care of the girls, and fall into bed.

My son, Wolf, was released before his father, Wolfram, and my sister and her husband Les, brought him home to me. This was Easter time and

117

the biggest season of the year for the business. My husband's brother Rob lent me $1,000 to help me over the rough spots. I didn't ask for the loan, it was nice to have the money, but I survived without it.

We had no insurance. I paid Wolfram's hospital bills and somebody paid my son's hospital bill at Fairview Park Hospital. I went to the hospital the day before he was released to pay the bill, and was told it was paid in full. To this day I do not know who did it.

I brought Wolfram home from the private hospital. He was not home more than two hours before the wealthy people who sold him Marlene's horse came for their money. How did they know my husband was home, or for that matter, that he was sick?

I did not know that Wolfram still owed them the money for the horse. I told them to take the horse back, but Wolfram kept telling them I had $1,000. The people acted surprised that I was holding back, but Wolfram pressured me until I wrote out a check for $850 to pay for the horse.

All this happened so quickly that I was left reeling. I had very carefully paid all the bills without dipping into the $1,000 and Wolfram hadn't been home more than a few hours, and it was gone.

In 1946 we laid the foundation for the last addition to the house. The contractor made a four-inch mistake, which made the building out of square. Wolfram laid ten floor joists before he discovered the mistake. Wolfram should have overhung the joists one foot in the dining area, but didn't do it, so now there are two mistakes.

I suggested that he pull the joists and square off, and then correct the error in the dining area at the same time. He refused to pull the joists and instead of squaring off, he continued the error in the whole building, even the stairs; and blamed the contractors for the whole mess. He never built the bay window in the dining area. My suggestions were never taken. I had no personhood. It seemed all these problems went against the training I had in college.

In September 1947 I offered my home as a meeting place for my church group in June 1948. I thought that surely Wolfram would have the living room finished by this time. I hoped he would at least put in the finished stair steps. But the months dragged on and nothing was done. The week before the meeting I cleaned the living room and carried out all the lumber and carpenter's tools that had lain on the living room floor for two years. The night before the meeting Wolfram decided to finish the stairs, and messed up the house again. There is no communication with Wolfram, none whatsoever. He yelled at me, "You wanted me to do this and nagged and nagged about it, so I'm doing it." And he did, but of course he couldn't finish the stairs because all the steps were out of square. I cleaned up sawdust, plaster and dust with a vacuum, then dusted all the furniture all over again before the women came for the luncheon the next day.

The first floor exterior of the house was stone rubble. Wolfram did a beautiful job of cutting and setting the stone. He left it in an unfinished state for many years with scaffolding in front of it. This stone work was started before our son was born, but it was my son who finally helped him finish it. It seemed that our house never made much progress after the plastering was finished; but he did make progress in the dog business, for now he was an AKC judge of Irish setters.

One of his first judging jobs was judging a show on Kelley Island, off the shores of Sandsusky, Ohio. To get to this island you took a ferry, flew in on an old Ford Trimotor Plane or chartered a private plane. Wolfram opted for the ferry, which was well on its way to the island when we arrived.

My husband was the judge: he had to be at the preshow banquet that evening.

We went back five miles to the airport and chartered a plane. We piled into this plane with an Irish setter and a Beagle hound. The pilot asked Wolfram to sit in the back with the dogs to keep them quiet. I sat in front with the pilot. This was the first plane ride for both of us.

Up we went and I could see the beautiful islands in Lake Erie below us. A plane ride wasn't so bad; I was thoroughly enjoying it. The pilot asked me if he should buzz a taxi. I saw the little phone hanging by the pilot so I told him to buzz a taxi.

That is not what the pilot meant! He buzzed the taxi driver's house with the airplane. The horizon went up on one side and then up on the other side and we were getting close to the ground. Wow! Are we going to crash? No, he just swooped down to buzz the taxi driver's house to signal him that he had a fare. My legs were rubber, but the dogs didn't seem to mind it at all.

The island is full of rabbits and pheasants, which are a little different from the usual habit of pheasants. These pheasants don't fly, they run between the bushes on the ground. The rabbits are everywhere. A Beagle hound is supposed to track rabbits, but this hound also was a bit different, he pointed pheasants just like his buddies, the Irish setters. A rabbit came out of a bush and bumped into the beagle's nose, but he just kept right on pointing a pheasant!

Both Wolfram and I saw it happen. I thought the situation was hilarious, but Wolfram was disgusted. He saw no humor in the event. We took the ferry back to the mainland that night.

I am finding it hard to write about these mid 1940 years. They seemed so mixed up that it is hard for me to unscramble them, but then those years were mixed up for me at the time. We were living like the poor people we were, but still giving an outward appearance to other people in the dog and horse crowd that we could afford all this.

It was about this time I asked Wolfram for money to buy boots for the girls His reply was to charge them at the department store. I told him that I didn't think they would accept any more charges because he owed money on the old bills. I suggested that he charge his dog feed instead. He replied that he never charges dog feed; that money comes out of his pocket before anything else.

Now the truth comes out. I was drawing house plans to be sure, but was never able to keep the money because Wolfram always needed it. He was short in his checking account. I was not winning at anything. He was accusing me of nagging, nagging. I would say he was right on that account, but where he was concerned, I had no personhood.

To make a marriage work, there must be communication. It was totally lacking in our marriage.

We took a trip to Kentucky to see Mammoth Cave and the Lincoln Memorial, which impressed me so much when I was young, because President Lincoln's cabin is encased in this building. We stopped off in Lexington to see horse farms. It was interesting until Wolfram saw a Palomino colt.

Wolfram had $175 for the trip, but he gave the owner of the horse $115 of it for the colt. We still had not been to Mammoth Cave or the Lincoln Memorial. Our car was a station wagon and we had a tent to connect to the back, so it only cost us 50 or 75 cents a night to park it for the night in a camping ground.

One night my husband opted for a tree trunk instead of an outhouse. The Irish setter that we took along probably thought the spot smelled like his owner, so he rolled in it. The dog got a bath before we went any further, and I didn't help with the bath.

The children did see Mammoth Cave, Crystal Cave and the Lincoln Memorial.

Our marriage was still having difficulties. Wolfram and I were growing very distant from each other. I didn't like to see this happen. I thought it was time we took our honeymoon. Wolfram agreed to a weekend in the Pocono Mountains in Pennsylvania. I made reservations for a weekend, and my mother said she would take care of the children.

Mom had already arrived when Wolfram decided that instead of going to the Poconos we were going to Kentucky to pick up the colt he bought. He said to cancel the reservations, we were going to Kentucky. At seven o'clock that evening, he started to build an enclosure on his trailer for the horse. He finished it at midnight, and we started for Kentucky. In the middle of the night the trailer broke away from the car and rolled into a ditch. Wolfram worked on the repairs for a few hours, then we were on our way again.

We finally got to Kentucky, picked up the horse and came right back. That was my honeymoon, Now another horse was added to the other animals. I'm trying to figure out how this helped our marriage (if it did) but it sure shattered my honeymoon plans.

The next animal Wolfram bought was a Shetland pony. It was in the dead of winter, and he thought our six-year-old son should learn how to ride a horse. It was 15 degrees above zero that afternoon and the snow was two feet deep when he put Wolf on the pony and sent him into a large field.

Wolf was not dressed for this severe weather; his boots were hand-me-downs from his sisters and too large for him. I didn't know my husband did this or I would have 'butted in' again. Wolfram knew that the pony wasn't the best mannered pony and he threw kids off at any chance he had. Wolf was out in the middle of the field when the pony threw him. He lost his boots. He yelled and screamed, but his father did not concern himself with the screams, and instead of examining the situation with his son, he came running into the house in a frenzy.

"The pony threw Wolf and is running away."

"Where is Wolf?"

"He's Ok. I can hear him. Where is Audrey? We have to take the car and find the pony."

"But where is Wolf?"

"Oh shut up, I told you he is OK."

"But where did the pony throw him?"

"In the field, he landed in the snow. He's OK."

"Did you bring him in?"

"Shut up. Audrey are you ready? We have to get the pony because he ran away."

Audrey came down the stairs on a run with her coat. She rushed past her father, then saw that Wolf was about 100 feet from the house. He was crying for help. Audrey rushed out to him, but her father caught her and tried to prevent her, because Wolf had to learn to be a man.

Audrey must have broken away from him, because I ran to Wolf and Audrey was ahead of me and picked him up. She rushed him into the house. He had no shoes or boots on. Audrey and I put him on my bed, and after a quick examination, we saw that he had frozen feet.

I phoned the doctor. By the time he got here, Wolf's toes were turning black. The doctor avoided Wolfram, and told me that it was possible to save most of the toes, but one. He had doubts whether it could be saved. He prescribed some new medication that had just come on the market. It increased the blood circulation.

I can't begin to tell you about the excruciating pain that Wolf went through. Audrey and I sat by his side constantly while his toes started to turn pink, all but one. I watched that toe like the doctor asked me to, and finally it too, turned pink. He wouldn't loose the toe

Late that night Wolfram came home with the pony. No one cared about the details of catching it. I just looked at him and said, "Get rid of that pony, and don't you dare to put another child on his back." I walked away from him. All the love I might have had for him at this time, left.

Audrey had a 'T' puzzle that someone had given to her in school. She had it sprawled out on the living room floor when her father came in the room. He looked at the puzzle and said, "I know how to do that puzzle let me show you."

Audrey said she wanted to figure it out by herself. Wolfram got mad and pushed her aside and said he would show her. Audrey said "No."

I asked him to let her do it by herself. He yelled at me and said "You are always butting in, I'm going to show her how to do that puzzle."

He threw Audrey on the couch and started to beat her and then started to choke her. I did all I could with this 220-pound man. I hit him on his head but it did no good. I tried to choke him, but my hands would not go around his thick neck, so I used a chokehold and dug my fingernails deep in his neck. He let her go and then cried and said, "I wonder why I do this?"

I had no answer. I do believe I should have divorced him at that time, but didn't do it. I have always believed I made a mistake. I didn't believe in myself enough to go through it. Divorce at that time seemed unacceptable; one believed in the marriage vows: for richer or poorer, in sickness or in health, for better or worse and a vow to obey."

I started to do my own thing. With my college training I was improving my love for architecture by taking the car and visiting historic buildings in the area.

I took the girls to the Cleveland Museum of Art, and to Severance Hall to hear the Cleveland Orchestra. Later in life these trips to Severance Hall had a definite effect on my daughters. They both took lessons from members of the Cleveland Orchestra; Marlene with her trombone and Audrey with her cornet. Both were good players, but it was Audrey who excelled this time for she was awarded a scholarship for a summer course in music at Kansas State University; an experience that she'll never forget.

Wolfram and I are drifting apart.

CHAPTER 13

OUR LIFE CHANGES

In 1947 I was president of the Parent Teachers Club in Mentor Avenue School. We had a nice sum in our treasury. The club decided to inspect the kitchen and look at the range, and the pots and pans that the cooks were complaining about. The cooks were right about the equipment, especially the range. It was in bad shape. We had enough money for the pots and pans, but not enough for an eight-burner, two-oven range.

I was elected to go to the Painesville Township school board for help. Little did I know what I was getting into when I went to the school board. They were very gracious to me and finally said they would buy the big range, if the club would buy the pots and pans. After the range was installed, I went back to them to thank them for the range.

The meeting was overrun with so many people that they had to go across the hall to a courtroom. By the time I got in the courtroom, the only chairs left were in the jury box. I sat near a local businessman.

The crowd was here because they heard about the school board's plans to build a new high school. We had no high school and our 200 students were sent to Painesville City or Mentor high schools. I had a daughter in

Mentor high school. The crowd didn't think that 200 students were enough to build our own high school, even though our six grade schools were overcrowded. The township was growing faster than the city and our students were forcing both Painsville and Mentor to increase the size of their high schools. The school board thought it was time we had our own high school. (Incidentally Don Shula, the famous football coach was one of our students attending Painesville City high school.)

This was the first time I heard about the building plans. I listened to these people. They were very angry. As I sat in the jury box, I reflected back on my own high school. We were in a tax-rich district, and so was this. The high school I attended had an enrollment of only 40 students with an excellent program. Out of my own graduating class of 14 members, eleven of us went on to higher education. My thoughts went back to this crowd; many of them were personal friends. I could see that the crowd thought I was one of them, and so did the school board. I felt like I was in the middle of a disturbance that I knew nothing about. On a quick assessment of the situation, I had the feeling that these people were wrong. We had to start somewhere, and in my mind 200 students wasn't too shabby.

By this time the crowd was ranting and yelling and things were getting out of hand. I couldn't stand it any longer.

I rose and was given the floor. "I want you, the school board, to know that I am not with these people," I said. "I came here to thank you for the new range you installed in the Mentor Avenue kitchen. I had not heard of your plans to build a new high school until tonight. I graduated from a high school that had an enrollment of only 40 students. I see nothing wrong with the education I received." That is all I said, then sat down.

127

The businessman sitting near me jumped the jury box rail and ran out of the room. Another went out and another and another until only a handful of people were left.

I was utterly amazed! I had no idea that I had the power to make such an impact. It frightened me for I realized that I lost some friendships, but I will always say exactly what I think.

I attended every school board meeting for the next year to give them encouragement to continue, despite such high odds; but the prospect was shaky.

I was appointed to a committee to serve the school board to help pass the bond issue for a new high school. We went door to door, wrote letters to the editor, made speeches at school functions; the bond issue passed. I was asked to make the groundbreaking speech. It was raining and the grounds were a mass of mud, only a handful of people attended, but the spirit was there.

In December a school board member resigned because of failing health, and I was asked to serve out his term. I refused the appointment because I didn't have a complete college education.

John R. Williams, the County Superintendent, told me a college education was not considered; they wanted someone with common sense. I accepted and held the position for eight years. (Mr. Williams was a former Speaker of the House in the Ohio State Legislature.)

The new high school was going up, then the progress slid to a stop! The Diamond Alkali plant that supplied the area with cement was on strike. It affected the building progress severely; the foundation could not be poured, the concrete blocks weren't manufactured, and even if we could get the blocks, mortar could not be made, and in fact, nothing could be built.

The workers who were department heads of the Diamond Alkali Company did not strike, but no one could get past the strikers to supply them with food. It was Wolfram who drove his truck past the strikers to supply them with food. The strike was eventually settled, but weeks went by and still no concrete was supplied to the school construction.

Wolfram called the CEO of the Diamond Alkali Company and asked him to send cement to the high school project.

The cement started to roll out for the high school. The mixing plant, the cement block plant and the contractor received all the cement they asked for, if the needs of the high school were met first. A salesman for the concrete block plant asked me if I knew which one of the school board members had the pull to do this. I took the 'fifth.'

The strike did set the project back so much that we put the opening date to the middle of October. Then the contractor started to drag his feet. He was using the strike as his excuse. We had given him that time; he had no excuse. He was told that the school would open in October and we were holding him to that date. The contractor didn't think we would go through with it.

The night before the opening of the new high school, about thirty people went into the school and cleaned plaster from the floors, swept the whole building out and threw trash out the windows. By that time we were so mad, we threw his sawhorses out the window.

He knew he had been given preference on the concrete, and so did we. He had no excuse for the delay.

The contractor was furious when he came on the job the next day. The school was full of kids, and he had to go looking for his saw horses. He finished the school working around kids.

Two years later we held our first graduation with 54 students in the class. My daughter, Marlene, was one of them.

I gave a speech in front of 900 people and presented diplomas with another board member whose son graduated in the same class.

Riverside High School is located on Riverside Drive and across the street from the house where I tried to raise chickens.

Within a few years this school was at capacity, and we added a new wing on the north side. It filled again, so we built a new Junior High School to the south of it. We built additions to 5 elementary schools and built a new elementary school. I was appointed finance chairman and signed bills amounting to over a million dollars a year.

Bronze plaques were installed in the entryways of the schools with the school board names on them. Years later when this was all forgotten, my granddaughter, Diana, told her mother (my daughter Marlene) that she saw my name on a bronze plaque in the junior high school, and tried to tell her classmates that it must be her grandmother. They didn't believe her.

I wrote a note to Diana and said that it was indeed her grandmother, and signed the paper. That shows that even though your name is on a bronze plaque, it is quickly forgotten. Incidentally, it is still there.

The Lake County Fair Board and the County Commissioners thought it a good idea to get harness racing in the fairgrounds, just about a mile down the road from my house.

We had a problem; horses drank water, lots of it, and the racetrack was constantly watered down. Our home was on a hill at the end of the waterline. This was the waterline that I worked so hard to get during the war. Now we had no water on a daily basis for eight hours at a time, and the racing went on for 48 days. The residents gathered to fight for our water.

A big turning point involved my son Wolf. In our bathtub was a portable shower hose connected to the faucet. Wolf drew his bath water through this hose. He jumped into the tub as it was filling with water. He had himself all soaped up when the water in the tub started to recede.

"Mom, the water is going down instead of up," he yelled.

"Close the drain," I answered."

"It is closed."

I ran up the stairs and picked up the hose, it was suctioning water instead of pouring out water. I called the water department and talked to the manager, Mr. Bowman.

"You must install a check valve or something to prevent this from happening," I said." He laughed at me when he said, "What you are telling me is impossible."

I talked to the race track officials. I begged them to help me by drawing water for the racetrack only in the night hours. They agreed to do this, but didn't.

We suffered through the first year of harness racing and nothing was done to improve the situation. The next year the residents met to weigh the possible options in solving the problem. We started with a 'letter to the editor' campaign, which I think did more to arouse interest than anything else we did. Other people were concerned with gambling, water shortage, noise, and fly infestation. The attendance at our meetings increased, and we decided that the only way to solve the problem was to get the racing syndicate out of the county.

We had no cooperation from the county officials, the fair board or other officials, so we decided to put the horse racing issue on the ballot in the fall.

Others joined the group who were more knowledgeable about legal matters, so they took over.

The election board said we needed 3500 signatures to get the issue on the ballot. We had over 3500 signatures and turned them over to them. The election board threw them out because we had too many. TOO MANY? We went over the heads of the local government and took the issue of 'too many' signatures to the Seventh District Court in Ohio. By this time the Cleveland newspapers were running stories about our problem. Wolfram had a friend in the dog business, who that helped us. He was a prominent reporter for the Cleveland Plain Dealer.

Under this pressure the election board put the issue on the ballot. Then found reason to take it off the ballot. On again, off again, but we kept on working with the Seventh District Court. The New Jersey Syndicate pulled out of the fairgrounds before it came up for vote.

In the winter of 1951, my brothers and sisters helped us finish an apartment in the warehouse for my mother and father.

Pop said he'd like to raise tomatoes on our vacant land behind the doghouse and horse barns. Wolfram had the land plowed and fitted in preparation for the project. My father was 73 years old and fitted with a wooden leg, but he set plants with the help of Wolf, who was eight years old. He gave Wolf a silver dollar as a souvenir of the first dollar he ever earned. Wolf kept this silver dollar in his pocket for many years and I think he still has it. Grandpa and grandson became very close friends.

My husband was very good to my parents and helped them in many ways. He helped with the heavy work in the tomato patch and then marketed the tomatoes at harvest time.

While this was going on, I built up a good business drawing house plans for building contractors. I needed better lenses for my glasses and had to buy my first bifocals. I told the optician I worked with large sheets of paper. The bifocals he made were tiny. I refused them, then the optician said, "Those bifocals lenses are large enough for any housewife." My personhood was taken away from me. I gave the glasses back to him, and told him to make them as I requested.

In 1952, Marlene earned an art scholarship and was scheduled to attend Kent State University. The scholarship helped with the tuition, but we needed more money for books and living expenses. The money I was making was not enough.

As the weeks went by, I was getting uneasier about the lack of money for college. Wolfram said not to worry about it, but I knew it wasn't available. I decided I would have to get a job to help put Marlene through college. An ad in the local paper looked good. A hydraulic valve company wanted a draftsman who could do artwork. I called for an appointment.

The president of the company interviewed me. The company, which had been in business for only a few years, was in need of a hydraulic valve catalog. A person was needed to draw technical drawings of valves, charts, graphs and circuits. The valve he showed me was so small it fit in the palm of my hand. I shook my head.

"I draw homes: there is no comparison." I said.

"I know nothing about mechanical things, let alone hydraulics." I continued.

"I know how to construct a house, frame it and design cabinet work. I don't think I can do it," I said.

"I will teach you in the first three weeks of your employment," He answered.

"I had very little experience in inking drawings."

"I will teach you."

"I can't set up a catalog for publication."

"I will teach you."

I refused the job. I thought hard about that job for three days. Finally the challenge got to me and I called the president and asked him if the job was still available.

"Come right over to the office." he said, "I want to talk with you." I went over to his office and he hired me.

"Report for work on Monday."

"Could we make it Tuesday, I must take my daughter to Kent State University for enrollment on Monday."

"Already you are too busy to work, "he said

I drove Marlene to Kent State on Sunday afternoon and started to work for Fluid Controls on Monday morning.

PART III

CHAPTER 14
MY CAREER

Don Stark, the president of Fluid Controls, did what he said he would do; he taught me mechanical drafting in three weeks. Then he taught me how to ink my drawings. The president, an excellent engineer, was also a fine draftsman. I could not have had a better instructor, for he knew if I was off by 100th of an inch.

Fluid Controls manufactured hydraulic valves and was only 3 years old: we would be making the first catalog. My job consisted of making pictures of the valves and pertinent data, order typesetting, and do layout work to complete the catalog.

The artwork I was doing was technical illustration. I felt a need for more instruction in this field, so went back to John Huntington Polytechnic Institute to study industrial illustration, two evenings a week.

I was 39 years old when I started this job and it was my first full-time employment. The year was 1951, Wolf was in grade school, Audrey was in high school and Marlene was enrolled in Kent State University. I thought having this job would solve the family's money problem. Not so, Wolfram took my paycheck as soon as I came home with it, because he needed it for his overdrawn checking account. It was not long before he came to the plant on payday to pick up my check.

Wolfram's dog activities increased so much since I was working, that it was costing as much for his dog hobby as it did to send Marlene to college.

It was difficult to pay for Marlene's college expenses. Nothing was working out; I stopped giving him my paycheck.

Marlene married her high school sweetheart, who was also attending Kent State University, during their first year in the university.

When the catalog was completed I had expected to be laid off, but the president asked me to stay on as his assistant and head the drafting room. I was an employee directly responsible for the accuracy of prints that were used in the plant for the manufacture of valves. The next step was to develop ads for industrial magazines.

The company was sending the employees who had responsible jobs to Fenn College in Cleveland for a course in Industrial Hydraulics. I was the only woman in the group and the men in the plant refused to take the course with a woman. This was the first time I experienced discrimination in the work force.

Mr. Stark told me about the problem and then eliminated me, but promised to give me the course in the future. A new engineer was hired, and we went together for the next session. Maybe the guys were right. I was the only woman in the class of 57 students enrolled in the Industrial Hydraulics class. It didn't seem to bother the engineer.

My participation in class was good, I learned things about hydraulics, but the engineer who went with me dropped out because he left the company for greener pastures. Before he left, he tried to talk me into taking a job with the United Shoe Company. He said it was an excellent company to work for, and he could get me in the company by his good references.

How could I move to Boston? I had a husband and three children. It was impossible for me to do this, but it was a temptation. I was perfectly happy with my job at Fluid Controls, but it gave my personhood a boost.

I finished the hydraulics course by traveling the forty miles to Cleveland by myself. The hydraulics class was located in one of the upper floors of a skyscraper at Fenn College. On the last day of class, I entered the elevator with some male students. As soon as I came in the men started to yell at me.

"Well, are you satisfied?"

"Do you think you learned anything?"

"Who do you think you are anyway?"

"Are you looking for a man?"

These yellow-bellied asses knew this was the last day of class and a report to the teacher couldn't hurt them. Nevertheless, the altercation frightened me. I was a woman alone in an elevator full of angry men.

With a forced smile I said, "I came to this college to learn about hydraulics, and that's just what I did." Then I shut up and let them continue their accusations. Why was I being treated like this? I certainly came to the college to learn. What was the reasoning behind all this taunting? Did they feel so threatened by a woman in this field that it took an elevator full of men to harass a lone woman who had no means of escape?

When I emerged from the elevator I was shaking with fright. I walked over to the pay phone booth to hide from the men and to give them time to get their cars out of the parking lot. I didn't want another altercation like the one in the elevator. I was worried about physical injury to me and perhaps damage to my car if I followed them out to the parking lot.

While in the phone booth I tried to make a long distance call to Wolfram, but there was no answer. I was sure he was outside feeding his dogs, so I tried again and again. Each time I hung up, I got my money back plus a quarter and a few dimes. I called so many times that I had a bundle of money, and was beginning to feel guilty about it. I never did get my husband, but the process got my mind off the altercation in the elevator, so that I was in better spirits.

My final grades were sent to the company. The president brought the grade report into the drafting room. He had a big smile on his face when he said that I got 'B' in the course. I could hardly believe it! The men in the plant were wrong about me, and so were the men in the elevator.

Everyone in the company of 35 employees brown-bagged their lunch because of a short thirty-minute lunch period. We all sat around two long tables. Mr. Stark always sat at the head of a table when he was at the plant. He came into the lunchroom on the day I got my 'B'grade with a big smile on his face. Oh, oh, I thought, he has something up his sleeve. He took his place at the head of the table and then arose and said, "I have an announcement to make." He asked the men from the shop one by one to say what his grade was in the hydraulics course at Fenn College. As each gave his grade I sat in horror, for not one grade was above a 'C.' Then to make matters worse, the president said to the men, "I want each of you to know that Freda's grade was a 'B.' He really knew how to dig these men, they had it coming, although it didn't do much for my popularity with them. In fact it did the opposite. Mr. Stark gave me personhood: I was somebody.

I didn't realize that I was an odd ball, or that it would be so hard working with men. Eleven years had gone by since I was the first woman accepted in the architectural class. The architects who accepted me in their classes played an important role in my life. Do you suppose that I was the first woman in the hydraulics class? I don't know.

Mr. Stark laid a valve on my drafting table one day and said, "We've been having trouble with this valve on and off for two years. The piston is hanging up. I want you to study all the engineering drawings, then make a blow-up ten times size to study the tolerances."

I reported back that the tolerances were Ok, and I saw no reason for the piston to hang up. "Now go into the shop and study the manufacture of the valve," he said, "go into every phase of the manufacturing procedure and be sure to study the jig." (A jig locates the drilled holes in the body of the valve.)

The first thing I did was to pick up the jig to measure the drilling for the holes. The plant superintendent, who had received a 'C' grade in the hydraulics course, was furious. "The jig is OK, you don't need to inspect it," he said.

I took the jig away from him and started to measure the hole locations. The first hole I measured was the one close to the piston that was hanging up. I found the error; the hole was off by 1/32 if an inch. The superintendent's hand shook as he was moving the ruler back and forth and denying any error. He was trying to prove that it wasn't so, but he knew and so did I that the jig was wrong at this hole. The piston was hanging up on the hose nipple that was screwed into the hole.

It was announced at lunch that Freda was given a new title: 'Junior Engineer of Tolerances.' A raise in pay didn't come with it, so it didn't mean much to me.

Mr. Stark almost fired me one day. I was working with the owner of a mining machine company. He was a practical joker and reversed the 'push' and 'pull' signs on the drafting room door. A salesman came through the door and pushed when he should have pulled. He looked at me and I could see that he thought I changed them. He turned around and went right back to report it to Mr. Stark.

Before Mr. Stark took the mining machine owner out to lunch, they both came into my room." Freda, you must know who changed the signs on the door." Of course I knew. The man was standing right alongside him.

"Someone could get their arm cut on the door with the signs reversed," he said, "now who was it?"

"Now Don, you wouldn't want me to be a tattletale, would you?"

"If you don't tell me by two o'clock this afternoon, the consequences will be serious."

"Well, I hope the guy I'm protecting buys me a box of chocolate covered cherries for keeping quiet."

I never got the chocolate covered cherries, but the boss didn't fire me either. The guilty person must have confessed over lunch.

An addition was to be built on the plant. Mr. Stark said that with my training in architecture, he thought I was capable of drawing the plans. The first phase was the employees' parking lot. I drew the plans and a bulldozer was hired to do the work. I was to supervise the bulldozer operator.

Mr. Stark gave me personhood when he did this, for the men in the shop wanted the supervising job. The bulldozer operator did exactly as I asked him to; I had no problem with him. The men in the shop lost precious time by standing in the open door to watch me, and Mr. Stark let them.

Aluminum bars would be stored in the new addition. They were 14 feet long and special made for the company. To make sufficient space for the bars, I moved the roof beam over one foot. The beam would be 'off center.'

The contractor, who was a personal friend of Mr. Stark, was sure that a woman knew nothing about roof beams and without asking about the 'problem', he placed the roof beam 'on center.' I was working only 15 feet away from him; it would have been easy for him to discuss it with me.

Mr. Stark and I weren't aware of what he done until the aluminum bars were put in place. Mr. Stark was furious, but not at me. He was angry with his friend the contractor for not following the plan. Again it was a man who thought a woman didn't have any brains. I lost my personhood.

My daughter, Marlene, was pregnant and would be making me a grandmother for the first time. I was in the maternity section of a dress shop buying her a dress.

Unbeknownst to me a toolmaker from the hydraulic valve plant was in the store, watching me buy the dress.

By some fluke, I wore a new dress to work the next day. Noontime came and during lunch the toolmaker got up and said he had an announcement to make.

"Mr. Stark, did Freda tell you that she was going to have a baby? I saw her in a store buying a maternity dress."

I sat quietly chuckling to myself. I had just told Mr. Stark that morning that I was to be a grandmother. I turned to the man and said, "Now why do you have to blurt out everything you think you know?"

Mr. Stark didn't smile, or maybe he did inside, but he took his time in answering, then addressed the toolmaker, "Freda was probably buying the dress for her daughter." The toolmaker tried to get me fired by informing Mr. Stark of my condition. In those days a woman would be fired if she were pregnant. He was another guy who got a 'C' in the hydraulics course. One by one, these men tried to take my personhood away from me, but they never seemed to win their fight.

I felt that my income should be invested, or else it would be spent with nothing to show for it. I bought a 120-acre farm. It was a beautiful piece of farmland with the back acres overlooking the Grand River.125 feet below the bank. These acres were densely wooded with oak, birch and a few second growth chestnuts. Wolfram and I planted small evergreen trees for future Christmas tree sales.

Mr. Stark came out to the farm with his wife and agreed, it was a good buy. We entertained many friends and relations with picnics and it was good for hikes or just sitting.

Wolfram organized field trials for dogs, and at times my farm wasn't so private. A large Irish setter field trial was held on the farm. I drove to the farm to see what it was all about. The farm was buzzing with activity. Dogs, refreshment stands, horses, horse trailers, special trucks equipped with dog kennels, and big cars, little cars and lots of people with lots of dog talk.

I wandered about for a while to find someone I might know, but they were all strangers. When I tried to be friendly and talk to somebody, the conversation only led to the action in the field, and Wolfram was very busy. To avoid the contestants, I walked along the banks of a creek to our Christmas tree field, which was off limits for the trial. I was stooped down examining a little tree, when a man on horseback came galloping toward me at high speed.

He was a field trial judge. He was yelling at me an ordering me off the premises. I tried to tell him I owned the farm and that he was off limits with his horse, and that he was trampling the little trees. He wouldn't listen to me; he just screamed and hollered at the top of his voice. I couldn't out-holler him so went back to find Wolfram. Whoops! There goes my personhood again.

Wolfram was as angry as I was about the incident; especially because the judge was off-limits and trampling the little trees. This was the last field trial that was held on the farm and it was Wolfram's decision.

In 1955 I bought my first new car. I owned a thirteen-year-old Plymouth when I started to work for Fluid Controls. The salesman gave me $600 trade-in for it on a new Buick. I casually asked the salesman how much he would get for the old car when he sold it. I guess he was trying to make the sale look good, for he said all he could get out of that old car was $15. I went into my purse and took out $15 and bought the car back again. I gave it to Audrey who was attending Hiram College.

With the new car came another problem. Wolfram wants to take it to dog shows and field trials. I should have been smarter and foreseen the problem, and given him the old car. I told him I didn't want a dog on the seats of the new car, but if he fixed the trunk so he could haul a dog in there, it would be OK with me.

Wolfram designed a cage of heavy screening in the trunk of the car and extended an iron strap to the lock so he could lock the dog inside. I told him it was nice, but then a thought struck me. When we had the old wooden station wagon, the exhaust came through the window in the back when it was open. I was afraid the dog would be asphyxiated. Wolfram agreed with me, so he suggested that he get in the trunk and I lock him in.

"Drive down the road about a mile," he said, "come back and open the trunk as soon as possible." This I did, well almost. I drove down the road and came back into our yard only to see a stranger standing alongside his car waiting for someone. I stopped the car and the man ran to me.

"Is your husband home?"

"Yes he is," I replied.

"Well, I knocked at the back door and no one answered, and then I went around to the front door, and no one answered. I walked into the barn and no one was there; I even peaked into the shop and garage. If he is at home, where is he?"

By the time the man got this far describing his problem, I was extremely worried about Wolfram. I heard no sound coming out of the trunk. Was he asphyxiated? I swung my car door open in such a hurry that I almost knocked the man down. I got out of the car, unlocked the trunk and Wolfram jumped out!

A surprised look came over the man's face as he glanced first at me and then at Wolfram. I thought the best thing to do was to say nothing, so I walked into the house. How could one explain something like that? Wolfram acted nonchalant about it and gave no explanation either. The man was selling insurance and never came back. Maybe he thought he had a good reason.

Wolfram always had a yen to own a fruit and vegetable market. He kept the wholesale business and made a big investment in the new store, which was an open space with a butcher. He was finding items missing and could only surmise the teenage sons of the butcher helped themselves, especially to chocolate milk, which was always missing. I tried to tell Wolfram to build a partition, but he was afraid to hurt the butcher's feelings.

One Sunday as we were passing through the town, we stopped in the store and caught the butcher in Wolfram's office rummaging around. The butcher acted nonchalant about it and made a weak excuse. At that point I would have demanded a partition, but Wolfram did nothing about it. After a year in this business, it failed. Wolfram was $10,000 in debt. He owed the property owner $2000 in back rent, and he put a lien on my farm. Wolfram told me it was my fault because I encouraged him to go into the retail produce business.

We were in a desperate financial condition. The hydraulic course gave me knowledge to broaden my responsibilities, but I wasn't paid enough for them. I was designing valve bodies, and made my own hydraulic circuits for the catalog. I was engineering librarian and had set up the library. I was head of the drafting room, technical illustrator and designer for the catalog. I formulated the mailing list for distribution and designed ads to be put in the industrial magazines. I knew I wasn't getting paid enough for all this, and it took a financial condition to make me realize it. Up till then I was thoroughly enjoying my work, but the fact that the pay was too low never entered my mind

I never had a raise as long as I was on the payroll of this company. I asked Mr. Stark for a raise, which he promptly refused. He said that he eventually would give me raises. But they would never total more than $25.00 a month more than my present salary because I was woman, and women don't get paid as much as men.

Then to add fuel to the fire, he said, "Why do you think I have so many women working in the plant as toolmakers and machinists? I pay them half as much as I pay the men and the work they do is just as good as the men's work."

I was never aware of this discrimination. I was shocked! I lost my personhood again and so did the women who worked in the plant. And this time from a man I really admired for all he had done for me, especially standing up for me in the hydraulic course, guiding the bulldozer and finding the problem with the jig. And now he was using discrimination against me. I was appalled with it all. I felt like he was deliberately using me to save himself a few dollars.

I rarely saw my paycheck; Wolfram always needed it. It seemed the harder I worked, we still got nowhere financially. It was hard to continue the payments on the car and the farm. I grew frustrated with Mr. Stark and Wolfram. I was close to a nervous breakdown. Mr. Stark put me on a pedestal, and then deflated me to save the company a few dollars.

I went to my doctor for my depression. He gave me shots and worked with me for a while, then told me that he had others from the same company that had the same problem. He advised me to quit my job. The money I was making was badly needed at home. The visits to the doctor dragged on another few months, then he told me I would have to quit the job or find another doctor; but I should have another job before I quit this one. So I went job hunting.

It was difficult for a woman to find a drafting job. The help wanted ads asked for a man, but I called on them in spite of the discrimination. The government aided the discrimination for they set a minimum wage for men at $1.35 an hour and for women it was 75 cents. This is what companies wanted to pay me, if I was lucky enough to be granted an interview. Most of them said they didn't want a woman in the drafting room.

My father was suffering from a series of strokes at this time. I went to his home every evening and told him of my progress in getting another job. He paid me a compliment by telling me that of all the descendants of his father, H.J. Ruetenik, I was more like him than anyone else. I think he knew this would help me in my job hunting.

I went to the building department of East Cleveland that had advertised for a building inspector. The man gave me a good interview and then said,"

You are well qualified for the job, but could you give a big burly workman 'hell' for doing something wrong?" I was truthful; I could not do that.

Then he told me of an engineering company that was looking for a draftsman to do ink drawings, a job right down my alley. It was Frank A. Thomas and Associates, the city engineers for Wickliffe and Euclid, Ohio. They were located in the Wickliffe City Hall.

On the way back home, I stopped at the city hall in Wickliffe. I was interviewed immediately by Ralph Thomas, without an appointment. The East Cleveland reference helped me and I highly suspected that Ralph Thomas had received a phone call from them. He told me they needed a draftsman in the near future to do ink drawings of maps, and would certainly give me a call.

On the next visit to the doctor. I told him of the interview and he said to stay on the present job until the new job was a sure thing, and that he would continue to help me. I was to remain at Fluid Controls for several more months and was beginning to think Ralph Thomas had forgotten me.

My father's condition was deteriorating fast. I went to see him every evening and he always asked me if I heard anything about the new job. He died one morning just as the sun was rising, and the room was filled with a rosy reflection of the dawn of another day.

I had been up all night with my mother and my father's sister, Lottie, who had come from Colorado. The next morning I was awakened with a phone call from Ralph Thomas. He wanted me to come in and see him; he had a job for me. I explained that my father had just died, and asked if I could I postpone the meeting until after the funeral.

I am sure that my father arranged this from wherever he was. I always felt he knew the job came through.

I went to see Ralph Thomas after the funeral, and he said he wanted me to start the next Monday. The pay was $100.00 a month more than I was getting at Fluid Controls.

The day I told Mr. Stark that I would be leaving on Friday, I heard him make the final announcement at the lunch table when he said, "Freda will be leaving the company to go back to what she originally trained to do, architecture." It wasn't quite right, I'd be working in civil engineering, but why fight it? On Friday I left the job I loved.

A NEW JOB

The first day on the new job I came into a room full of men, most of them civil engineers, and a woman secretary. Near the close of the day the field crews came in, and more engineers. This totaled 42 men, but the atmosphere was different from the company I had just left. There was no discrimination. I was treated as a peer. Even though I was hired at a salary that was $100 more, I was given two more raises within three months; and I was learning a new profession.

My fellow employees said they sensed I had been having problems and was depressed, so they tried to make me laugh as much as possible. It worked, and the depression along with the 6-hour sobbing spells left me immediately. The doctor was right, I did need a change in jobs.

I was accustomed to carrying my lunch on the old job, so continued to brown bag it on the new job, even though the other employees went to a restaurant. I ate my lunch out in the back of the building where picnic tables were set up on beautiful grounds. Another draftsman soon joined me. I didn't know this was the first time he didn't eat in a restaurant at noon. He later told me he sensed something was wrong with the last company and he wanted to make me feel accepted in this one. When the weather turned cooler, he asked me to join the rest of them in a restaurant. I hope these guys knew how much I appreciated their concern for me. This was something new to me after the way the men treated me on the last job. All his employees called Frank Thomas, who owned the company, 'Dad.'

Wickliffe City Hall is an old mansion that was built by a multimillionaire for his home. The floors were marble throughout the halls, bathrooms main rooms and staircases. The woodwork is walnut, and there are several beautiful fireplaces. The grounds are spacious and beautifully landscaped. I can't imagine anyone living in such large rooms. Our department was in a bedroom so enormous that it contained at least 12 large drafting tables.

Dad Thomas was also the city engineer for the City of Euclid. I was locating sewer and water lines on the road maps for this city, and inking them for permanent records. I set the elevations of houses in subdivisions so the sewers would have sufficient drop into the existing sewer line. I finished this work and drew topography and subdivision maps.

The only draftsman, who did not like me, sat behind me. Steve was always harping at me for showing him up. "We will run out of work if you don't slow down," he said. I heard him say this so many times that one day I replied, "I bet when you get home at night, you tell your wife that you've had a hard day. So she gets your slippers, removes your shoes for you and puts your slippers on your feet, even though she also has a full time job outside the home." I hit it right on the mark because his face got as red as a beet.

When I went to the restroom, Steve went into my purse for gum. One payday I had my check in my purse, and when I came back from the restroom, Steve came over to me as mad as a hornet.

"How do you like that?' he said, 'I've been here two years longer than you, and you get the same pay."

"How do you know how much I'm paid?"

"I saw your paycheck in your purse."

"What business did you have going into my purse?"

"I was looking for gum when I saw it."

"It was in an envelope."

"I know that."

I took my problem home to ask for help. Audrey's boy friend came that evening. He and I worked out a scheme to catch him. He bought some hot gum in a joke store. I bought a package of Teaberry gum. Both gums were pink so we exchanged wrappers; we even broke one stick in half because I only chewed a half stick. Steve took a whole stick.

The next day I went to the restroom and came back into the drafting room in time to see Steve nonchalantly putting a stick of pink gum in his mouth as he was talking to Dad Thomas. As he chewed it, Dad was asking him about the job he was drafting. Steve glanced over to me with a weird expression on his face. He couldn't spit it out with Dad watching him, and his face got redder and redder. I didn't pay any attention to him. When the boss left, Steve came over to my table and swore at me.

"Gosh, what's this all about?" I said.

"You know what it is about, "he said, "you planted that gum in your purse."

"Do you mean to tell me that you went into my purse for a stick of gum while I was out of the room? How terrible that you should go ransacking into my purse without my permission." He never went into my purse again.

About this time I was running for reelection to remain on the school board. I had been very ill when I worked on the last job and had no interest in working hard to get reelected. I lost the election.

Dad Thomas had a nice talk with me about it then asked me to run for county commissioner; he would help me. I refused because I had enough of politics. But that wasn't the only reason. I knew I could be a good county commissioner, but when I was serving on the school board, my husband often said he was going to run for county commissioner.

The storm sewer trunk line for the City of Euclid was my drafting job. One of the men told me that the one who worked on a sewer had to walk the sewer. I knew he was pulling my leg, but went along with the game. WOW! I had to go down a 35-foot ladder to where the sewer emptied into Lake Erie, walk through the dark tunnel for one-mile and climb up a 15-foot ladder at the end. I chickened out at the last minute. The men took a camera with them to take pictures for me. This was a Saturday morning. When they came to the 15-foot ladder, they could see the new construction beyond. They noted that the bracing had not been put in, or was lacking altogether. They snapped many pictures. Sunday night the tunnel collapsed. For once it paid to chicken out! Our company avoided a lawsuit.

Wolfram and I were having problems with the IRS, who said my husband's income was not in order. They would not believe that he lost $10,000.00 in one year, and still could spend all the money he deducted for the dogs. It was the dogs they repeatedly questioned. Our accountant was scared stiff, and showed it. Out of the clear blue sky, the IRS man said,

153

"Who owns that new Buick in the backyard?"

"I do, "I said.

"Where did you get the money to pay for it?"

"Look at my income tax records you have in your hand."

"Oh yeah, you work."

"Do I make enough money to buy a Buick?"

"Yeah, you do. Do you see that old car parked alongside it? That's the car I drive."

That remark made me angry, so I replied, "Mister, when you get as old as I am, I can only wish you make enough money to buy a Cadillac."

Wolfram and the accountant were angry with me for this impertinent remark. Didn't I see how he was questioning the dogs? The consequences could be serious. It was I who was paying the income taxes by withholding them from my pay. Wolfram repeatedly told me how much he was helping me by deducting the cost of the dogs. Did he think I was stupid?

The outcome of the meeting was that the IRS decided that my husband owed the government $130.00 which he refused to pay. The IRS confiscated my savings account and took everything I had in it. I felt like I was being penalized for saving a little money.

I missed the inkwork I did for Fluid Controls, and now there was very little of it to do in this organization.

I went back to Fenn College and enrolled in a technical illustration course. I followed that with an advanced course with the same teacher. To add to this, I went to a private class in airbrushing pictures of industrial products.

The work at Thomas' called for lessons in calculus if I wanted to advance. I taught myself trigonometry when I worked at Fluid Controls, but I needed more math than that for subdivision work. It was not more math that I wanted; it was illustrating mechanical products. One of the engineers brought an ad over to my table one day. He knew I had been going to college for technical illustration and airbrush lessons.

Addressograph Multigraph Corporation was looking for a free-lance illustrator. I applied for the free lance job and got it. I moonlighted at home illustrating for the Addressograph-Multigraph Corporation. Among the drawings I did for the company was the first credit card machine. I came into the plant on the day they received their first two million-dollar order for those machines, so I was included in the happy occasion. I brown bagged my lunch on the days I picked up and delivered the artwork. The plant was very close to the Thomas Company, and the arrangement was excellent.

It wasn't long before I went back to Fluid Controls and asked for free-lance work. They had not been able to replace me in the catalog department, so Mr. Stark hired me to work on Saturdays. I asked for and was paid without question, three times the amount they paid me when I was on their payroll.

No more did I hand over my money to Wolfram. I paid for my car and the farm without worrying about it. I hired a woman to do my housekeeping, (which I hate to do anyway) and hired a window washer to clean the windows. I still felt it was a woman's responsibility to take care of the house. In my generation it was hard for me to change my idea of what woman's work was, and the only solution I could see was to pay someone to do it.

Fifteen years had gone by since we started to build our house. The house was unfinished and no work was done on it for several years. It was hard to keep the rough sub floors clean. More finish work was accomplished, but we still had no trim on the doorways, and very few doors were installed. The attic was full of beautiful unfinished new doors with hardware just waiting for Wolfram to find time to install them, and the trim was in the basement. It would have been better if he too, would have paid someone to do some of his work, but he refused to do it.

I decided to hire someone to hang the doors. I talked to the carpenter when he came. Wolfram sat in his chair with his hands in his pockets and wouldn't talk to the carpenter. The carpenter never came back.

Wolfram and I are drifting apart. I went to a marriage counselor who talked to us separately. She told me, "Your husband seems to be satisfied the way things are, even though you aren't. You both admit the problem isn't sex. You say that you have a good job, but you complain. Your husband can keep his dog hobby as long as you have a good job, so there's no problem." Nothing for me, I was to work for his fancies. That marriage counselor was a bummer. This woman had cost me my personhood!

Well, I had a good job. The marriage counselor seemed to think I could be independent, so I applied for a credit card at the May Company department store. I was given a credit form to fill out, which I did.

"This application for credit states that you are married," said the credit clerk.

"Yes I am."

"Your husband will have to fill out this card, not you."

"I want the card in my name, only, "I said, "look at my wages, I make good money."

"Your husband's wages are the only ones that count, we can't consider your wages."

"But I want the card in MY name."

"We can't issue a card to a married woman in her name only. We must have her husband's record and his signature, and the card must be in his name."

"If I were single, could I get a credit card on my salary?"

"Yes, you could."

WOW! Maybe I should get a divorce. I could get a credit card, I could have a car in my own name, which I wasn't able to do. I could have a savings account that couldn't be attached because of my husband's decision not to pay his bills. I could establish credit in my name only, I could, I could, I could!! Things would be much simpler if I were single.

If I were single I wouldn't have to obey my husband, no matter how much I disagreed with his thinking, like when he said, "When did you start using eyebrow pencil?"

"About two years ago."

"Take it off."

"No, if you hadn't noticed it for two years, what's the point?"

I refused to go to dog shows anymore, but this didn't stop me from entertaining his dog and horse clubs in our home. Wolfram had progressed far in the dog world and was an AKC judge of field and show. He does have recognition for all his persistent efforts with dogs.

I started my art courses because my whole life was involved around dogs, and I was an artist. Dogs came first in Wolfram's life; I came second. I was a person, and I too, had a life to live.

Dogs were never my cup of tea. I did enjoy some of his friends who visited him, but when I invited my friends to our home, he was always too busy to visit with them. Even though he knew days ahead of time that I was inviting them to dinner, he made dates with some of his friends and spent his time in the kennels causing me much embarrassment.

I had a two-week vacation coming. I asked Wolfram to go to Colorado with Audrey, Wolf and me. He wouldn't go, so I included my mother and sister.

The road to Colorado was paved all the way. A far cry from what we experienced 30 years ago in 1927. Although the modern double lane highways with overpasses didn't exist.

Aunt Lottie and Uncle Ernie had moved out of the high country, and lived in Wheatridge. Aunt Lottie warmly greeted us and told me to say hello to Uncle Ernie who was in the garden. I happily ran to him with Audrey, who was 20 years old, and Wolf, who was 12 years old. I said, "Hello Uncle Ernie," but he didn't reply to the greeting, he only saw Wolf. All he said, "You brought a young boy with you."

"Yes, this is my son Wolf."

"Now all my kitty cats will go away and won't come back until you leave. They don't like boys." Uncle Ernie grumbled.

I didn't get along with Uncle Ernie after that remark, and that was the rest of the time we stayed in their home. Uncle Ernie said, "Let's go for a mountain drive." I suggested we take my big car so we all could ride together. He would not hear of it, he had to drive his small car, and suggested we grown-ups would enjoy ourselves more if Audrey and Wolf stayed home. I protested and took my car with Audrey and Wolf in it, and followed him.

He proceeded to try to lose me in the Denver City traffic. I knew he was headed for Buffalo Bill's grave, so I looked at my map. There were two ways to get there. Lariat Drive, which was so scary in 1927, and Mount Vernon Canyon. I took Mount Vernon Canyon. When we met at the top of

Lookout Mountain, Uncle Ernie took me over to look at Lariat Drive. It was no different than it had been in 1927. Our whole stay had similar instances to this, with Uncle Ernie always grumbling that Audrey and Wolf were spoiling it for the grown-ups. Aunt Lottie was an angel to put up with this man all these years.

Audrey fell in love with Colorado, and thought it would be great if she and Tom could live here after they were married. She loved the mountains, and experienced the same feelings I had when I first saw them in 1927. I still wanted to live in those hills.

When I got back to Ohio, I had serious thoughts about my life and where I was heading. I was angry about Fluid Controls and their attitude towards women. I still loved that job, but it was impossible to work with men who harbored discrimination against women. I could not progress at Thomas' unless I studied calculus. If I ever made progress in the field I loved, I would have to do it on my own, in my own business.

I talked it over with Dad Thomas. He realized how Steve treated me, and wanted to establish in his own mind that this was not the cause of my leaving the company. I assured him that when I had a problem with him I was able to deal with it. Then Dad gave me some pointers about going into business.

CHAPTER 15

I GO INTO BUSINESS

I opened a one-room office in Mentor, Ohio, with two clients, Fluid Controls, Inc. and Addressograph-Multigraph Corporation. I named the business 'Freda R. Stumpf and Associates, Technical Illustrations for Industrial Publications.' I had no associates yet, but had high hopes.

When I worked for Fluid Controls, I met a woman who owned the print shop that printed the Fluid Controls catalogue. Her clientele included many industrial businesses and she gave me many leads for my business. One of the leads was Euclid Road Machinery, a division of General Motors, who were revising their parts catalogs.

I made a cold call on them and they hired me as a freelance artist. I was given the blueprint of the electrical system of their new sixteen-foot wide bulldozer. The bulldozer was in two eight-foot halves, so it could be transported. It was extremely difficult, but I did complete it. When I delivered it to Euclid Road, the head artist smiled and said the blueprint had been given to four other artists and I was the first one able to complete it correctly. Then they gave me so much work I had to hire another artist,

Dave, who was a classmate of mine in Fenn College, when I studied Technical Illustration.

When I hired Dave I changed the name to 'Stumpf and Associates.' Using a woman's name in the title was hurting me. The problems were with the men in the lower echelon; the company heads were open-minded. After that I picked up work from many small companies.

I received a phone call from my former instructor at Fenn College; he wanted to meet with me. We met in my studio. He said he would like to go into business with me as a partner. I started a new business and got the customers, and then he wants to come in as a partner? I told him I could handle it alone.

In a few months the business grew so much I had to move into larger quarters. I was doing illustrations for garden tractors, brake press machinery, loaders, marine rubber products, bicycle parts, and of course, hydraulic valves and business machines.

Dave and I had our own room plus a conference room. We did drawings of new products and for competitors. Some clients were nosy and wanted to see what their rival was making. The conference room kept them out of our illustrating rooms.

We did illustrations for magazine ads drawn by using blueprints, because the product was nonexistent. I airbrushed the drawing to look like a photograph. If the client had good reports from the ad, he made the product.

The business grew and it now included displays for industrial shows. This was fun work! I was ready to hire another artist. One of the applicants had four years of art in college. I told him that a drafting course was necessary as a prerequisite to Technical Illustration. He complained that no one wanted to train him for a job. I paused, and thought about my first job.

Mr. Stark trained me. Maybe I was too harsh with this man, but then I had drafting, plus art when I applied for that job.

I was thinking about this and was considering hiring him when he made a statement, "Boy, lady you have it made." Then I knew I didn't want him as an employee.

I joined the United States Chamber of Commerce, and shortly after, the Mentor Chamber of Commerce, who voted me in as a director.

I am the only woman on the board. The men wanted to serve refreshments. I thought it was a good idea until the men said they would buy the doughnuts and coffee, if I made the coffee and did the dishes. I told them, "I hate to do dishes, let's take turns with coffee, doughnuts and dishes." The refreshments didn't last too long. I guess the guys didn't like to do dishes either.

Being a member of the Chamber of Commerce meant civic gatherings in a large restaurant. One evening I sat next to Mr. Bowman, the head of the water company. I engaged in casual conversation him and he asked me where I lived in the county. I said that I lived on Fairgrounds Road. He looked surprised and said, "Oh, that is the road that had all the water problems, because of the horse racing." I replied, "You have that right."

Then he said, "Do you know what one woman told me when she called and complained? She said that her son was taking a bath when a hose he was using to fill the tub started to suck water back into the line. Have you ever heard of anything so ridiculous? You sure get all kinds." I looked at him square in the eye and said, "You know I don't think it was so ridiculous, it really happened, I was the caller. "His face got all red as he apologized, but I kept right on and said, "You should have installed a check valve in my line if you had no intentions of doing anything about the situation." I told him I obtained most of the signatures to put the water issue on the ballot, and if we had more cooperation, the problem would have never gone as far as it did. Well, I retrieved my personhood, but it sure took a long time.

I added an ad agency to my business. I was invited (with my husband) to cocktail parties given by industrial magazine publishing companies in Cleveland. Here I met industrial designers, other people involved in the industry and artists who painted the magazine covers. Mr. Stark invited us to cocktail parties at his country club, and there was a drastic change in my life. I had added a little sophistication into it. Where was the meek little housewife, who did all her husband's bidding, because my marriage vows demanded that I obey him? I had come out of my shell.

A printer's convention was scheduled to be held in New York City. The woman who owned the printing company and I decided to go to the convention. Before I went on this trip to New York City, Wolfram said we should make out wills.

Wolfram told the lawyer that I was going to fly to New York the next week, and I was going to will everything to him. The lawyer was shocked. I didn't do as he asked. Maybe he had good reason, for this was before the large airliners. We had to skirt a thunderstorm, which was a frightful experience.

One never knows what goes on in the little companies on Saturday. My clients would have found me scrubbing the floor and polishing the furniture in the reception room. One Saturday I drove to a small company to deliver a rush job. A woman was on her hands and knees polishing the marble floor in the reception room. I gave her the drawings and she said, "I suppose you don't know who I am."

"I'll bet you're the president's wife."

"You're exactly right."

Then we both laughed when I told her I just got through doing the same thing.

One of my clients owned a rubber manufacturing company. He did not wear designer clothes, for sure. He was always dressed in old clothes that had rubber residue on them, for he also supervised the workers in the plant. He came into my office one day when Dave, my illustrator, was alone. When I came into the office, Dave said, "Some dirty guy was in and wanted us to do a catalog for him. I didn't give him any encouragement because I didn't think you wanted to do his work; he probably didn't have the money to pay you, anyway." He handed me the man's card.

It was the president of the rubber manufacturing company. I had called on him many times in an effort to pick up his catalog work. I was flabbergasted. I went right to the phone and called the man and told him I would be right over. Then I chewed Dave out. "Don't you ever again treat a customer as if he is a nobody. This man owns a large manufacturing company, and heads a savings and loan firm." Dave took this man's personhood away from him because of his clothes.

It had been three years since I landed the Euclid Road Machinery account, and their parts catalog is nearly complete. I went on the road to pick up more clients, and did acquire a few but not enough to fill the empty gap caused by the loss of Euclid Road's business. I had to let one artist go and then I let Dave go.

Just before I let him go, I found a high stack of pictures in the storage case in his room. The stack was of a sports nature and I knew it did not pertain to the work we did in the studio. There were twenty pictures all mounted on white mounting board. I turned around and asked Dave about them. He said he mounted them for a friend. "Did you use my white mounting board, adhesive sheets and electric mounter?" He said he did.

Dave knew the work was slow. He had no intention of paying for the materials and the use of the expensive mounter. I told him, "Dave, you probably don't realize that when you do this, you don't take the cost out of a company, you take it out of my pocket. I paid for them." Dave had a key to the office. He might have been moonlighting and using my expensive Strathmore paper, or just doing some more mounting for his 'friends.' I didn't know, nor did I care at this point. I had to let Dave go.

I moved to cheaper quarters down the road, in a building with a doctor. This proved handy, for I cut my hand severely on the paper cutter, and I knew it should be sutured. I walked next door and the doctor took one look and started on it. He did a good job for I don't have a scar.

Wolfram was having chest pains. Dr. Stephens told him that he had angina pectoris, he could not do any lifting and it forced him to sell his business. He came into my business as a contact field representative. Now I was free to devote more time to my illustrating work. He did bring in several accounts, but it wasn't enough so he sold industrial lighting along with my work.

My mother came down with cancer. She was living in my home when she died. With as much help as I could hire, and two sisters who came to help, I was trying to care for her and my business too. I'm afraid I didn't do a good job at either one. My mother was a deeply religious person. I remember her most from a Biblical quotation she liked:

"I will lift up mine eyes unto the hills, from whence cometh my help.

My help cometh from the Lord, which made heaven and earth."

Psalm 121 verses 1 and 2

Audrey and her high school sweetheart attended Hiram College. They were wed on the day Tom graduated from Hiram College. They eventually moved to Colorado and had two little girls, Kathleen and Heather.

While visiting at Audrey's home in Colorado, I had a gall stone attack. When I returned home, Dr. Stephens said I must have an operation as soon as I could get my business in order.

I asked my son, Wolf, who was attending Riverside High School, if he thought he could do some exploded drawings of a garden tractor in pencil. He said he had some training in drafting at school. He came into my studio every afternoon after school and his work was so good, I asked him if he had done any inking. Of course he had. I said, "Why didn't you tell me that you could do this kind of work?" He replied "Because you never asked me," a typical teenager answer! He went into my studio every afternoon after school, so I was free to go to the hospital. Wolf was to work for me for several years. I feel proud to have given him his first job. Today he is an engineer.

Wolfram wasn't making enough money selling industrial lighting. His take-home pay was anywhere from $20 to $50 a week. I had been after him for about two years to get another form of income, but I think he liked being on the road, and was able to visit with some of his dog friends. A living wage didn't seem important to him. When the gall stone operation came up I was happy he had a hospitalization policy that went with his job. I asked him for the policy so I could make arrangements.

Two days before the operation, he quit his job because, as he put it, "You've been after me for a long time to quit and I did." "But what about the hospitalization policy?" I said. "Well that stopped when I quit my job."

I was shocked; I didn't know what to do. I called the company and explained my predicament. They also wondered why he quit at the time he did, but after much conversation, they asked me to send them three months payment on the policy and I would be covered.

The night before the operation I had a visitor in my room. It was a patient from the next room. "Hello, Freda, remember me? I met you at the high school when you were on the school board." I faintly remembered her as the mother of a woman I worked with when the high school was being built. "They tell me you are going to have a gallbladder operation tomorrow," the woman said. Gossip in this hospital sure did travel around. Then she said, "Do you remember the cook who worked at your school when you were on the school board?" I remembered her. "Do you know she passed away?" I remembered about it. "Well, she died of a gallbladder operation and I thought I better tell you to cancel that operation for tomorrow morning."

This woman was no harbinger of good news. I should have told the doctor, but I didn't and spent a wearisome night. The next morning I had a successful operation. In the afternoon the patient from the next room came in. "I see that you had the operation in spite of what I told you about the cook." I told her that she could see that I came out of it OK. Then she made this prime statement. "Well you may think that you came out of it OK, but it took the cook nine months to die after the operation."

She upset me so much, that I vomited all over her, and the lady in the next bed called the nurse. That was the last time I saw THAT woman.

Dr. Stephens assisted in the operation. He referred me to Dr. Downing, who was an excellent surgeon. While I was in the recovery room I saw a doctor at a table making out a report. I recognized him as a brother of a girl friend in high school. I called out to him; "Gordon is that you?" "Yes it is, do I know you?" He came over to my bed and said, "Why you are Freda, one of the Ruetenik twins!" I told him that I was sorry to hear that his sister had passed away, because we were good friends in high school.

The next day I heard the familiar click of my surgeon's heels as he came down the hall. He was a snappy fellow and I liked him. He came into my room and said, "Hello Fritz, how's Skinny these days?" I was very puzzled. I hadn't been called Fritz since my high school days, and my brother Arden lost his nickname long ago. How did he know Skinny? After a good laugh I said, "You were talking to Gordon."

He said he was, "But don't you know who I am?" No, I hadn't recognized him.

"I was one of the kids who run around with Skinny when we were young."

"Were you one of those kids who ran away from home and went to live in the shack behind the railroad tracks?"

"I was one of those kids."

"Oh, oh, you aren't going to like me; I was the person who sent the railroad detective out looking for you. I'm sure glad you did the operation before you knew that!" The laughing made up for all the bad conversations I had with the next door patient. I knew then that he was the right sort of a guy.

I went back to work just two weeks after the operation. The good doctor, who had an office next door, came over to see me.

"It's so good to see you Freda, but how long has it been since the operation?"

"About two weeks."

"Freda, you better go right back home."

"Yes, I think you're right, I thought I would come over and pick up my mail, but I'm so weak." It was nice to have a professional concerned for my welfare.

I went home for lunch one day only to find that Wolfram's champion Irish setter was loose. The dog did not come when called, and no one was at home to help me catch him. So here I was all dressed up in red high-heeled shoes, running through the fields chasing a dog. I caught him. It had cost too much to make a champion of him to let him go. I didn't ruin my new red shoes, but I had to change into some new stockings and remove the prickers from my dress before I went back to the office.

Wolf was drafted into he Army when the Vietnam War was in full swing. My husband was selling real estate. And I took a course in silver smithing at the Cleveland School of Art, and a gem cutting class in Cleveland.

Marlene had done some layout work for me in the studio, but now she had three children to care for; Diana, Kandi and Kris. She loves the blue iris as much as I do, and also plants the blue iris wherever she lives. The tradition lives on.

The United States Department of Highways was designing a new east-west freeway, Interstate 90. It will go through the farm I bought. I was buying this land on land contract, so it was not recorded in the courthouse. Instead of trying to find the owner, they sent a survey crew on the land, then a bulldozer to knock down trees. The surveyors were trespassing to be sure, but a bulldozer knocking down trees? The persons holding the land contract were not contacted either, so the highway department really didn't do its homework.

Wolfram and I went out to the farm and ordered them off the property. We are now fighting the government. We told them that unless we are contacted, they had no right on the land, especially with the bulldozer knocking down our trees. The men would not go. They said that stories about the new highway had been in all the newspapers and that should be notice enough.

We told them that no notice was in the paper to specifically find out who owned the property, and that is what mattered. They still insisted on trespassing. Wolfram went home and got his shotgun. With the gun he chased the men off the property. Then we took turns guarding the entry with the shotgun. This forced them to contact us to buy the property and start negotiations, which is what we wanted. They were land locking 120 acres of the farm by this construction.

A woman a few doors away wanted to move out of the area, and sold her land below market value. This set the price for our property. This resulted in the government paying me exactly what I was paying for the land. I was left with only one acre of land that had access to a road. The landlocked property over-looked the Grand River 135 feet below and the other side a creek was nearly as deep. The new evergreens were not considered, nor the work involved, because they were not big enough to market. I imagine the government employee who made this deal received lots of brownie points for his efforts.

Several years later an investor who wanted to buy the land locked farm contacted me. He had acquired much of the property in line with ours, which was also landlocked, and one of the parcels bordered a road. My farm was last in line. I sold it and put the money in Wolfram and my names, but in an account that needed both of our signatures. I was able to pay for the $2000 lien that was put on my farm when the produce store failed, and most of the mortgage on our house property.

I made regular visits to the eye doctor for stronger lenses. Every eighteen months I needed a new set, for techincal illustration work. Besides all these glasses, I still used a magnifying glass. The doctor limited me to five hours a day on the board. I couldn't support my husband on five hours a day of work, so I moved my studio into our recreation room at home. Wolfram installed good lighting, and tiled the floor, and the door opened up to our parking lot. It was an excellent set-up.

The menagerie in the backyard not only consisted of lots of dogs and horses, but also pigeons, ducks and bantam chickens. The chickens did not use their coop for roosting; they used the axle of my car. Being the person I am, I start the car put it in gear and away I go. This particular day I was in a hurry to get to downtown Painesville before the drug store closed. I forgot to chase the little chickens off the axle of my car. I put the car in gear, drove out of the yard and saw no cars on the street, so without stopping I turned into the street and drove three miles to town. I didn't stop the car until I pulled into a parking space. I stopped the car, pulled out the key, opened the door and dashed around to the back of the car, only to see the street and sidewalk full of little bantam chickens. A second look at them told me they looked awfully familiar.

Bantam chickens in downtown Painesville, Ohio

I knew what happened, and while I was standing there collecting my thoughts, a large crowd was gathering, looking at the little chickens. I tried to explain to them what happened but they just looked at me in awe. Then after they collected their thoughts, they helped me catch them and put them in the trunk of my car. With a red face I drove them home. I often wondered about those little chickens. They must have had a thrilling ride with heads into the wind holding on for dear life. Do you suppose some of them made that ride with their rears towards the wind with all their feathers flying backwards? I'm surprised that none of them were running around naked!

Fluid Controls hired a new engineer, just out of college and put him in charge of the catalog. On his first visit to my office, he told me I was much too feminine to work on his company's catalog, and grabbed his work and went out the door. I ran after him and took the work away from him. While he was standing there still surprised, I went back to my office and called Mr. Stark. I asked him what was wrong with my work, hadn't I done a satisfactory job for him for many years? He didn't know the engineer tried to release me, and straightened out the problem. I lost my personhood and gained it right back.

To add to my income, I applied at the Erieside Institute in Willoughby, Ohio for an instructor's job. I would be teaching evening classes. Mr. Duchon, the director hired me to teach technical illustration. I was added to the staff of instructors.

My class enrollment was all men and one woman, who left after the first lesson, because she could not take a course of this nature under a woman. Hey! This was a funny way for me to loose my personhood!

The director told me he could add two more men for the course in airbrush instruction, if I could qualify as an instructor under a John Huntington Polytechnic Institute scholarship. He said it would be difficult for I must fill out a stiff application. I told him that I didn't think it would be a problem, so he called them on the phone to send the application. He said they laughed when he told them who the instructor would be, and an application was not necessary. They knew me well, for I had attended their classes for many years.

One of my students was a milkman. Door to door milk service was being discontinued and he needed another occupation. He showed promise, but didn't take the advanced course to round out a good illustrator. This was not the last I heard of the milkman.

In my efforts to look for new clients, I answered an ad in the paper. Cleveland Trencher Company wanted a free-lance illustrator for their parts catalogs and service manuals. I called on them. My account with Euclid Road Machinery should help me obtain some of their work for it was similar. I was given a good interview then the interviewer surprised me. He said he could not let me do their work, for he just noticed the wedding ring on my finger.

"Are you a married woman?"

"Yes, but what has that got to do with this interview?"

"We have a policy in this company, that we do not hired married women."

"You aren't hiring me. I have my own company, but what does your company have against married women?"

"They have babies and quit."

"But I have my own business, I wouldn't have a baby."

"I don't want a woman in my art room."

"I would do your work in my studio. I am sure if I can do this for Euclid Road Machinery, I can do it for you." But this is the way it goes. I lost my personhood again, but this was not the last time I heard from this company.

A few months later the milkman, who was a former student of mine, called and wanted to talk with me. The milkman came to my studio and we sat down for a talk. He asked me if he could take some private lessons in technical illustration. I agreed to give him lessons. Then he told me the whole story. After I applied for work at Cleveland Trencher, he applied and they gave him a full time job because I was his instructor. They told him they interviewed me, but I couldn't work for them because I was a married woman, and if he was a student of Freda's, he must be good.

Then the milkman made a mistake. He laughed at me because I was a woman, and he was able to take the job away from me, even though I was superior in the profession. He then said that after working at the place for a while, they told him he needed more training and asked him to go back to Freda as a private student. Well, here goes my personhood again.

I sat there for a while, just doing some hard thinking. I couldn't go back on my word to accept him as a private student. So, I told him, "I will train you in all you need to know to do the work for Cleveland Trencher, but the check for my instruction must come from and be signed by Cleveland Trencher." I never again heard from the milkman. I did not like my personhood taken away from me, so I retrieved it. The milkman should not have laughed.

In my effort to keep my head above water, I applied for a job with the United States Government. I was trying to get to Colorado, and was hoping for an opening in the Federal Center in Denver. I felt there was nothing holding us in Ohio any more. The application for a GS rating took two days to fill out. I was granted a GS 11 rating, but they told me no jobs were available in Denver, but that there was an opening in Washington D.C. I didn't want to go to Washington D.C. I wanted to go to Denver.

Wolfram was not making enough money to support us, and now, neither am I. As I was glancing through the Help Wanted ads one evening, I saw an ad for a draftsman at Sidley Precast Company. This will be going back to architecture, and would be easier on my eyes. I applied for the job and was hired. I will be a senior draftsman at Sidley Precast Company in Thompson, Ohio, and moonlighting at home for the clients in my own company.

CHAPTER 16

BACK TO ARCHITECTURE

Sidley Precast was a good place to work much like the Thomas organization. To get to work I drove Interstate 90, which took me over the farm I owned and then farther out into the country. It was a beautiful 20-mile drive.

I had a woman boss who was head draftsman. I worked with structural and architectural plans in this job. I had a good position and it wasn't long before I had junior draftsmen under me. I earned the title of senior draftsman.

Precast panels are beautiful exteriors of large buildings. The draftsmen drew plans for the molds and did the math to fit the panels to the building. I worked with the men who built the molds and other men in the plant, so I was not continually on the drafting board. This job was kinder to my eyes than any job I had since I started to work. This work was interesting for the result of our efforts was so beautiful, and it made me proud to be a part of it. I progressed to a well-rounded knowledge of precast buildings.

Our drafting rooms were in a building that was an old farmhouse. The offices were downstairs and the draftsmen worked in the bedrooms upstairs.

A new building was in the planning stage, so not much was done to make the building look like a commercial office. My room upstairs was papered in pink roses, and Jeanie's room had other flowers suitable for a bedroom. Jeanie and I sure got a lot of kidding because we worked in bedrooms!

The wind whistled through the cracks in this old house. When I found a crack that let in too much cold air, I taped it shut with industrial tape. One day the president of the company came into my room and remarked about the tape in the corners and under the window. I surmised he knew the answer, so I told him, in a dry type of humor, that I was trying to hold the building together.

The precast company was in Thompson, which is the place where I lived in 1938; it is now twenty-eight years later. After work one day I ventured out to where I lived so long ago. The old house looked the same. Nothing had been done to the outside. It was still enclosed in the same crummy asphalt shingles.

The lawn was over-grown with high weeds and I thought it might be deserted until I noticed the electric and phone lines. The road is now paved instead of the two muddy ruts I remembered. I reflected back on the life that I lived since I left this little house, so many years ago. So much has happened.

I lived in my own unfinished house. I always felt bad about raising our children in an unfinished house, but it was still much more pleasant than this house.

Now my girls are married and my boy was drafted into the Army, because of the Vietnamn War. I glanced back again at the house I lived in so long ago. It now has electricity and a phone, but it looks like that is the sum of the improvements. I wondered if the pot-bellied stove was still in the living room.

I drove past the Strava farm where I bought eggs. The farm has a new barn; both of the children are in agriculture. The daughter is a county agent and a friend of mine. We both were members of the Quota Club, and she is the only member who knew me when I was very, very poor. Nothing is ever said about it except that she asks about the two little girls that I brought along with me when I bought eggs. I'm dreaming ... let's get back to my story.

All my work was on large commercial buildings. The job I really liked was the American Automobile Association building located on the shores of Lake Erie.

William McVey, a well-known sculptor, designed the window panels on this round building. When I was taken to his studio to pick up his model of the building, he showed me around his studio. He is the sculptor who sculpted the statue of Winston Churchill with the cigar in his hand, which drew so much publicity. The high point of the visit was when he showed me the original model of the hand with the cigar. He also had a model of the Idlewood Airport building, which in the shape of a shell. His reasoning for this structure was that if a snail could build it, so could man.

I was privileged to meet him. The model of the window is small, but the panels are actually 30 feet high. I designed the casting mold for this window.

I was job captain of the precast part of the American Automobile Association building, which was the entire exterior. It was due to be completed before fall, so a college could move into their building on Euclid Avenue. The architect's drawings were incomplete, so I worked almost entirely with the structural engineer's drawings. I set the exact perimeter of the building with my self-taught knowledge of trigonometry, then to make sure, a surveyor and I mapped out one full window segment. The window precast fit exactly right. Erection time was near, and I was given the power to use any facility in the plant I needed to push the job as rapidly as possible. I was in charge of the erection itself, and attended the job site meetings with the other contractors.

The executive vice president of our company went with me to a meeting in Cleveland. He told me not to tell anyone who he was. I did all the negotiating with him sitting alongside me, not advising me or talking to anyone. I negotiated with the steel erectors to use their crane at times our crane would not be on the job. I did this with questions to our crane operator who also attended the meeting. Even the crane operator addressed himself to me, instead of the vice president.

The job superintendent for the main contractor called me the next day. He said, "Freda, you had another man with you at the meeting yesterday besides the crane man, and I neglected to get his name." I told him it was the executive vice president of Sidley's. "Freda, why didn't you introduce him?" I explained to him that this was the way he wanted it to be, because if you knew who he was, you would have directed your questions to him, not me." He understood. This was the first time I had a responsibility of this magnitude, and my work on the building was successful.

I received an invitation to the opening of the AAA building. I was all alone and looked out of every window. It was a thrill just to wander through the whole building, and to see what I had done. In the middle of the second floor, was a large round balcony that overlooked the first floor. As I was on this balcony, the insurance agent, who wrote my life insurance policy, when

I worked for Frank A. Thomas Associates about fifteen years ago, came up to me.

"Hello Freda, what a surprise to see you here. I didn't think you had any connection with the Cleveland Automobile Club. You still live in Painesville, don't you?"

"Well, hello John. It's been years since I have seen you."

"But you must have had an invitation to come here today."

"Yes, of course, I was job captain of the exterior of the building. I work in precast now, and designed the forms for the precast, set the exact perimeter of the building and administered the manufacturing schedule and the crane setting."

The insurance man gave me a disgusting look and said, "Oh yeah?" Then he took his wife's arm, gave me a dirty look and walked away.

A few years later his company wrote to me and said that John was elevated in his company, and that it would be nice, since I had the policy so long, if I would send him a note of congratulations.

I wrote back to the company and told them what happened the last time I saw John at the AAA building. Then I told them to verify what I did on the building by calling the president of the Sidley Precast Company. I received an apology from John. Sometimes it takes years to get my personhood back.

Wolfram and I were having severe difficulties. I work five and six days a week and he is never home on weekends. I was trying to get him to understand that he should find some kind of a job, but his old excuse for not working was his heart. I told him to get a job in the dog profession he knew so well. He did get an offer from a dog food company, but turned it down because he wanted to be a judge, and it would be against the rules of the American Kennel Club. He was running dogs in the field trials, showing dogs in shows and training dogs in the field for free. One of these free customers was Steve, who was the draftsman who sat behind me when I worked for the civil engineers. He was the guy who ransacked my purse when I left the room. How he got acquainted with him I don't know, but Wolfram thought I should come and greet him. I refused. I hardly ever saw Wolfram; he was too busy with dogs.

I came home from work one day and a man, who was buying a puppy, was in the living room with Wolfram. I sat down at the table with my usual cup of coffee to relax after a day's work. After they finished the pedigree papers, they came through the dining area with his puppy. Before he went out the door, the man turned around and said to my husband, "What kind of work do you do for a living?" Wolfram replied, "I raise dogs." The man said, "Come on now, you can't make a living raising puppies."

Why Wolfram said what he did when he answered him, I shall never know, but he told the man, "Why should I work, my wife has a good job." The man gave me a side-glance and walked out. I just sat there with raised eyebrows. It made me feel like a fool. Wolfram always told me that he couldn't work because of his heart, but he could train dogs in the field for friends. When he had his own dog trained, it cost him over $100 to get it trained in the field.

Despite the fact that even though it had been seven years since Wolfram had a steady job, he had not found time to finish the house. The beautiful doors and the nice hardware are still in the attic, where they had been gathering dust for many years.

In the fall an Irish setter club planned a clambake at our house. It was Saturday, and I was working overtime to get a job out. I was to pick up the corn from a farmer for the feast. I worked so late that the farmer thought I wasn't coming to pick up the corn, so he sold it. The farmer and I went into his corn patch and picked more corn for the clambake.

It was about 8 o'clock when I drove into our yard and it was full of strangers who came for the clambake. A group of women was standing close by, so I opened the trunk and told them that I had the corn. They just looked at me and went on talking. So I left the trunk open and went to the picnic area and saw a keg of beer. I thought, "Oh well, why not?" I knew nothing about pumping a keg of beer and all I got was a tiny amount of it and the rest foam, so I sat down at the picnic table to wait for the foam to go down.

One of the club members came over to me and told me that not all of the club members had arrived as yet, and we should go easy on the beer until they all had a chance at it. I was already feeling sorry for myself, and no one talked to me except for this remark. Poor me.

The cook arrived as I was sitting at the table. He was just starting the bake. I thought I'd have some food when I got home, I hadn't had anything to eat since noon. I was very tired after working ten hours on the job and then helped pick corn. I was really feeling sorry for myself. The cook was a club member that I was acquainted with, and so he struck up a conversation.

"My wife broke her arm this week."

"I heard she did."

"I lost my assistant when she broke her arm."

"I'm sorry to hear that."

"Now the first thing I want you to do is get me some salt and butter."

I suppose the most gracious thing to do was to help him, but after the beer episode, I was indifferent, hungry and exhausted. I wasn't a member of this club. There were many club members who could help him. I paid for someone to clean the house for them. I felt I done my part, so I replied, "The salt is on the stove in the kitchen and the butter is in the refrigerator." Then I went up to my bedroom and cried.

Now that I think about it, the refrigerator had a bungi cord around it because the latch wouldn't work and the door wouldn't stay closed. I had recently asked Wolfram to hold the door and I would put some C washers under the hinge so the latch would work. He got very angry, accused me of always nagging and slapped my face one way and then another, throwing my head around like a basketball. Well, maybe his dog friends got mad at the bungi cord too.

I was lying on my bed in my tears, then I thought better of the whole matter, so I phoned my son, Wolf. I told him I was hungry and there was no way to get my car out of the yard, and the clambake wouldn't be done until midnight.

He said to meet him at the mailbox in front of the house. Wolf and Susan, his wife, picked me up and took me to Arby's. We had a long talk over the sandwich. They wanted to go to Colorado to live and so did I. We made a pact. Whoever got to Colorado first would invite the other, and we would meet at the Red Rocks Amphitheater in Denver for Easter sunrise services.

I came home and went into the house unnoticed. I went to my bedroom and climbed in bed. I had not even been missed. About midnight, Wolfram came in the room. He said the clambake was ready to eat, and that he had been looking all over for me. I told him I wasn't hungry, but he said I HAD to eat it, because he paid for it. So he brought it into the bedroom and went back to his friends.

One day a friend asked me about Wolfram's horses. I told him he was mistaken, because Wolfram hadn't had any horses for about ten years. Then I got suspicious and stayed home from work one day. When he left the house I got in my car and followed him to a horse barn in the fairgrounds. I walked into the barn and watched him cleaning out horse stalls. I was surprised to see that he had not one horse, but two of them. How he could afford to rent stalls in a barn for two horses, I don't know, for we had a horse barn with two stalls at home. He was deliberately keeping them here so I would not know he had them. I was so shocked I couldn't say a word. I just watched him do his work.

I had talked to my lawyer about a divorce several years before this, but told him I wanted to make a go of our marriage. Slapping my head around, the clambake, the remark to the man about not working because I had a good job, and the horse situation was the straw that broke the camel's back. Wolfram followed me home after I saw his horses and just sat in his chair. I called the lawyer in his presence and told him I was ready for the divorce that we had talked about.

I had a vacation coming up at Sidley's. Before I left, the president of the company told me that he had a funny feeling about my going to Colorado for a vacation. He wanted me to take administrative head of the drafting room. I couldn't tell him about the divorce.

I was going to Denver to apply for a job. I had interviews at two companies. The job I really wanted was Mack Precast that made beautiful precast buildings, but that company said to come in again when I got to Colorado. The other company would hire me. I took the sure thing with Prestressed Concrete of Colorado.

After I had my job secured in Denver, I drove to Grand Junction to visit my daughter, Audrey, her husband and my two granddaughters, Kathleen and Heather. I stayed with them a few days, then back to Denver to pick up the travel trailer I had pulled for the trip.

On the way home while in a campground in Iowa, I fell out of the trailer and tore all the ligaments in my leg. I went to the manager's office and called a doctor. His receptionist said he was booked until Friday. I told her my leg was either fractured, or the ligaments were torn and I thought it was an emergency; but she didn't think so. Friday was three days away, so I got in the car and pulled the trailer to Chicago to my brother Don's place. We decided I could get home in one day if I left early the next morning.

When I got home the doctor took an X-ray, no broken bones but a bad ligament tear.

I told Wolfram I had a job in Denver. I was going to move and would like him to come along, but he told me his security was in Ohio. I said it would have to be a divorce. He said he also wanted a divorce.

I went to my lawyer and started proceedings. The hearing was set for December 27, 1968.

I talked to the president of my company and told him of my move and divorce. He said he knew something was wrong, and he understood why I couldn't say anything. He also told me that if things didn't work out in Denver, I always had a job at Sidley Precast Company.

I needed money for the move, so sold most of my rock collection and my rock cutting machinery. I told Wolfram to take all the photos he wanted out of the albums, but got no cooperation from him. I had those decisions to make. I divided the furniture the best way I knew how, and by the time of the divorce hearing, I was ready to move.

Grounds for divorce were required. The lawyer, who was a friend of both of us, said he had so many grounds for divorce that he didn't know

185

what to use. Five minutes before the hearing he said he would use the dogs. The judge was concerned about my welfare. The lawyer told him I was employed in the engineering field, and was able to take care of myself. I was granted the divorce.

The divorce papers said Wolfram could live in the house until it was sold, but had to live in it alone with only one dog in the house. We gave him the listing to sell the property because he was a real estate agent.

I was on my way to Colorado on December 29, 1968. I forgot to take a root of the blue iris.

PART IV

CHAPTER 17

I MOVE TO COLORADO

I departed for Colorado just two days after the divorce. I wondered at myself for starting out during the winter season, for the road from Cleveland to Columbus, Ohio was solid ice. I was in line traveling 35 miles per hour. Someone who thought he knew better tried to pass the whole line, and when he came up alongside me, he disappeared. A quick glance told me he was going around and around down the median, always upright, so they were OK; but I'll never forget the woman sitting in the front with a big Christmas package on her lap.

I stopped at the next rest stop and went to the ladies room. A woman was inside with a Beagle hound that crept under the door of my enclosure. I screamed, "Get that dog out of here. What do you mean by not leashing him?" When I came out the woman said, "I don't like the way you screamed at my dog. I want you to know that we are on our way home from a dog show and he won Best in Show." I replied, "Lady, don't you let that dog touch me, or Ill kick him so hard, he'll be good for nothing!" I meant it and she knew I did. She hurried out the door with her dog.

189

The road from Columbus to the Mississippi River was clear. After I crossed the river, a freezing rain hit, and the road was in worse shape than Ohio. I stopped at a motel, then went out to dinner. When I returned, I heard a dog howling in the next room as if his heart would break. I stood it for about an hour, by then he was crying so hard that I went to the manager's office. I asked him to do something about it, then told him of the divorce and the dogs. He told me to stay in my room he would take care of it. He did.

The next morning I continued on my way to Abilene, Kansas. It was six degrees above zero. I stopped at a motel and told the desk clerk that I wanted a room away from dogs. They gave me a room in the far corner of the motel. The room never got over 55 degrees. I went out to my car and got my electric blanket and a religious book that my sister, Gertrude, had given me. I read this lovely book until I fell fast asleep.

The next morning it was too cold in the room to wash. I loaded the car and when it warmed up, I turned the heater switch on, and the cable broke. I had no heat in the car. I called a garage and was told that they opened up at 8 AM. The mechanic looked at the heater cable and said they would have to get another cable from Denver. It would take two days. I told him I was headed for Denver, was there some way I could get heat in the car? He asked me to put my head under the dash, and he showed me how to operate it manually. I had heat in the car.

This is a lonely road to be sure. I had a sleeping bag alongside me for emergency. I set it upright and placed a hat on the top of it to look like I had a companion.

I arrived in Denver on New Year's Eve. I was fortunate to find a motel room. On New Year's Day I drove south on Pecos Street, looking for the

190

place I was to pick up my job. Someone above must have been guiding me, for I only drove a mile before it came into view.

I started my new job as a senior draftsman at Prestressed Concrete of Colorado on January 2, 1969. The vice president seemed upset about me working in the place. I was the first woman in the field ever hired by this company, and I surmised he hadn't been told about me. I probably didn't look too promising, because I was still using a cane because of my sprained ankle.

When I applied for the job, the drafting room head said he would find an apartment for me, and that my moving expenses would be paid. This was not in writing, so tough luck; no apartment, and no moving money.

I went apartment hunting for I would soon be out of money if I remained in the motel. Denver was experiencing an apartment shortage. Everywhere I went it was a four weeks to two months wait. In desperation, I parked my car in a doughnut shop parking lot, and started to cry; then thought better of it and put my head down on the steering wheel. With my face in my hands I prayed, "Dear God, I have been unable to find a place to live, and I don't know what to do. My life is in your hands completely. Amen."

After my prayer, I looked up, turned my head around, and there on 71st Street was a big apartment building with a large sign on it, 'NOW RENTING.' I drove over and rented a nice two-bedroom apartment. They only had one more apartment, but it was very tiny.

The contract with the moving company was for the same amount that I had left after paying the rent. I moved into the apartment with a cot, a sleeping bag, a few pieces of luggage and my grandfather's iron clock with mother of pearl. I bought some food and had a phone installed. I knew that my last paycheck should arrive from Ohio in a few days to make up the difference. I called the moving van company to deliver my furniture. He told me that my moving papers were all mixed up, because the man who was to pick up my furniture was killed in an accident. On top of all this, my ex-husband kept calling me collect to get my furniture out of the house.

A knock on the door, and I opened it up to an Avon lady. I had no furniture, so invited her to sit on the floor with me. She told me about a shopping area and after inquiring about a church, she told me where I could find one behind the shopping center. I thought I had a new friend, but I never saw her again.

I needed my last paycheck from Sidley's and it hadn't arrived. When I left them, I had no other address other than Prestressed Concrete of Colorado. The mail girl who received the letter sent it back as UNKNOWN. The vice president came up to my table and told me the president of Sidley Precast Company had just called him. He said my paycheck came back; he wanted to know if I was employed there and if I was OK.

The next day the movers called and said my furniture would be delivered at 11 o'clock, and that if I wasn't there I would have to pay them $35 an hour. I told my boss and that I didn't have enough money because my paycheck had been sent back to Ohio. The draftsmen in the room had been listening to all the conversations and started to take up a collection.

Then my boss dug down in his pocket and gave me the money as a loan. He was responsible for the problem, because as he admitted, he neglected to tell the mail girl I was employed there.

The movers told me it would cost me $55 more because my apartment was on the third floor. I did not have the money. I showed them my contract that said nothing about a third floor delivery. They said that they would leave the furniture, but I'd be billed for it. I was billed for it, but argued the case with the company. That was the end of that.

I was assigned a drafting table in a far corner, far away from the men. It was hard enough breaking into a male dominated atmosphere, but I had an additional problem, I was still crippled with a sprained ankle.

Three weeks after I started to work, another woman was hired. Fran Nichols was given a drafting table near me in the corner. After our handshake, she said, "It looks like they don't know what to do with a woman to stick us in a corner like this." Then she said that she was hired because it worked out so well with me. It would have been nice if my boss told me that too.

Fran was a registered architect, so she knew what a problem it was when a women entered the engineering field. She told me that she was refused admittance to the American Institute of Architects' chapter in Denver, when she moved from Kansas. I felt that Ohio was twenty years ahead of Colorado with their acceptance of women in the business world. Fran was my first friend in Denver.

My work in this plant was different than what I did in Ohio. It was a big disappointment, but I had a job and accepted it. I was a senior draftsman in this company.

A junior draftsman was hired and assigned to me. The man was black, and was hired to prevent racial discrimination. He was working on drawings that would go out in the yard for manufacturing. They must be correct. It was my job to check them. He made many errors, so I red marked them. He would not correct his errors because I was a woman. He had to be put under male supervision.

I was given a 20-story apartment building. When the job superintendent was erecting the building, he phoned my boss. He said that I made a four-inch mistake, so he had problems setting the second floor. I was sent to the job sight. Fran overheard the conversation, so she asked to accompany me. It was good to have an architect with me, but the job was my responsibility.

When we arrived at the building site, the superintendent was no where to be seen. He knew two women were coming to meet with him at 2:30. "Oh, there he is," said Fran, "but why is he walking away from us, should we tell him who we are?"

I agreed, so we called out to him, but he continued walking. We YELLED to him. He stopped and turned around. "Oh, I didn't see you," he said. Oh yes he did, for he turned around and walked the other way when he saw us.

I had the plans with me so he opened the back of his station wagon. I laid out the plans, and he proceeded to show me where he was having problems.

"The floor isn't fitting, we are four inches out," he said as he opened the plans to the first floor. He pointed to the place where he thought I was wrong.

"Are you setting the floor with this sheet?" I said.

"Yes, of course I am," he replied

"But why are you setting the second floor with the first floor plans," I asked, as I turned over the sheet to the second floor layout and showed him where the four inches were. I was angry, and Fran was just as angry as I. This man was so sure a woman couldn't read plans, let alone drafting them, he came to the conclusion that I was incapable of doing my job.

"So," said the job superintendent," I see that you don't need to go up on the second floor to inspect.".

"Oh yes I do. I was told to inspect the floor slabs to see if they were manufactured right.

The job supe found a handmade ladder. He put it on the outside edge of a balcony. Alongside the ladder was a deep twenty-five foot excavation, which was dug out for an underground garage. A safer position would have been on the edge next to the building. I looked at the situation, and am unashamed to say I was frightened to go up that ladder. To make matters worse, the rungs were about 14 inches apart. Fran and I had on business suits with tight skirts. Companies at this time prohibited wearing pantsuits to work, but Fran and I were so angry at the job supe for doing this to us that our adrenal glands activated so we knew we could do anything! We knew he didn't expect us to go up that ladder. In Ohio I was treated with respect when I went on a job. Here in Denver, I was really going back twenty years.

Fran looked at me and I told her there was only one thing to do about the matter. I pulled up my skirts to my hips and climbed the ladder. Fran did the same thing and followed me up. I'm afraid of heights, but I did it! If it wasn't for the bricklayers giggling underneath us, I think I would have gone down again, but they gave me courage. We both knew it was the job supe they were laughing at, for he couldn't look up. Fran and I were thankful for the new invention, panty hose.

Job Supe gave me a homemade ladder to use

We arrived safely to the top and to my surprise the architect and the engineer were also called in for the 'mistake'. No wonder the job supe didn't want us to go up on the second floor. I graciously greeted them and asked, "How in the world did you get up here?" By using the ladder in front," the engineer said. "Oh, there is another ladder?" I said. Then he showed me the ladder the job supe set up for them. It was a new aluminum ladder and rested on the balcony next to the building; it was only 7 feet from the ground.

I took the engineer to the back of the building and showed him the ladder Fran and I climbed, that was 14 feet above the ground with a deep hole right alongside it. Then to the business at hand. I explained to the engineer that the job supe had set the second floor by using the first floor plans, so there was no error. As I was inspecting the double tee floor slabs, I moved over to the elevator shaft. The shaft didn't look right to me; it was not my problem, but I thought it should be brought to the engineer's attention.

"Please come over here for a minute," I said to the engineer, "I am sure that when I read your plans, rebar extended from the first floor concrete pour to the second floor of the elevator shaft. Am I right?"

"Of course it should," the engineer said.

"Well look here, where is the rebar?"

I turned around and told the job supe I was ready to go, and walked back to the ladder I climbed. I let the engineer deal with the job supe.

"You're not going down that ladder are you?" said the job supe.

"Of course I am. You put it there for me, didn't you?"

I gave him my big white purse and my set of plans to take down, then Fran and I went down the ladder. I was shaking all the way and couldn't look down. Fran was as satisfied as I was, and we kept the personhood we almost lost with that job superintendent.

When the building was up ten stories, my boss asked me if I would go to the job site for an inspection trip. I said, "Ok, but don't expect me to go too close to the edge." Bart, another draftsman came along this time.

We arrived at the site and were shown the elevator. I had never been on a construction elevator before, and had no idea what I was getting into. The elevator was connected to the building to the outside of the balconies. It had been nicely enclosed with plywood for my visit. Bart and I rode up with a load of bricks. I thought the elevator would let me off at the outer edge of the floor. WRONG! I had to walk a plank without a handrail. The man who ran the elevator held one of my hands and Bart the other, until I was safely on the building. No exterior walls were on the building at this height, so I was glad that I inspected the interior section of the building and Bart the outside edge.

Before I went down, I surveyed the beautiful view. We were above the smog, and the city of Denver lay sprawled below us with the mountains in the background. Mount Evans and Longs Peak made the view spectacular! Then we walked the plank back to the elevator, AND THAT'S THE LAST TIME I DID THAT!!!

Wolf and Susan had made a pact with me that no matter what happened to our lives; we would meet at Red Rocks Amphitheater in Denver on Easter Sunday. They flew out to make that date! Easter Sunday, 1969 will never be forgotten.

Audrey and her family were a wonderful addition. They came from their home in Grand Junction, Colorado. For two weeks I had a house full of people.

The night before Easter, everyone climbed into sleeping bags. The floor was a mound of people. We set the alarm for 3 AM and everyone scrambled to make the date at Red Rocks. The only party pooper was Audrey's husband. He refused to get out of his sleeping bag, so we left him.

It was dark when we arrived at Red Rocks Amphitheater, and it was already filling up with people. We groped around and found some seats and then bundled ourselves up in blankets. The amphitheater faces east and seats 7000 people. It is situated between two high red rock walls. A perfect place for Easter Sunrise services.

The eastern sky behind the stage started to glow with the rising sun. Behind the stage on a mountain were three crosses silhouetted against the rising sun. You have no idea how beautiful that sunrise was with all it's splendor! It was a sight to behold!

It was worth the plane trip Wolf and Susan made from Ohio. It was worth the 325-mile trip Audrey and her family made from Grand Junction, so I felt a warm relationship with my family. We got back to my home. Tom was still asleep in his sleeping bag. We made plenty of noise to get him up with our preparation of bacon, eggs and toast for breakfast.

The next morning Wolf called on a company he had been in contact with for a job, and was hired. They will be moving from Ohio in April, and will live with me until they find a home. It wasn't easy going through the divorce and then coming out to Colorado all alone. Now I have family near me.

By this time I had made many friends, including a neighbor who lived alone in a house across the street from the apartment. She came over one day for a visit to welcome me into the neighborhood. She told me that her son was missing in Vietnam. For a moment I reflected back on Wolf, and how close he had come me to being sent overseas to Vietnam. Several times he was pulled out of a line-up at the last minute. The last time he was pulled out, he was sent to school for training with the FBI. He remained in this type of work for the duration of his war service. Even though the neighbor had hopes, we both seemed to know the answer.

Wolf and Susan had been living with me for about a month, when they found an apartment closer to his work. So once again I'm living alone. If the weather cooperated, I painted pictures of the mountains.

I usually stopped in a little restaurant high in the mountains for my Sunday dinner. They served excellent meals. I especially liked the homemade pie. If I was lucky I got a table by a large window facing the high mountains. It was a perfect picture of the high range with Mount Arapahoe in full view.

A few years later I found another restaurant in the mountains over looking a mountain stream. In season, zillions of humming birds came to feed at the feeders on a balcony. I called this my white tablecloth restaurant, and I could buy a cocktail with my meal.

I was painting in the mountains one day when a man came up behind me and said, "You are painting my house." I looked around and it was a structural engineer from the plant where I worked. I was surprised and said. "Do you live among these beautiful mountains?" "Yes, you see that road you put in the picture? If you follow that road to the next crossing, I live on the corner. Please come over for a cup of coffee when you are through."

I did take him up on his offer and met his wife and children, then she invited me to stay for a quiche supper. What a nice family

I went back to the same place to finish the painting. Another man came up to me and said, "Did you paint that picture all by yourself?" I thought I would make a joke out of the silly question, so made an issue out of it by looking around to see who else could have helped me, and replied, "Yes."

"Even the clouds and the sky?"

"Yes."

"Can you paint dogs?"

"Yes."

He ran to his car and brought me a dog! "He's out of champion stock, do know what that is?"

"Yes."

"What would you charge me to paint him?"

"At least $50 if I would do it." Again he said, "He's out of champion stock."

The dog reminded me of my marriage and recent divorce. Won't I ever let those memories go? I did not want to get involved in another dog relationship, no matter how sincere, so I replied," My ex-husband is an AKC judge. I doubt that I'll paint him." He left without any further questions.

I was far away from Ohio. The house that my ex-husband, Wolfram, and I owned still was not sold, and I needed the money from the sale to build my own home in Denver. Wolfram, who was a real estate agent, held the listing for the sale.

A friend of mine wrote that Wolfram had a woman with five kids living in the house with him. I called my lawyer in Ohio, and he found it was true; he also had four or five dogs in the house. The divorce decree said that he must live in the house alone with only one dog. I was fortunate to have a good lawyer, for he asked the woman to move out of the house.

Wolfram had met the woman in his real estate office when she came in to rent a house. They couldn't find one, so he told her to come to live in his house. Because of this incident, it looked like we had no action to sell the house, so the lawyer and I decided it must be put in the hands of another realtor who had no personal interest in the matter.

In the fall of 1969, I told Fran I would like to transfer my Quota Club membership to the Denver chapter and that since she was an architect she was qualified to join. We went to a meeting together. When it came time to vote me in, they had my address wrong. I had no idea where that was, but Fran did, and it was in the worst part of town. Fran rose and told them that I did not live at that address and the woman who made that announcement knew it. She said she came along as a potential member, and that she was an architect. Fran also said she wanted nothing to do with them, then told me what they did, and we both walked out.

After this episode Fran and I joined the Colorado chapter of Women in Construction. In this club, I was made cochairman of a model building contest. This was open to high school girls to encourage them to go into the building trade. I met Flo in this club, who was the executive secretary of Mack Precast Company. She said she remembered when I came in their office when I was looking for a job, and they still had my application. Their head draftsman had moved to Texas, and they probably would be calling me right after Christmas to take his place.

Wolf, Susan and I went to Grand Junction to spend Christmas with Audrey and her family. Early on Christmas Eve we embarked on this 325-mile trip. We drove the Mount Vernon Canyon road and as we neared the high mountains we came upon a large sign, 'Chains required on Loveland Pass.' After several unsuccessful attempts to get the chains on over our snow tires, Wolf finally succeeded. We drove on again and found a motorist stalled along the side of the road. My son said, "It's Christmas," so he got out and managed to start the man's car. We drove on again and another motorist stopped us. "The pass is closed, if you would rather turn back," he said. We figured would add another 250 miles to go back to Monarch Pass, so we decided to continue and take our chances. Below Loveland Pass a line of cars greeted us. Most of them had already waited two hours. An avalanche had closed the pass. We waited another two hours.

The highway patrol came by and inspected our chains, shoved trucks and trailers off to the side, and let us proceed up the pass. We drove through a high wall of snow as we were going up. How these men who manned the snowplows knew where the road existed is beyond me. I did find out that the men who manned these plows do nothing but go up and down the pass all winter long. The avalanche was at least a quarter mile long; no wonder that it took them four hours to clear the road. We followed the plows with their blue blinkers single file. After we got over the pass, the whole trip was like a beautiful Christmas card. We were tired and tried to find a place to have a cup of coffee. Bars were open, but they had no coffee, only beer and liquor, so we asked for water. We finally arrived in Grand Junction at 5 o'clock in the morning on Christmas Day.

After the Christmas holiday, Mack Precast called. I started my job as head draftsman on January 5, 1970. Now I had a job like the one I left in Ohio, those beautiful precast buildings. When I came on the job, I found only one draftsman, and he was a deaf mute. This was his first job since leaving drafting school. He had not been trained in lip reading, I had no training in sign language, so now I was educating myself in sign language; and I had thought my school days were over. Besides this problem, he knew nothing about precast or its construction. I was doing all his phoning, and drew pictures of everything he was talking about. I had very little time for my work. It is difficult enough to train someone who could hear and speak. I motioned to him about his training in lip reading. He had no training in lip reading, and no intention of learning it.

203

The problem is his, but I was learning the sign language to compensate for his lack of lip reading. I was drawing pictures and doing his phoning and trying to show him what precast is all about, then I discovered he could not read or understand what was written on the plans. In trying to find out what he could do, he wrote and motioned that he was a star basketball player and had medals in skiing. It seemed to me that this was the extent of his education. I called his instructor of drafting and told him I was having difficulties with him. He understood, and said tests at the school showed he had the mentality of a fifth grader. And he was trying to do precast work?

I talked to the president of the company about it and we both agreed, we would have to let him go. The deaf mute cried bitter tears and wrote that I was just like his father. His mother was kinder to him. I suspected that his mother babied him.

Two new men were hired. One was a 'business man' and the other had been a safety engineer, who immediately tried to take over the drafting room. He went into the file and proceeded to throw out papers that he thought were unnecessary. I stopped him. He knew nothing about the papers. Then he tried to be the boss. I asked him if he knew that he would have a woman for a boss before he took the job. He said he had been told. I asked him if he was hired as a draftsman under my control. He admitted he was told. I told him to keep it that way, and leave the files and everything else alone.

One payday the sanitary engineer, Harry, flaunted his paycheck in front of me. It was $25.00 a week more than I was paid. I went to the president and complained. He said the 'business man' had owned two businesses and so he was worth more. I told him I also owned a business and it was successful, but both the businessman's projects failed. Then I asked him if he knew what kind of an engineer Harry was, on the last job he had in a big manufacturing plant. He didn't know so I told him that he was a safety engineer. His answer was that they were family men, so were worth more money. I was a 'family man' too and a sickening feeling came over me, when I realized that a woman doesn't count in this plant. Harry only supported himself, like me. I never resolved the problem. I lost my personhood.

Because of the problems Harry made when he tried to take over the drafting room and flaunting the check, I decided that he didn't need training. Harry complained to the president that I would not show him how to do the job. The president called me in.

"You and Harry aren't getting along together, I'll have to let one of you go." he said. "Harry complains that you won't show him how to do his work."

"That's right sir," I said, "You are paying him more than you pay me even though I'm his boss. If he is getting paid more than I, it should be Harry who is showing me how do the job, not the other way around." I knew by this remark that I was putting the president on the spot, for I forced him to realize who was important.

"I will have to let one of you go."

"If you want me to go, I will."

I knew the man couldn't perform and so did the president, for hadn't Harry admitted it? The safety engineer was fired. Herman, the 'businessman' was kept on, but would not do as I instructed him. One day I took him to the job site to help me do some measuring at a crucial spot. The superintendent of the building construction accompanied us. I asked Herman to measure from a tight corner to the center of the column, not the outer edge. He continually went to the edge, one or the other, never to the center.

The superintendent knew I was in charge of the exterior precast on the building, and he also knew why I asked Herman to measure to the center of the column. He watched Herman a few minutes, then yelled at him, "Why in the hell don't you do what she is asking you to do?" After this I had very little trouble with Herman.

In the fall I did some house hunting in Northglenn. A vacant lot interested me, and it had a FOR SALE sign on it, so I went to the middle of the lot and looked around. On the east I could see the rolling hills of the prairie, on the south I could see the whole city of Denver. On the west I could see Mount Evans jutting its peak towards the sky. Then at a closer look to the south, I spotted Pikes Peak 90 miles away. It was a perfect view!

I called the number on the sign. A builder, who owned the lot, said he had only one plan that would fit on the lot. It was similar to the house we owned in Ohio, only much smaller. I had enough money saved for a down payment, even though the house in Ohio had not been sold. I signed the contract. The builder said it would take three months to build the house. Only three months? Unbelievable!!!!

CHAPTER 18
I BUILD A HOUSE

January 1971. It's fun to inspect the house that is going up. My visits are after work, or on weekends, so I never see the men who are building my house. It seems like little elves are doing it, for every time I see it more construction has been done, and it's being finished! After living in a house for 28 years, and watching every board and every nail go into the project, this is hard to believe. I chose the brick and other materials. I didn't see them again until they were in place. I was like a child with a new toy.

I moved into my new home in Northglenn, Colorado on March 1. The first thing I did was to open the closet door next to the kitchen. The same closet in the kitchen, in the Ohio house had never been finished. As I opened this door, I was shocked to see that the floor was carpeted. I got down on my hands and knees and ran my hands over it, then I lay down on the floor, and laughed and cried, laughed and cried … it was unbelievable! I went from room to room. Everything was finished! The doors were hung!

Then I wondered about the house in Ohio. Were the beautiful doors still in their protective wrappings, gathering dust in the attic? I've been getting word from Ohio that Wolfram was finishing the house to get it sold. Maybe the doors were hung by now.

It had been three years since leaving Ohio and the first time I was living in a place where I could once more plant my blue iris. I wrote to my daughter, Marlene, and asked her if she had a root of the blue iris. She didn't have it, but thought she could get it from a friend, who was living in a house she had formerly lived in. Her friend shared it with us. I planted the blue iris in the backyard, under the garden window, of my new house. It is now fifty years since I was a small child, and watched my father plant the iris at the head of the fishpond. This is a beautiful memory of my father, who planted it, and of my mother, who kept it weeded.

Back at work, the new issue of the Precast Magazine was brought into my room. It featured the American Automobile Club building in Cleveland, Ohio. The executive secretary and the president knew I was job captain and in charge of the precast part of the building.

The president came into my room with congratulations. He told me that he also worked on some buildings in Cleveland, but a long time ago. He did the polished marble staircase in the Palace Theater. I looked at him very startled, for I had gone up and down those steps many times. One never knows who they may meet in later life, who were involved in something you thought was so beautiful.

A visit to the doctor confirmed what I suspected; I should have an operation. On a follow-up visit, he told me he also suspects cancer. That operation supercedes the first one. I had been living in my new house only a few months, when this came up. The date for the operation was set much earlier than I had planned, for I wanted to take a vacation trip to Alaska, not the hospital.

I couldn't believe it, so went to a clinic to see another doctor for a second opinion. He came into my room in a big hurry. He put on an air of being very busy, did the exam and hurried out again. After I left the room I went down the wrong hall, and here was the doctor sitting on a desk with his arms wrapped around his knees, gabbing to a nurse. My, but he was in a big hurry! I gave him a look of disgust, and never went back to him.

To get my mind off the operation, I took a weekend drive down to Westcliffe. Coming from Pueblo, I came over a high hill. I stopped the car, and looked down into a big valley. I could see the big expanse of the Sangre De Cristo mountain range, which is only twenty miles away on the other side of this valley. How beautiful! I followed this beautiful valley, for many miles, then turned towards home.

The operation was on a Saturday morning. Audrey, who came from Grand Junction and Susan, my son's wife, accompanied me and waited during the three-hour operation. I woke up as they were transferring me onto a gurney. A red-headed man leaned over me and I said, "Hi"." He smiled at me and said, "Today you are the luckiest woman in the world, no malignancy."

I was not recovering as I should, my bowels were paralyzed, my condition worsened, and by Thursday I was near death. I was too sick to know that my family and friends were saying prayers for me. Audrey stayed faithfully by my bedside and whispered in my ear, "Mommy, you have done many wonderful things in your life."

I faintly remember answering, "Yes, but I didn't know they were wonderful until the job was done." I remember going down into the shadow of death. It was very dark, but I was not afraid. I saw a bright light. It was casting purple shadows from behind a pillar. It was the brightest light I had ever seen. I knew it was Christ. As I waited in the dark for him to light my way to Him, He moved, but never lit the way. I faded out of the catacombs.

I awoke to find doctors and nurses working around my bed. One was constantly taking my blood pressure. A specialist was at one side of my bed and across was my doctor. He and my doctor were saying nothing, but talking constantly with their eyes. I was scheduled for another operation, the next morning at ten o'clock. All the prayers that were said for me were answered at eight o'clock the next morning. Miraculously, the paralysis left my bowels and they opened. Suddenly the room was filled with nurses, who were all smiling and laughing while they attended me. My doctor came in and said, "Do you know we almost lost you yesterday?" I told him I knew, and explained what happened to me. He said, "That is the way it is when you are near death."

A few days later I was released from the hospital. Audrey took me to her home in Grand Junction. I wasn't at Audrey's house too long before my skin turned yellow and then orange. She took me to her doctor, who put me in St. Mary's Hospital in Grand Junction. The doctor didn't think it was an ordinary case of hepatitis. He told me that it looks like I was allergic to something, and even though it was rare, he thought I might have been poisoned by the anesthetic.

The doctor said, "Did you ever have an operation using Fluothane anesthetic?" I told him I had an operation in 1964, he could call the surgeon. He called Dr. Downing in Painesville, Ohio. Yes, he used Fluothane for the gall bladder operation. I had an allergic reaction to this anesthetic, and was near death's door again. I am one of 500,000 persons who are allergic to Fluothane. Not a pleasant statistic to have. Another dose of that anesthetic would have been fatal. I would have had that dose, if I had not avoided the

operation for a bowel obstruction. Yes, the prayers were answered again.
God is all-powerful; no one can tell me any different.

I was in this hospital two weeks, and then back to Audrey's house for
another two weeks. While I was at Audrey's home, my brother Donald and
his wife, Arlene, visited me. At this time I was sleeping 20 hours a day and
I fear I wasn't good company for my visitors, because I was falling asleep as
they visited.

I came back to my home in Northglenn. I found a police summons on
the front door. I must do something about the weeds in my yard, or I would
have to pay a fine of $300 or spend three months in jail.

I wrote a letter to the mayor, and told him of my illness and hospital
stays, and that I couldn't afford the $300, so they could put me in jail, but be
sure to have all the medication I needed while there. A policewoman came
to see me. She apologized for the summons. She said a neighbor had told
them I went on vacation and was out of town quite a bit and hadn't done
anything to my yard, since I moved in the house. Then she said the police
force offered to help me in their spare time. I had already signed a contract
for a man to rock my yard, and contacted a high school boy to help me with
the weeds and landscaping. She said to call if I needed any help. After that,
the police waved to me every time they passed by.

The same neighbors complained that children would throw the rocks in
their windows. I thought this might be a problem. I was too weak to control
a bunch of kids, so I invited all the neighbor kids into my yard. I had packs
of plastic eyes that rolled around. I gave each kid a pair of eyes and some
glue and told them to pick out a rock from my yard and make their own 'pet
rock.'

Pet rocks were very popular at this time. Soon about twenty kids were coming for rocks, and showing off their handiwork. The idea grew so much they gave ME rocks that they found in the mountains. Being the rock hound that I am, I thought I got the best of the bargain, for one of them was a piece of marble from Marble, Colorado.

I made a friendship garden, and put the donor's name on the back of their donation with India ink. They brought visitors to see their rock in my garden. Of course each visitor was given a pair of eyes and told to pick any rock in my yard for their pet rock. A rock was never thrown to break windows in the neighborhood again. I made lemonade out of a lemon!!!

The doctor ordered me to do a lot of walking. All these kids followed me up and down the street as I walked. The gang called me 'Freda' as I asked them to. One day a little visitor called me 'Grandma.' One of the kids said, "Would you stop calling her Grandma, you'd think she was old enough to be our grandma." The rest of the kids said "Yeah." I let it go at that; why spoil it? I never forgot that bunch of kids.

Four months had passed before I was able to go back to work. By this time the house in Ohio had been sold, so those ties are broken, for which I was grateful. I needed the money for expenses caused by the illness. The precast company I worked for was down, no work. I was still very tired, so the doctor told me to go on a vacation.

I went to see my daughter in Ohio. This was a restful vacation. Marlene did what people in Ohio usually do in the fall. She picked apples from her tree and we took them to the cider mill. This was the kind of thing I needed to do. On my way back to Denver the plane stopped in Chicago, so I stayed with my brother Donald in Chicago for a day before boarding again for Colorado.

When I was finally able to go back to work, I found that blinds had been put on the windows in my office. I was happy about it until I found that they had been screwed shut. I could not open my window, which was on the south side. The room got very hot. I shared an air conditioner with Mary the bookkeeper, but she closed all the vents that serviced my room. I didn't say anything about it. I just bought a new pants suit and had a new hair-do.

The plant manager came in and told me that he had been ordered to screw the blinds shut, or loose his job. The men in the plant were mad about it and felt sorry for me. He also said that he was told that Mary, the bookkeeper, had complained that I looked out the window too much instead of working. One day I was out in the plant, and found the manager standing in the middle of the plant, with his hands in his pockets. I asked him what was wrong and he said "I've been looking around and thinking what a rinky-dink outfit this is."

Maybe he was right, for the president asked me one day to live in the apartment he has at his golf club. I told him I was happy in my new home.

Winter had come, and I came home one day, and found all the sidewalks shoveled off, and I live on a corner! After the problems I had in the plant, it made me cry with joy to know the neighbors cared about me.

Mack Precast was still lacking work, so I attended a real estate school in hopes of eventually leaving Mack Precast, for I wondered who would hire someone as old as I, except to sell real estate. I sold real estate on the days Mack had no work for me.

I heard of a man who owned a lot of real estate and called on him. He was eighty years old, and was interested in selling some of it. I researched his property and came back for a listing. He got off the business at hand, and asked me why a woman like me was single. I just shrugged my shoulders, and then he asked me to marry him. If I would marry him, he would buy me a Lincoln car. He was wealthy to be sure, no doubt about it, but I inquired as to his reasons for the proposal. He said he needed someone to drive the car for him, and his family was trying to put him in a senior citizen's home, and he didn't want to go.

I looked around and asked him who planted the vegetable garden, who planted the beautiful bed of pansies, who mowed the lawn and who cleaned his house. He said he did all those things himself. I told him that his family was nuts. And went out and never came back for a listing. My son said some young chick would grab at the chance some day, for the man was desperate. I didn't want to mess with his family. I saw nothing but bickering.

In June, Mack Precast had very little work, so they loaned me out to an architect as an 'expert on the skin of buildings.'

Executive Tower Inn is a 32 -story skyscraper and I was in charge of the technical work on the exterior. I met an architect, Arnie Vollmers who introduced me to his wife, Audrey. Arnie worked on the interior of the building. Meeting his wife started a close friendship with the couple.

By the time I was finished with this building, I knew I needed another operation. I told the doctor I wasn't ready for another hospital trip, I still wanted to go to Alaska. But to the hospital I went. But not before being hired by another engineer in Boulder.

The operation was done in the delivery room to prevent any contact with the fluothane anesthetic. A new mask and tubes were used. Even with all these precautions, I couldn't help looking for yellow and orange skin afterwards, but it never happened.

The hospital was crowded and they were putting on a new wing. I was put in a section that hadn't been used for a long time. The curtains on the window were torn, the window looked out onto a brick wall. The room was so small, the bed was put in a corner.

I had a strong suspicion that the rest room down the hall was a multipurpose room, where bed pans were emptied in a large sink. The bed pan sink was equipped with the only faucet in the section. I was sure it was used to draw our bath water, and even our drinking water. I complained to the doctor, who thought I needed a psychiatrist.

The psychiatrist came to my room, and I told him what I suspected was true, and I wanted him to leave, because I didn't hire him, so I wouldn't pay him. He said he'd talk with me for nothing. I began by asking him questions, and he finally told me I was cross-examining him instead of the other way around. I told him to be happy, I wasn't charging him either. I took him into the rest room. I showed him blood that had been on the toilet for four days, and the slop sink had the only water faucet in the room, and it was used to clean bed pans and draw our drinking water. There was no other water faucet in this section of the building.

That night a nurse came into my room and closed the door. She sat on the bed and said she had something to tell me. Everything that I suspected about the water faucet was true, and she wanted me to know that: Gosh, I'm not nuts after all. I was glad to be released from that hospital. I suppose that more people than I were glad to see me go, for I wrote a nasty letter to the head of the hospital.

I went to work for the engineer in Boulder. I had a raise in pay, and more benefits than the last job. When they hired me, I was told that they had a large precast building in Salt Lake City to engineer. I didn't know that they did not have a contract for the job. I worked for several months when they informed me that they lost the contract. It was granted to another firm. I worked for them a year. They tried to give me enough work, but no work is no work. So they let me go.

I wasn't out of work too long before I got a job with Ken R. White, an engineering firm, south of Denver. The man who hired me said he was told that I was a precast expert. I told him that I didn't say that, but he said the people I worked for said it. "You are a precast expert," he said.

Summer came and the company went on a ten-hour day, four days a week. This was very hard for me to take, so I worked an eight-hour day. It gave me only a 32-hour week. I lived twenty miles from work, and drove through heavy downtown traffic to get there.

A young engineer dated me a few times, ate his lunch with me, and came over to my house one evening, and said he wanted to marry me. I told him that our ages were too far apart, but why? He said he would like to continue his education, and thought WE could manage this if he married me. Well, that one was a bummer, too.

Colorado Shockbeton asked me to work for them. This company was close to my home and is a division of Prestressed Concrete of Colorado. I left Ken R. White to work for a company close to home, but with a stipulation that I first take a trip to Alaska. Fran Nichols had a lot to do with them hiring me back, for she is now heading the drafting room.

I went to a travel agent in Northglenn to get my plane tickets for Alaska. They said I should have made my reservations a month before the trip. Of course that was impossible. They said all they could get was a one-way fare from Seattle to Anchorage, but a guided trip was available. They also recommended I not go to Alaska alone. I had a suspicion that a two-way fare was available, but that they made more money on a guided trip. I told them, "So I stay up there for three months; give me the one-way ticket to Anchorage, Alaska." I bought it and went home to pack my bags.

CHAPTER 19

ALASKA AND HAWAII

I left Denver on August 17, 1973 for Seattle, Washington, where I boarded an Alaska Airlines plane. Looking down from my window seat, I could see the channel dividing the mainland of Alaska from the mountainous islands, jutting out of the sea. My eyes traveled to the Coast Mountains on the mainland. They are covered with snow and ice from many glaciers. Away in the distance I could see more mountains, which also looked like solid snow and ice. This is August, how could that be? Little wonder that no road traverses this snowfield.

I landed at Anchorage and got a taxi, which took me to the Westward Hotel.

What time is it? Well now, that is a problem. Alaska encompasses five time zones: Pacific, Yukon, Alaska, Bearing and USSR. Alaska is the most northerly, eastern and western state in United States because the 180-degree meridian line bisects the Aleutian Islands. It was on a game show, that an answer to the most eastern point in the United States was off the coast of Maine. Someone didn't do his/her homework.

I held reservations for all my flights, except the flight back to Anchorage, because the agency had no return flights available. The travel agency also gave me these reservations in an expensive hotel. I took the room for the first night and asked for a cheaper room. I was given a tiny room that faced a brick wall. I walked over to the Holiday Inn, and registered with them. The bellhop from the Holiday Inn came for my luggage and put them in the bellhop closet, for I will be boarding the train to Mount McKinley today

The train trip to Mount McKinley was an eight-hour ride. I seated myself, and then a woman asked me if the seat next to me was taken. She was also traveling alone, so this started a wonderful friendship with Jacqueline Fogel, who is a sculptor/artist from New York City. Jackie designs full-life figures of famous people out of old furniture. Years later, she was commissioned to paint one of those famous cows that adorned the New York streets.

The train tracks are laid on tundra, and a few feet below is the permafrost, which thaws unevenly, so we have a slow 35-MPH trip. The landscape is flat except where the mountains jut up, and they go up violently to about 4000 feet! Black spruce grows here, the limbs are sparse and the trees look small and skinny, but we are told they are 100 years old. The roots cannot penetrate the permafrost so they fan out sideways, and it prevents the trees from growing tall. The farther north we travel, the permafrost is closer to the surface and goes down deeper. At Mount McKinley it is only two feet below the surface and is 900 feet deep. The tundra is hard to describe. One cannot walk around it in the region of Mount McKinley, for the ground water cannot penetrate the permafrost, which makes it very swampy.

When we arrived at the lodge near Mount McKinley, it was a mad house. The first thing we did was to get in line to put in our reservations for a room and hope for the best. The hotel had burned to the ground the year before. They built a new lodge, and added four Pullman cars on stationary tracks. Jackie and I met Leona, a schoolteacher from Massachusetts, in the lobby while we waited for assignments. One by one we were called to the window for our room locations. I was assigned an upper berth in a Pullman car, Jackie had a roomette and Leona a hotel room with two double beds.

I was putting my luggage in the upper berth, when a Japanese man proceeded to put his luggage in the lower berth. He couldn't do it because my ladder was in his way. He was trying to tell me something in Japanese, and I was trying to tell him something in English. We both started to laugh. The laughing continued as he tried to hoist his luggage over the ladder, and then crawl underneath it to get to the other side, bowing in Japanese fashion all the way. Even if we had a language barrier, we both had a sense of humor.

Back in the lobby, I was telling Leona and Jackie of my experience with the Japanese man. They decided it was not good for me to share a curtain with a man, so Leona offered me the extra bed in her room.

I spent the night in Leona's bed. We must rise at 3 AM to catch the 4 AM bus to view the highest mountain in North America, Mount McKinley. Our room was missed for the wake-up rap. At 3:45 Jackie was at the door. She missed us at the bus stop. We dressed, packed our bags and went down to the lobby in record time. Jackie informed the dining room, so they had breakfast waiting for us, and we were at the bus stop with a cup of coffee and rolls in our hands at 4AM. Thus started the ten-hour bus trip to the big mountain.

We hadn't been riding for too long before we spotted Mount McKinley 60 miles away, with the red sunrise on it. The sky was clear with no cloud cover on the big mountain, and the guide said he only hoped that it would remain cloudless, because this was only the fifth day that year it was clear.

I saw my first snowshoe rabbits. We stopped on a bridge. Below us was a grizzly bear with her two cubs fishing in a stream. As we drove through this bleak, almost treeless wilderness, moose and elk made an appearance. Higher up, we spotted Dall sheep. The scenery was remarkable ... glaciers, glaciers, glaciers. The timberline in this part of Alaska is 2000 feet, which is about the altitude we were traveling. Then it was a barren tundra wilderness. I don't understand how the wild life can exist under these conditions, but they do.

Mount McKinley was only 20 miles away when we arrived at a rest stop. We ate lunch as we viewed the big 20,320-foot high mountain rising from an altitude of about 2000 feet. What a tremendous sight to behold! It is solid ice above the 6000-foot level. By the time we were ready to return, the clouds were starting to surround the mountain. On the way back to the lodge, we saw more animals, plus a golden eagle. A proud little ptarmigan was slowly walking across the road in front of us. He was so slow the bus driver had to stop for him.

Jackie and I parted when we arrived back at the lodge, for she will continue on to Fairbanks. I will return to Anchorage. While waiting for my train on the platform, I noticed Jackie's bags were on the same cart as mine. I inquired about it, and Jackie was called from the lodge. Her luggage almost went to Anchorage. I was able to repay the kindness' Jackie did for me, when she missed me at the bus stop.

In Anchorage the next morning, I boarded a bus to see the Portage glacier. The road followed Cook Inlet and Turnagain Arm. We stopped at

Mt. Alyeska for a salmon buffet lunch. A doctor and his wife joined me at my table. They had rented a car and were on their way down the Kenai Peninsula. They invited me to accompany them, but my luggage was in Anchorage, or I would have taken them up on their offer.

We arrived at Portage Glacier, which was named after the trail Indians used to portage over the mountains to Prince William Sound. The glacier is big and beautiful, with many icebergs dotting the water. We were told that the icebergs are blue because they are compacted so hard that the air is removed. I saw other glaciers on this trip, but none so large.

On the return trip, the bus driver recited poetry all the way. He was good at it. This is what I call a 'super-dooper' bus driver. Again we rode along Turnagain Arm, which is laden with silt caused by glacier movement. Turnagain Arm is named for Captain Cook when he tried to find the Northwest Passage. He had to turn again to go out of this inlet to the sea.

The next morning I had reservations for a crab boat in Seward. I would have eaten the crabs I caught, but the trip was canceled because of rain in Seward. I was disappointed, for we would have traveled by train to get to Seward, and I love trains!

I found another bus that was loading passengers for a trip to Matanuska Valley. I arrived too late along with a few other people, and the bus was full. It was decided to put on another bus for the trip. Some passengers from the crowded bus came on our bus. Among them was a man with a big camera around his neck.

Matanuska Valley is very fertile, and the long summer sun favored the cabbage, which grew to six feet in diameter. While on this trip, the man with the big camera was taking pictures. I forgot to bring my camera, so I asked him if I could hold back some leaves so that he could take a picture of the enormous radishes.

That little question started a whole new life for me. I was holding back leaves of other vegetables, and stood by vines of enormous peas. Everywhere I went I would peek around, and see him taking pictures of me. Pictures by Indian graves, pictures by giant flowers, pictures, pictures, pictures!!!! I think something was happening.

By the time we toured the state experimental farms, the man with the big camera around his neck and I were buddies. We went into a cow barn. The cows were bedded down in tundra, not straw. On second thought, where would they get straw? Alaska did not lend itself to growing grain. The barn had a dirty look to it because of the gray/brownish tundra, but it was really clean. Bill St. Clair, the man who was taking pictures, wiped his feet on the grass when he left the barn.

I said to him, "You must be from a big city, a man from the country wouldn't wipe his feet like that." He looked at me and laughed when he told me he had been born and lived in Honolulu all his life. I laughed too, when I told him I was from Denver, but was born on a farm. Then he laughed again, when he said he had just come from a photographer's convention in Denver.

Just before we boarded the bus back to Anchorage, we stopped at an Indian graveyard. Small houses on top of the graves were painted brilliant colors and covered with blankets. In the houses were the personal effects of the deceased. It was a unique part of the trip.

On the return trip Bill and I sat together. The bus driver knew something was happening, for as talkative as he had been, now he was silent and had an ear turned our way. Bill and I exchanged addresses, then he invited me to come to Honolulu the next June. No wonder the bus driver was so quiet! I waved goodbye to Bill as the bus stopped at his motel, and wondered if I would ever see him again.

When I got back to Anchorage, I bought a plane ticket to Juneau. In spite of what the travel agency said about being unable to get me a return trip from Alaska, I was happy to just do my thing about getting back. After this was settled, I went shopping. I bought a leather cape in a fur store. The storeowner said,

"Would you consider moving to Alaska and work for me for $15,000 a year?"

"Why do you ask me?"

"You have such a happy glint in your eyes."

"No, it's too cold and damp."

"I'll outfit you in fur at no cost to you."

I refused again. I could not live in the damp cold of Alaska, even though the salary was a lot of money for 1973. I suppose the happy glint came from meeting Bill.

The next morning I boarded the plane for Juneau in the rain. I didn't see anything but clouds below, until I spotted Canada's Mount Logan jut its 19,860-foot peak through the clouds. Soon after this, the plane dipped below the clouds and I could see Mendenhall glacier, and the Capitol City of Juneau below us. We landed at the worst airport imaginable; it was either being renovated or built, but it was an awful mess. I wandered around on planks and boards until I spotted a limousine outside. My luggage was loaded and I was taken to my hotel. I wandered back into the street. I found a travel agency where I bought a ticket for the ferry to Ketchikan, but I had asked for a ticket to Prince Rupert in Canada, because I wanted to take a bus through Canada. They told me that the bus drivers in Canada were on strike. I thought I shouldn't trust my luck any further, so purchased a plane ticket from Ketchikan to Seattle. Back in Denver, when I purchased the one way ticket to Anchorage, I made lemonade out of a lemon, to return to Seattle like this.

At the visitor's center I was told of a salmon bake that evening. I bought a ticket for the bake and was informed that a limousine would pick me up at my hotel. The limousine turned out to be an old school bus. On the bus a man sat next to me. I'm Art Lowe from Burlington, Colorado, and who are you?" "I'm Freda Stumpf from Denver." What a big laugh came out of him! He invited me to join him and his wife at the Red Dog Saloon after the bake. I accepted, but I did not sit with them at the bake since I wanted to meet more people. I sat alone at a large table to see what would happen.

Soon the table began to fill up with a group of people, who seemed to know each other. The table was full of people from the Alaska Health Department. They were doctors and nurses from all over the state. I sat next to a nurse from Point Barrow. Each one asked me as they sat down "Who are you and where are you from?" I gave them a standard answer, "I'm Freda from Denver." I could see they thought I was a new employee of the health department. I told the group that I probably sat at the wrong table, but I'm having such a good time, I'm staying. On the way back, Mrs. Lowe sat with me and I joined them at the Red Dog Saloon where we were entertained by a pianist playing songs from the early 1900s on a 'rinky dink' piano.

The next day as I was entering the elevator in the hotel, a girl with a big smile on her face called out "Hello Freda from Denver." As I walked down the street someone called from the other side, "Hi, Freda from Denver." I guess they didn't care that I crashed their party.

That afternoon I visited Mendenhall glacier. This was the big glacier I saw from the plane. I thought Portage glacier was large, but this one is colossal! It is two miles wide. Try as I might, I couldn't get the whole glacier in my camera with one shot. On the way back I saw salmon spawning and then dying as they do. It was sad to see this, but it's part of nature. In Juneau I saw an original Russian church. It was topped by the typical cross. A cross bar was tilted up or down, depending how you looked at it.

Time to turn homeward again. I boarded the Alaska ferry, Matanuska, for the 20-hour trip to Ketchikan. I was unable to get a cabin, so slept in the lounge like everyone else. It was raining most of the way, but once in a while it lifted, and I could see the island mountains jutting up from the sea on either side of the boat. No wonder that a man was sounding the depth of the water in front of the ship. We made stops at Petersburg and Wrangle, where I saw many shrimp boats. We arrived in Ketchikan at ten o'clock in the evening. I was driven to my hotel immediately. I was happy to slip into a nice bed and fell fast asleep.

The next day I took a bus trip to Saxman Park. The Tinglet Indians, who are the descendants of the original owners, reconstructed the totem poles. Most of these people live in the Saxman Park area, and I saw totem poles in various stages of repair, in their yards. The poles symbolize the ancestry of the carver. Many of the streets in Ketchikan are built on wooden stilts, for the town is built on the side of a steep mountain. At a point where the mountain drops down to the sea, a tunnel is built to get from one side of town to the other. This was my last evening in Alaska.

I inquired around, and was sent to the finest restaurant in town. After a lovely dinner, I was shown into the lounge and sat around a piano bar with a cup of coffee, and a shot of brandy. A musician was playing the organ and piano. I was sitting there for a long time listening to this wonderful music, but had to leave to get ready to fly home the next day. As I left, he played a number I knew was especially for me. I stopped and looked around and sure enough he was watching me, and singing to me. The song was so appropriate. How did he know that I'd met someone special? Maybe I still had that glint in my eye. The next day I boarded a plane to Seattle, and then home to Denver.

I started my new job with Schokbeton, but because Pretressed Concrete of Colorado owns it. I was working in the same drafting room I worked in when I first came to Colorado. Fran had been elevated in the company, so now I have a new boss, who was a recent graduate with an engineering degree. He was very young for a supervisory job.

When I took this job, I made arrangements for a three-week June vacation.

Bill and I were corresponding. The letters and tapes are flying back and forth from Denver to Hawaii and back. The bi-weekly letters are getting more 'loverly' all the time. The sound of Bill's voice on the tapes made the waiting until June seem so long. His voice had a distinct British accent, so common to the native people who lived in close relationship to the missionaries, who came to Honolulu from Boston in 1820.

Bill had a collection of 200 Hawiian records. He sent me tapes of his favorites, the enchanting melody, 'Lei Aloha, Lei Makamae' is the traditional wedding song of Hawaii, and the haunting sounds of this tune still make me melt with emotion. I think 'Lei of Stars' was Bill's favorite, for he sent me a tape of at least ten renditions of this song performed by different musicians. It was 'our song.'

I bought my plane tickets for the 22nd day of June, 1974. I was taking this trip at a good time, for the company was low on work for the draftsmen. I went to my boss to arrange for my absence. Before I left him he asked,

"Are you flying to Hawaii in a 747 plane?"

"That is the plane scheduled for the trip."

"Well, how do you like that? Here I am your boss and I have never been on a 747."

"You fly for the company, why don't you ask your secretary to schedule you on a 747?"

The remark showed his immaturity. Too bad, for he was put in this job because of his engineering degree, but schooling doesn't always give a person experience or maturity for managerial work.

HAWAII

June arrived, and I boarded the plane for Hawaii. I never thought I'd like to visit Hawaii, but this is different. I had a good reason to go. When I landed, the airline hostess put a lei around my neck then gave me one for Bill. When I met Bill, he put three more leis around my neck, and I put one around his with kisses of course.

He took me on a short tour around the city. Flowers, flowers, flowers, even on the trees hanging down in soft folds. I had never seen so many flowers! Then he took me over to meet his father and mother. His father with a little twinkle in his eye sang a little ditty about a girl from Denver. It made me like him immediately.

The next morning Bill told me he had bad news for me. A few months before I arrived, he was told he had cancer and was getting radium treatments. He was sure they caught it in time, but it was too early to know. He was a little weak, but felt that he was strong enough to continue with my visit to the islands. We decided we would have three wonderful weeks together. We never mentioned the cancer after that. As the weeks progressed, he got a little stronger.

I remember the time we were waiting in a line for a table in a restaurant. The couple ahead of us was watching us. The woman said, "You must be celebrating an anniversary or something, you both look so happy!" I said, "No" and Bill said, "Yes."

I bought a muumuu, then as a present to Bill, I bought him a shirt to match. Bill said, "People will think I'm a visitor with these matching outfits." His prediction was right, for as we were riding up in an elevator to a nightclub on the top floor of a hotel, a woman asked where we found the matching outfits. While we were talking the man who was with her, asked Bill where he was from, and Bill told him, "Texas." Then the man asked what he did in Texas. Bill told him, "I'm in oil." I kept quiet until the nosey couple got off the elevator.

Bill was enjoying his role as 'tourist', or 'visitor' as they say in Hawaii, until one day when he took me to a park that was unknown to visitors. This is a park where the Hawaiians have their picnics. As we were about to enter the park, a Polynesian woman started to quiz us. Bill told her that he was a native, but that I was a visitor. She accepted this, but turned to me and said, "Put some Coppertone on your skin." I did feel a little odd being a blonde with white skin.

The park is tucked into a little corner of the city. Above the jungle of trees, one could see the tall buildings of downtown Honolulu. Many flowering trees surrounded us, and a beautiful stream flowed through the park. We came upon a swimming hole with many little golden bodies enjoying themselves by diving off the brink of a falls, and swimming below in the pool.

We crossed the stream on a footbridge, and then came upon a woman sitting on a mat, drinking beer. As is the custom, her family was doing all the cooking for a picnic. As we passed her, she called out to me in Hawaiian. Bill was telling me he couldn't speak Hawaiian, and now he was speaking to her in Hawaiian. I was laughing to myself as he took my elbow and guided me away saying "Mahala, mahala, mahala," very politely. I knew he was thanking her for something. He said she was inviting me to drink beer with her. Then I teased him because he knew how to speak Hawaiian.

My visit to Hawaii was perfect because I had a guide, who knew just what to do, to make it enjoyable. One day he drove down a short street and we came upon a little Chinese restaurant. I told the Chinese woman waitress that I would like some iced tea. Every time I tried to make her understand, she kept saying "Hut, hut, hut." I didn't understand what she was saying so I turned to Bill, and told him to tell her that I'd like iced tea. The woman still kept saying, Hut, hut, hut." Bill said, "She's trying to tell you she only serves hot tea." We did a lot of laughing when we got back in the car ... hut, hut, hut. In fact when we needed cheering up, one of us would say, "Hut, hut, hut," and Bill would remind me that I needed Coppertone.

Next it was to a Japanese restaurant, where he taught me to eat with chopsticks. I did very well indeed. Maybe it was the cups of saki that steadied my hands, but I ate the entire meal with chopsticks. He gave me the little saki cups to take home as a souvenir, because he was proud of me. I still have those saki cups. The little girl in me never washed those cups until last year when I decided 28 years was a long time to keep unwashed dishes!

Bill was a good host. The next restaurant was Hawaiian, where he showed me how to eat poi with a spiced fish.

Then on to the Polynesian Cultural Center. The Mormon Church sponsors this and the participants were students from the islands in the South Seas, Tahiti, Samoa, Fiji, Tonga and New Zealand. The setting was a beautiful lagoon surrounded with flowers. The entertainers and their boats were also adorned with flowers. Each islander danced the native dance of their island, each was distinctive and beautiful; the fast Tahitian hulu, the dance of New Zealand done with balls on a string, the soft dance of Hawaii and the expressive dances of Fiji, Samoa and Tonga.

Bill with his camera reminded me of the meeting in Alaska, where he took pictures of me. Again he took pictures everywhere we went. He had them developed for me and inserted them in containers for my projector. His photos were like a picture post card; there is no doubt in my mind that photography was his profession.

He took a little side trip one day, where we came upon the little Kealiiokamu Church. The doors were open, so we went inside. The church was decorated with orchids. Bill said it looked like they had a recent wedding in the chapel. Bill with his camera again, asked me to go up on the pulpit. I looked in the Bible. Nothing was printed in English. I picked up a hymnal, and it too was printed in Hawaiian. I was able to find the song, 'He Aloha Ko Iesu,' (Jesus Loves Me This I Know) and proceeded to sing it in fractured Hawaiian.

We left the church and drove on until we got to a lovely bay, where Bill took some 'loverly' pictures with his arms around me. Then up, up, up a mountain road. Bill had never been on this road, so we went exploring. He stopped the car on the top and we got out. The scene below us was spectacular. The sun was shining like a spotlight on the sandy beach and bay where Bill had taken the 'loverly' pictures.

Flowers once again surrounded us when we visited Foster Gardens, where many exotic flowers and trees are grown. I saw ginger flowers with long stems so tall I smelled the blooms without bending over. The orchids, plumeria, flowering trees and shrubs and ferns made me feel like I was walking through a fairyland in a children's storybook.

Way up above Honolulu is a rain forest, where we could view the whole city. Then we came down again, and to an extinct volcano where he showed me the little house on top where the man was stationed who gave the warning of the Japanese planes, when Pearl Harbor was bombed. He would not take me to Pearl Harbor, and I sensed he did not want to talk about it, for I knew he had experienced the Japanese bombing raid on Hawaii.

Bill and I were to fly together to the big island of Hawaii, but first he must take his father to the doctor. His father was having serious problems with his throat. His father was told he had cancer of the throat. Bill took his father in for more tests, so I went to the big island alone, for Bill needed this time to be alone with his family.

I landed in Kona and was taken to my motel room, which had louvered doors opening out upon a rocky seashore. I fell asleep that night listening to the comforting sound of the waves smashing against the rocks. The next morning I found the driver of our limousine fishing along the shore and putting little fish in a shallow water pool. He said he ate them raw.

After breakfast I boarded the limousine. The high point of that trip was the Kilauea Volcano. We were driven down into the cauldron where it was wired for rumblings. The guide told us of a ranger who was caught in the last eruption, and showed us the road he used which was blocked by a high hill of lava from that eruption. I asked him how they got the ranger out. He said the ranger had a two-way radio. I looked at all the wires inside of the cauldron and wondered about the ranger. Of all people, he should have known about the rumblings, if these wires really worked. Then I asked the guide if he had a two-way radio in the limousine. He said, "No," so I told him to get out of there. The volcano started to erupt three weeks later, and has been erupting ever since.

That night at the Hilo Hotel, Bill called me and said that my son had called from Denver. My house had been broken into.

I went back to Honolulu the next day. Bill and I had some serious talks after that, especially about his father. The cancer was inoperable, and he only had a few months to live.

We visited with his parents that evening, where I met Bill's sister, who had come from the mainland, where she lived. Bill bought a bottle of Scotch for me and told his mother how to mix the drinks with lots of ice. She kept filling my glass as if it was lemonade. I didn't know how to stop her and neither did Bill. I let the drink stand and she thought she hadn't mixed it right, so she took the glass out to the kitchen and filled it with fresh Scotch. You could tell his mother knew nothing about alcoholic beverages. My politeness caused me to become a little tipsy.

We lingered over our final Mai Tais in the revolving restaurant on top of the Ala Moana shopping center, where we said our good-byes. Our love for each other had strengthened. I didn't want to think about Bill and his cancer.

CHAPTER 20
A BREAK IN

I entered my home and found that a stranger had gone through every nook and cranny in my home. I felt violated, and the house was a mess.

My projector was gone and all the pictures that Bill had taken of me in Alaska. That broke my heart for they were precious to me. My stereo was gone. The things that were taken and not replaceable were my grandfather's iron clock, my mother's clock and all my sterling silver flatware. Among the silver were two silver spoons that belonged to my grandmother, Emilie Clara Martin Ruetenik, who was the daughter of the founder of the Martin Guitar Company. The silver jewelry I made is gone. I had taken a lot of it along with me, so I still had that, and a tray of 60 opals that I cut. The detective insisted he declare the stolen wedding ring.

The thief had entered my home by way of the garden window. He trampled the blue iris I had planted there, so I removed it and planted it by the fence. Then filled in the space with yucca and prickly cactus.

I went back to work and had worked only two days, when the new young boss fired me. The reason? They were low on work, and he had to let someone go. He said I was the only one in the drafting room, who had enough money to go to Hawaii, so he chose me. Word came to me that he was fired soon after that, but it was too late to save my hide.

I applied for unemployment and was considering Social Security, but applying for it at 62 years old, is a bummer. I had to do something until I was 65. I went out looking for work and picked some free-lance drafting work from Mack Precast. I did part time work for a job shop, and then got a job drafting for a cabinet shop, that built store interiors.

In the meantime, Bill had made a trip to New Zealand, Fiji and Australia. He had been around the world twice, and expected this to be his last trip. He came to visit me soon after Christmas. He was looking forward to meeting my family, and said he was feeling good. He stayed with me for ten wonderful days.

Bill was anxious to see Colorado snow and a real Colorado ghost town. I told him that it was almost impossible to get to them in the wintertime, for most of them are high in the mountains. I remembered the drive I took to Westcliff. It was not completely a ghost town, but close to it.

The trip took us through Colorado Springs, where we stopped to buy him an overcoat. We drove through Pueblo, then turned west through the Wet Mountains. When we came to the top of the pass we could see the beautiful valley below us, with the snow covered Sangre de Cristo Mountains in the background. On this pass Bill spied a small ski run. This was a family place and not at all pretentious. Families with children were there with sleds, skis and tubes, just having fun. He was impressed with the ski run and the view, so again, pictures, pictures and pictures.

We went down into the wide valley. We went into a restaurant located in one of the old buildings. Then I drove around the town and showed him the old buildings, and he had enough of THAT! I guess the old ghost towns weren't as glamorous as he imagined. Then we drove through the beautiful valley under the Sangre de Cristo Mountains.

We stopped near a ranch with red painted roofs. "Ah, Santa Clause lives here," said Bill. So he went out to take pictures of the red roofed buildings with the Sangre de Cristo Mountains for a background, and round haystacks with high mounds of snow on their tops, he called 'cupcakes.' We came back across the 10,000-foot high plateau of South Park, and down through the Front Range and home. It was dark when we got home, and Bill would not believe that we traveled over 300 miles. On the island of Oahu where he lived, you can scarcely drive 70 miles before you find yourself back home. The next day it was hard to take him back to the airport.

In April 1975, I signed preliminary papers for the Peace Corps. Bill wanted to wait a few years before we made any further plans for our relationship, because of his cancer. His father had passed away from cancer, and it was hard for him.

I was doing well in the cabinet shop, and had junior draftsmen under my control. They wanted to train me for project manager and had given me a raise.

In September 1975 I was accepted for Peace Corps work. They told me I was excellent Peace Corps material, but because it was hard to place a woman in the drafting field, it would not be too soon. I read that the Peace Corps were looking for a drafting teacher to introduce the profession in Samoa. I asked them to place me in that job. They told me over the phone that the Samoans would not accept a woman to teach drafting. This remark always made me wonder about that job. If I would be the first person introducing drafting in Samoa, how would they know it was a job usually given to men, unless the Peace Corps told them so?

235

In the meantime I was very active in the church. My group wanted to do something of an outreach nature. I suggested they contact Lowry Air Force, and ask for their choir to sing in our church. Then we would invite them into our homes for a Sunday dinner. I was sure the members of the Air Force would appreciate something like that. The group went along with my suggestion.

Three men and a woman came home with me after their program at church. I made a good dinner for them. During our conversations, I discovered that none of them had been in the mountains, which I thought was disquieting for they lived right below them. I suggested that I take them to Central City in the mountains.

Up in Central City I took them every place I thought they should see, and then stopped outside of an old saloon. I told them that I'd like to take them inside to see all the junk hanging from the ceiling, and some of the tables that had toilet seats. I reminded them that they were in uniform, and I didn't know the rules of the Air Force, but I knew they could order a soft drink. After conferring amongst themselves, they decided they could go inside just to see it.

A hostess dressed in an old fashioned costume met us at the door. I asked her to show them all the stuff, which she did, and then she escorted them down in front next to an old-time band, that was playing Western music. We were down in front so far I knew that everyone in the place was watching us, and it worried me. The next thing I knew, we were served coke on the house.

To our surprise, the band struck up the Air Force Anthem. The Air Force people stood up. I didn't know what to do, so I stood up. To my amazement, the whole crowd did the same thing. My guests were flabbergasted and so was I. The Air Force Anthem played on a rinky-dink piano by a Western band, is something one doesn't hear every day. The crowd clapped, then the band continued with their regular music, until we had to leave to meet the Air Force bus in Northglenn.

The next week the group from Church met. We all wanted to know what the others did to entertain their Airmen/Airwomen. One by one they told of the wonderful time they had with their group. Some took them to concerts, others took them visiting, others took them to a show, and then it was my turn. I said I found out that none in my group had been in the mountains, so took them to Central City. I related what happened in the old saloon. Their reactions were mixed. Some roared with laughter, and some were flabbergasted that I would do such a thing! But one airman wrote to me from far-away places and said he would never forget that afternoon. THAT'S all that mattered!

In April 1976 I finally received a packet from the Peace Corps. It had been a year since I applied for Peace Corps work. I was advised that I would not go to the South Pacific, which is what I wanted, but I would go to San Pedro Sula in Honduras as an advisor to drafting for the city. The job sounded excellent, right down my alley. There was so much to do, what about my house, my furniture? I didn't know what to do about it until the Peace Corps had a definite date. I was busy filling out forms, pages of them. I got my birth certificate and passport and then went to the Armed Forces Examining and Entrance Station in Denver for a medical examination.

I was 64 years old, when I took the medical exam at the Armed Forces Medical Center for the Peace Corps. I was old enough to be the grandmother of the girls who were here for the same examination. I wondered if I would pass it. The girls were joining various branches of the armed forces, I was the only one joining the Peace Corps. I went in for the hearing test, the blood test, and everything the girls did. The final doctor complimented me, because I was in excellent health for my age and in good shape for the Peace Corps. Some girls were twittering about me, an old woman taking this exam, but I defiantly waited for the outcome. The doctor came in.

"I will take you one at a time," the doctor said, "Peace Corps, will you please stand up?" I stood up. "You have passed the examination with flying colors. You will take your papers across the hall for processing." She gave me the papers and then addressed the girls "Will the rest of you girls please stand and salute Peace Corps as she leaves the room." Wow! As they saluted me, I was flanked on both sides with young girls. I went across the hall and gave them my papers to process. They sent me to an office at the end of the hall with more papers. As I was going down the long hall, people in the Armed Services came out of their offices, shook my hand and congratulated me. What a send-off! I don't know what happened to the other girls, but I doubt that they received the same treatment. The doctor must have been aware of the twittering and had done some phoning.

It was June 1976. I should be leaving for basic training in August. The last part of June, I received a letter from the Peace Corps. This must be the information I needed, so I thought. I opened the letter; it was short. I was told I was disqualified from Peace Corps work because of multiple medical problems. I put a call in to Washington D.C. I was not given any satisfaction about the medical problems, and they said the Armed Forces Examination had no effect on the Peace Corps decision.

I asked them to return my passport. They would not. What good is it to them? It was never returned to me. I do not know what they did with it. When the Peace Corps had an opening in Samoa, they refused to give me the job, because I am a woman, and now this. Were the Peace Corps themselves discriminating? I know that if a country discriminates against women in any kind of job, the Peace Corps must pull out of that country. This was the hardest blow to my personhood.

The owner of the cabinet company was very ill, and was unable to spend very much time in the plant. He asked me to teach his granddaughter drafting, which I did. She gave me a gold pencil for teaching her.

The owner told me I could have use of his office at any time. The phone in his office was private. In one conversation he asked me to be a liaison person between him and the plant. I agreed. The manager of the cabinet company called me into his office. They heard that I was joining the Peace Corps. I said it was true, but I had been disqualified.

They accused me of making a big mistake on a Pueblo store. I told them I had nothing to do with that store; it was not my job. (I knew who did the job, he would never put his initials on a drawing because he didn't want to take the blame for a mistake.) I told the manager that my initials are on all my drawings; they won't find them on that job. (No wonder the drafting room head kept putting the mistake on that job on my desk to correct it.) I never had time to do another's work and I told him that. Something was going on! Then they said the mere fact that I was thinking of leaving them to join the Peace Corps was reason enough to let me go. So again I lost my personhood.

The company had a clause in the retirement program that I could not collect retirement if I was younger than 65 years old. I was only a few months younger than 65, but lost that retirement.

I applied for unemployment. The accountant phoned me.

"I see that you have applied for unemployment."

"Yes, of course, I can collect it under the circumstances."

"Well we want to give you your retirement, but we can't do that if you apply for unemployment. So what do you want, retirement or unemployment?

"But you told me I was ineligible for retirement."

"Well we decided to give it to you, if you dropped unemployment."

"I don't think you can legally give me that choice."

I gave him no answer. The unemployment was greater than the retirement. I didn't trust them so did not withdraw my unemployment.

I was hired as an instructor for technical illustration and drafting, in the Adams County Vocational School. While the class was working on an assignment, I was scanning the new textbook we had just been issued. I got to the hydraulic valve drafting section and found several drawings that I did for Fluid Controls. The odd part of this is that I gave the class those very drawings to work on until our new books were issued.

When I told the class about it, one student hollered out across the classroom, "There you are Paul, and you said Freda wasn't too bright." I don't know if I gained personhood or not! But it was this class that gave me my credentials for vocational teaching in the State of Colorado.

I applied for Social Security, but they told me it was all messed up. I would not receive it for five months. I asked them what I should do for money. They said to get food stamps. I applied for food stamps, and was refused because my car was only two years old. I guess I shouldn't have been so honest about the age of my car.

January 1977 and Social Security had not sent me any money. The money from teaching was not enough to keep me alive, so I applied for work with a job shop company.

I still had my real estate license, so I also sold Boise-Cascade Homes for a real estate company.

March came and still no check from Social Security. It was seven months since I had applied. I will be sixty-five years old in April. I hoped that the money I received from all the odd jobs I was doing would pull me through, but it was hard to make my mortgage payments.

April 1977, and Social Security finally came through with my first check. It had taken eight months. In 1999 a report from Social Security said I got my first payment in August 1976. I should be getting a higher Social Security check. After much corresponding with them, they wrote that they couldn't look into the problem, because computers weren't in use in 1976.

Even with the Social Security check and all my odd jobs, I still had a hard time meeting my mortgage payments. A woman who was a school principal rented my spare bedroom. She had a home in the mountains, so was not with me on weekends. This helped me financially, but it seemed like all I was doing was to make enough money so I could keep up the payments on my house.

I was visiting my daughter in Colorado Springs, and she told me of a real estate company that was looking for someone to sell new homes. I had an interview, and was asked by the owner of the company if I had a goal. I said I wanted to go to the South Pacific sometime. I was hired. I suppose he thought a person with a goal like that would make a good salesman.

Then I looked for a house to buy in Colorado Springs. I found a four plex. I liked the construction of the building, so bought it on a contingency. I thought renting three of the apartments would at least pay for the mortgage.

I went back home in Northglenn and with the help of my brokers, we set a price on my home. After we set the price, I added $4000. The broker didn't think I would get it, but my home was in good repair with beautiful landscaping. It sold for the higher price in 5 days.

My broker was good to me, I was charged no fees for selling my home, and he and his wife came down to Colorado Springs and sat in on the closing.

With the money from the sale of my home, I assumed the loan on the four plex. I moved into the four plex with my blue iris, and planted them in front between the walk and the building.

My four plex is near Peterson Air Force base, so my renters were mostly airmen/airwomen. When I assumed the loan on this building, I had enough money left over from the sale of my home to put several thousand dollars into the four plex to bring it up to a better standard. I took up my job selling new houses and sold a house right off. I may get to the South Pacific yet!

Things were going very well with my new job until they hired a new head salesman. He was a hard-sell salesman and put severe pressure on us at the sales meetings. After every sales meeting, my stomach hurt. I was afraid my ulcers were returning. Nevertheless I continued until my fellow salesmen were trying the hard-sell tactics on each other. And stealing sales.

I was working with a couple, who was undecided about a house, so I told them. "Here is the key to that house across the street. I want you to go in and think about it." I knew if they opened the door, they would feel like it belonged to them, for it had a pretty entrance.

A fellow salesman followed them over and sold it to them. The couple was unaware of real estate practices, and had no idea we were working on commission.

The next day the salesman asked me if I would help him, he didn't know how to do a VA loan on the house, and he knew I had it all worked out with the couple. He wanted the information without offering me any part of the commission. I didn't help him. I gave him a sidelong glance and walked away. I couldn't take the sly tricks and high pressure any longer, so quit the job.

A job shop company hired me to do technical illustration and drafting. I was in there for almost a year. My boss was always asking me to finish a job for someone else.

One of them was a drafting job for an architect. He already had sent two draftsmen to do the work. They both quit because they couldn't get along with the architect. I was asked to finish the job.

When I got to the architect's office I couldn't see anything else that the other two draftsmen did. I was starting all over again. The architect gave me two black ink pens and asked me to ink the drawings after I penciled them. The drafting paper he gave me was mineral oil base vellum, which didn't lend itself to the ink and it bled. I called the architect over and showed him what was happening. He said he never did architectural drawings in ink, and asked me if I had ever inked them. I told him that I had inked many drawings, but the paper was unsuitable for inking. Then he said, "Well why did you ink it?" "Because you gave me the pens to do it." "Well that doesn't mean you had to ink the drawing."

I was furious, so went to the rest room to quiet down. After a half-hour in the rest room, I was still angry with the architect, so went back into the drafting room and grabbed my purse and coat. As I was leaving, I felt the architect looking at me, so I turned around and looked at him. I was right, he was watching me, so I picked up my stool and threw it at him and walked out the door.

When I got back to the office my boss said, "Come in here I want to talk to you. Is it true that you threw your stool at the architect?"

"Yes it's true, and now I know why the other two left that guy."

My boss couldn't believe that I would do such a thing, he said I didn't look like the type. But he didn't fire me and I could see he was enjoying the incident.

An opportunity came to do technical illustrations for a large company in their plant. I wanted the work, so I asked the boss to review my resume. He wouldn't give me the job, then said, "Look at you, I can't send anyone to a company who is over-weight and old." I knew if I had been a man who was over-weight and old he wouldn't have hesitated to send him. I asked again to be sent to the job because it had a three-week time limit on it, and I knew I could do it.

He sent a young inexperienced man instead. Three weeks later my boss called me. "The man I sent on the technical illustration job has been there for three weeks and he is only one-third finished with the job. Will you go to the company and finish it for them?"

I refused even though I could use the money. I lost my personhood with his put-downs.

I put an ad in the local paper for a companion. I picked up a letter at the newspaper office in answer to my ad. I liked what I read in the letter. The man was a retired engineer. I called the number and it was Walter Firm. He came over the next evening and took me out for a lobster dinner. We liked each other from the start and I never went back to the newspaper for more letters, if indeed if there were any. I knew with our engineering backgrounds I had met the right companion, for we were never at a loss for words.

Walter retired from a firm in Minneapolis, and had come back to spend his days in his old stomping ground. He was born and raised on a ranch in La Veta, and was a true cowboy in his youth. He had many interesting tales of the old days. After listening to his tales, I didn't think the life of a cowboy was a glamorous as the movie want one to believe, for he rounded up cattle in ice and snow for great distances. It was fascinating to hear tales about his mother, who gave food and staples to the starving Apache Indians, who came to the door.

The high mountains known as the Spanish Peaks were just south of La Veta. I painted a picture of them, for Walter. My easel was set up close to Walter's boyhood farm while I painted, so I knew that the painting went to someone who really appreciated it.

Walter never forgot his cowboy ways, even to chewing a quid of tobacco now and then. When you have a friend who is kind to you, and one who has a good heart, you overlook things you don't like about him. It's like a grain of wheat, you save the kernel, and blow away the chaff.

Walter came to my house almost every day, for there was always something to do on the building. He loved to paint walls. It took up a lot of our time. The apartments were in tip-top condition before the new tenants moved in.

Most of my tenants were personnel stationed at Peterson Field, but they get transferred. It wasn't too long before I got acquainted with the tenants who lived next door. They gave me a new nickname, "Momma." Walter and I shared many good times with them.

I moved into one of the small upper apartments because the tenants in the owner's apartment were moving into their own home in May. When they moved out, I moved right in with the help of all the airmen and airwomen, and their spouses. The next evening three couples were at my door and said, "This is the night we paint your living room." Paint they did and a beautiful job mixed in with lots of fun. No wonder Walter came so often, this was a busy place.

In the apartment building next to mine, lived an airman and his wife. He was born and raised in Guam. His mother and father came to visit him. He brought them over to visit me because she was a professional organist. She played my Baldwin organ and his father played his melodica, and the airman had a beautiful voice. More airmen and their wives followed them so we had a wonderful party with professional entertainment. I'll never forget those people.

Walter loved to fish. I went along with him one day, for this was the day he was teaching me how to fish. He taught me the art of casting so well that I caught three trout, my pants in the back, my sweater and my shoes. Coming home from fishing one day we got lost. We tarried too long at the lake and it was dark, very dark. He went down the wrong road, and ended up in open cattle range. The road narrowed down to two ruts. Here we met a herd of cattle that wouldn't get out of our way. A few tried to buck the side of the Jeep, then one big bull decided we were something he didn't like, and did a lot of damage to the front of the vehicle. We eventually found our way out, but Walter was on the receiving end of a lot of teasing from me after that. I told him he was better herding cattle with a horse than a Jeep.

When he took me for rides in the mountains, he drove on shelf roads that scared me so badly; I sat on the floor until he was over the high places.

I brought Walter to a dinner at my church one day. The church building is over 100 years old and the architecture fascinated me. I wandered in the sanctuary with Walter and showed him the unusual construction on the ceiling. With his engineering ability, I knew the construction would be of a special interest to him. Walter's left hand and arm were partially paralyzed due to a football injury. As we were concerned with the bracing in the ceiling, Walter was suddenly quiet. He looked down on me and said, "The feeling is coming back in my hand." We stood there in silence for a while. In the days that followed we both worked on his hand, and it grew stronger.

Christmas 1978 rolled around. Even though Bill, in Hawaii, had not written to me for several years, I never failed to send him birthday and Christmas greetings. This Christmas, Bill responded with a letter. He said he was very ill and on dialysis three times a week. He wanted to see me for the last time, would I come over to Hawaii?

I talked it over with Walter, and he didn't hesitate when he agreed that I should go over to Hawaii to see Bill.

I flew to Hawaii in February 1979. Bill was on dialysis three times a week, and cancer had spread to his brain. He was not the man I had known for it had affected his personality. He didn't write because he didn't want me to know that the cancer had come back. It was a shock to see him this way.

He couldn't drive his car, so I drove it for him. We went for rides around the island, and visited the places we knew so well. The little church we liked so much was locked up. This was a disappointment for both of us.

One afternoon we drove to a beach and I picked up some puka shells. We always kidded ourselves that when we retired, we would make puka shell necklaces. I brought them back to the car and gave them to him. He

247

remembered the dream we had. We went to another beach and I recorded the sound of the waves as they smashed against the rocks. He helped me take pictures as he sat in the car giving me instructions.

We went back to the little Chinese restaurant where the waitress was trying to tell me she only served hot tea by telling me, "hut, hut, hut." This time I was a little wiser, I drank hot tea and used chopsticks with ease.

Many times I picked him up at the hospital and visited him while he was on the dialysis machine.

He gave me a credit card for gas and the keys to his car, so I was free to do what I wanted to do on the days he was not home. I had brought my easel and paints so spent my time painting the beautiful green mountains and the deep blue and turquoise sea.

One morning Bill asked me to marry him. It was heart breaking to hear him ask me. I thought he had forgotten me, because he had not written for so long. I told him that we should have married four years ago and then we would have had four wonderful years together. He agreed. I reminded him that I had offered to care for him if we married and the cancer came back. I was sincere about taking care of him, but the years of silence made me wonder if he had changed his mind about our relationship. I didn't tell him about Walter, he was too ill.

The time had come for me to go home, and the United Airlines pilots were on strike. I had a United Airlines ticket that I managed to exchange for a Pan Am, and then they went on strike.

I called United to get on one of their emergency flights, but they only went to Chicago. I tried a last ditch effort at 6 AM. I was told I could get on a Continental Airlines flight as a stand-by, if I came to the airport immediately. I called a taxi, and by the time it arrived, I was packed and ready to go. I had just enough time to give Bill a hug, and kiss good bye. It was 1 PM before I was able to get on a flight to Los Angeles. An announcement came over the loud speaker that they had only one seat available, then called my name.

At Los Angeles I waited until 3AM to get a flight to Denver. While I was waiting I got acquainted with a Marine and an Air Force cadet, who both were going to Colorado Springs. I called Walter to pick me up at the airport in Denver. Walter was waiting at the airport and gladly gave the Marine and Air cadet a ride with us.

The servicemen told Walter it was so kind of him to take them along, but Walter told them, "No problem, Freda is always doing something like this." I came home feeling that I didn't ever want to leave the mainland again. After living in the wide-open spaces in Colorado, I felt cooped up on the little island of Oahu, especially because of the airline strikes. It made me realize how hard it was to get off the island without air passage.

I owned the four-plex for two years, when I decided to paint pictures, not walls. I lived about 20 miles from the mountains on the eastern edge of Colorado Springs, on the western edge of the prairie. It was a long ride through Colorado Springs to get to the mountains.

I had worked very hard to get the four-plex up to a higher standard. I put in a lawn with the servicemen helping me. I was watering constantly. I planted evergreen trees and had the building painted. I replaced several cracked windows and carpeted the balcony to make it quiet. The four-plex was now very attractive. I decided to sell it and move to the mountains.

I was working for another realtor, so knew the four-plex was worth at least $15,000 more than I paid for it. I set the price, but just before I put the ad in the paper, I added $5,000. This money, if I got it, would pay for a trip to the South Pacific. Again the building sold in five days for the higher

249

price. At the closing the buyer told me, "You made a big chunk of money on this property, I looked it up." "Yes," I said, "but I spent a big chunk of money in repairs, and if you would do the same, you also will make a big chunk of money."

I hadn't expected that the place would sell so fast, but I always had the belief that if you kept your property in good repair and painted, it is always in selling condition. I still believe this to be true.

I looked at manufactured homes and bought the finest one on the lot. I had no place to put it, so went to Woodland Park and found a beautiful spot snuggled in amongst the mountains. The house was installed on my lot, and I moved in before the workmen left.

It felt good to be so shrewd with my property. I put the ad in the paper on the 13th of the month, moved onto lot #13 on the 13th of the month and the money I had left after the closing ended with 13 cents. I felt lucky!

I planted the blue iris in front of my home with some iris and tiger lilies Walter had given me, and with the Ohio violet from Marlene. As my eyes wandered above the blue iris, Pikes Peak was large and in full view, for I was located in the foothills of this beautiful mountain.

PART V

CHAPTER 21

WOODLAND PARK

I moved my new manufactured home to Woodland Park in September 1979. The large floor to ceiling bay window by the dinette, had a full view of Pikes Peak. Of all the places I lived in Colorado this is the first time that a transformer didn't block the view of the peak.

My home was tucked into a mountainside of enormous pine trees at an altitude of 8500 ft. The sliding glass doors in my living room opened up onto a deck only 8 feet from the mountainside. I sat in my living room to watch the black tufted ear squirrels, rabbits and lots of beautiful birds on this deck.

I took advantage of a path that led to an open valley, and trees where the bears sharpened their claws. I know they visited me at night once in a while. On the edge of this big valley I came upon a pair of blue grouse. I never bothered them, I just walked by. It was on this path that I took my paint box and easel, and did a beautiful painting of Pikes Peak. I didn't have that painting too long before it was sold. Like all my fellow painters, I wish I still had that painting.

Woodland Park is in a Snow Belt and it snowed and snowed, making the whole area seem like a fairy wonderland. The snow was piled so high, that it wasn't too unusual to be snowbound. Digging out a sixty foot long path to my car was a major operation, which took about three days to remove the snow. After all that work I cleaned off two feet of snow from the roof of the car. A man probably could do the job in one day, but I'm not a man.

A pigeon came to visit me one day, and sat by the glass doors. I thought he had an injured wing or lame foot because he hobbled back and forth across the deck. I fed him and gave him water; he stayed about a week and then flew off. A few days later he came back with ten or more pigeon friends. He strutted back and forth in front of the glass doors as if to show his friends where he had been for so long. I was beginning to think I'd have a whole flock to feed, however they only stayed for about an hour and left forever. Maybe they were just thanking me for taking care of their friend.

Old friends came to visit and I made new friends. To show my appreciation for their friendship, I entertained them with a Christmas Tea. I made 500 German cookies from recipes used by my mother and grandmother. Some of the recipes were over 100 years old. Do you suppose Grandmother brought some of them over from Germany on the sailing vessel, that brought her to America? An item on one of the recipes called for five cents worth of citron. Another called for 1# of Brazil nuts (in the shell). I bought a pound, shelled the nuts and measured them to change that recipe

I sent invitations to forty-six friends, never expecting all forty-six to show up, but they did. It overcrowded my small home. It's a good thing my friends had a sense of humor; they laughed about the situation I put myself into and had a good time. When it got too crowded some would leave to make room for the next bunch. This started a tradition of mine that lasted for over twenty years.

Walter and I continued our cribbage games. One evening during one of the games, Walter was talking about his wife who had passed away. He started to cry. I just sat quietly for a long time. Finally he said, "This is the last time I'll do that." And it was.

Sometimes we went to our favorite nightspot for dinner and an evening of dancing. The entertainment was Wes Jones at the organ and piano. Wes lived in Hawaii sporadically, and I had told him about my friend Bill in Hawaii, and asked him to play 'Lei of Stars" which was our favorite song. He surprised me one evening by playing and singing the song as I entered the bar. This started another tradition.

In January 1980, word came to me that Bill had died. This saddened me. The last time I visited him, I helped him record tapes of Hawaiian music from his 300 record collection. When he was doing this, he was so sick he could hardly work his equipment. I have very fond memories of Bill, for it was like a Cinderella story; but with a sad ending.

The next time Walter and I were dancing, I started to cry. I laid my head on his shoulder and Walter just slowly danced until I was finished. Walter was a very understanding person, he still mourned the death of his wife, Violet, and now it was me with Bill. The understanding was mutual.

· A new life was now in store for me. I was still searching for some way to get to the South Pacific. I wanted a trip that would let me mingle with the natives. An organized trip was not the answer. I remember the Alaska trip, when I saw people sit in the hotel lobbies, just waiting for their tour conductor. Waiting is a waste of time. I want to go, go, go and meet other people.

The May 1980 AARP News Bulletin came in the mail. On the front page was an article looking for seniors to participate in Earthwatch Expeditions. I wondered if they also went to the South Pacific. That $5000 CD is still in the bank, waiting for me to find a way to get there. An expedition seemed to be a way I could meet people and be part of their customs. An expedition would be just the thing! I subscribed to the Earthwatch magazine.

The first issue came, and in it was an expedition to the South Pacific in the Society Islands. The expedition was on the little island of Huahine in the Tahiti group. I sent in my application and the required two hundred-dollar retainer fee. A reply came back that the expedition was filled. I wrote back and asked them to hold that retainer fee for the 1981 expedition. They sent two volumes of reading material plus a list a list of recommended books to read about the islands. The Woodland Park library was able to get them for me, so I read and read and read.

I had over a year to wait for the expedition. I was happy to get some free-lance work at the Colorado Springs airport doing technical illustrations for a manual. The work was secret; it's a good thing I have a poor memory. I was nearly through with the airport work, when Walter started to do some free-lance work for Honeywell. He got me a job as his draftsman, so we both were working in the engineering room. This was good work with nice people, who didn't seem to mind two old people among them.

My two sisters, Elenora and Gertrude, came for a visit. On the last day of their visit I just blurted out, "Let's go up to the top of Pikes Peak on the cog train." I am terrified of heights; I had to do this on the spur of the moment. Up on the cog train we went! The ride was beautiful until we got higher than timberline. I couldn't look out the window, just down on the

floor. My sisters looked at me and said, 'What's the matter, are you afraid?"
"You're durn tooting I am, just leave me alone."

It was winter when I received a jury summons. The Teller County
Courthouse is in Cripple Creek. To get to Cripple Creek I must drive a high
mountain road, which I try to avoid in summer, let alone a snowy high road
in winter. I wrote back and told them I cannot drive the high road in winter;
that they should send a patrol car after me. They tabled my jury duty until
summer.

Fran Nichols, the architect who was my first friend in Denver, was now
terminally ill. The last time we had lunch together in Denver, she told me
she had a lump on her shoulder that was cancerous. We sat in the mall for a
long time just talking and doing a little crying. One day I had a persistent
urge to call her at the hospital. Fran's daughter came on the line and told me
that her mother passed away 30 minutes before I called. Fran and I had a
wonderful relationship with ESP; we always knew what the other was
thinking. This was the last time we used ESP.

Life goes on despite all the sorrow. It must. It was a good thing for me
that I had the South Pacific adventure to keep me going.

A new letter from Earthwatch informed me that the 1981 expedition had
been canceled for lack of funding. This meant one more year of waiting for
the South Pacific adventure, but I answered the letter and asked them to hold
my two hundred dollar retainer and put me on the 1982 expedition.
"Persevere," I said to myself, "I'll get there yet, by golly."

I had another year to wait for the expedition, so I thought I might as well
get into shape and loose some weight. A neighbor walked with me every
morning. Martin had a fast pace, and the walking starts every morning at

6:30 AM sharp! He was patient with me, for sometimes I had to rest along the way, but we stuck to the three mile walk.

I drove up high in the mountains near Cripple Creek in the gold mine district to paint. This was my favorite place, for to the east, Pikes Peak was in full view, and towards the west you could see the Continental Divide about forty or fifty miles away.

One day I was alone when a motorcycle gang stopped. Two men got off their cycles and ran towards me. I had a palette knife I had sharpened for such an encounter, so grabbed it and looked at the men. I knew I was licked before I even started to defend myself. They came within ten feet of me, turned around and got on their cycles and rode off. I was too shaken to paint any more so went home.

The next time I went up, Walter went with me. We were in open range country. Two cowboys came up to us and tried to chase us off. We were on BLM land and I didn't think they had that right. Walter got upset. He stood up and asked them who wanted us off the land. They said their boss ordered them to do it. Walter told them to go back to their boss and tell him we had a painting to finish, and we would be gone in two hours. The cowboys never came back, even though it took longer than two hours. I trusted his ability to deal with the cowboys, for in his younger days, he had been a cowboy and a dance hall bouncer. If I had been alone with those cowboys, I probably would have gathered up my paints and hurried away.

My friend, Dolly, accompanied me the next time I painted in this area. A security guard for a gold mining company chased us off the property. We were on the county sand storage lot. I told the man he had no right, but we were told to get off anyway, for he said the open mines in the area were too dangerous and we might fall in them. Instead of going home, Dolly and I went to the Teller County Courthouse, and after much research, found that no land was recorded in the name of the mining company.

Walter got interested in the problem and took me to the United States Bureau of Mines and the Bureau of Land Management (BLM) in Denver. We couldn't find the name of the mining company in those offices either. We were given mine ownership computer read-outs and many maps of existing mines. Some mines were over 100 years old.

We discovered that legally the mines had to be fenced, and eventually after much research, Walter said to the men who were helping us, "It looks like we uncovered a big bucket of worms." The men nodded their heads. Leave it to me to get into a bucket of worms. I expected to be shot someday for poking my nose in other people's gold mines.

I went to the county commissioner's meeting and told them that painting the beautiful scenery in the gold mine territory was part of my livelihood, and it wouldn't be so dangerous if the mines were fenced like the law says. I persisted, then in a few days I went back to the spot to finish the painting I started. This time I noted that all mines had new fencing around them.

In the summer of 1981, I received a letter from Earthwatch. The 1982 expedition to the island of Huahine in Tahiti had been funded and it is now GO!! I immediately answered to put me on this expedition. By October I had my acceptance, so now I know for sure that I will be leaving for the South Pacific in August 1982. I went to travel agencies and got as much information about the little island of Huahine as I could find. Little did I know that I would be meeting the same natives who were pictured on the brochures.

I sent to the Bishop Museum in Honolulu, Hawai, for a book on the Tahitian language. A neighbor gave me a set of tapes on the French language. I studied and studied, read and read and walked and walked. Walter is not too happy about the whole thing, but this is my life. I must go on with my dreams and ambitions.

Earthwatch sent new material. My life was full of excitement. I had to get a passport, and didn't know what problems I would have because the Peace Corps kept the last one I had. But it was issued to me. I went through another physical examination, which I passed. Some people told me how lucky I was to be going on an expedition, but I think trying for eight years and having the perseverance to stick with it, is not luck!

In February 1982, Walter was not feeling well. The circulation in his lower extremes was almost nil. The plastic artery going from his heart to his legs is blocked. He must have a new plastic artery, and it is a major operation. I took him to the hospital in Pueblo where his surgeon is on the staff. One thing led to another, and after three major operations within a week, he was in a semi-coma. It was hard for me to see him this way, and hard for me to travel the sixty miles to visit him.

Walter's family was constantly coming from Minneapolis, and I went along with them to visit him. Walter was in intensive care for five weeks, then lost his battle for life. I lost a wonderful companion. The cribbage games, fishing, dancing and so many things we did were lost; everything was so silent. I lost a good friend. Both Walter and Bill are gone. It was almost too much to bear.

The day I came home from the funeral, which was held in Minneapolis, the travel agency called me about my plane trip to Tahiti. So much had to be done. Even though I missed Walter very much, I had to dive right into the plans for the South Pacific trip. But fond memories of Walter were still lingering.

In May 1982, I never gave it a thought that I had just turned 70 years old and would be traveling alone on an expedition!

I bought a Nikon camera. My son had given me a strobe light. I bought eleven rolls of film and six long tapes for the recorder, and bought film for my Polaroid Camera. I made cotton clothes for the hot humid weather in Tahiti.

Then came serious planning for the plane trip. I could find no direct return trips to Hawaii from Tahiti, for they all went by way of Fiji. I mapped the trip with a four-day stopover in Fiji. I remembered the book 'The Dove' where a honeymoon was spent in the Yasawa Islands in Fiji. It sounded so beautiful, so I included a three-day cruise throughout the Yasawa Islands. Everything was shaping up, I could have a four-day layover in Hawaii, and I took it. I will go in early August and return in late September. I went to the passport office in Colorado Springs and registered the camera, strobe light and recorder. I had my passport and the only thing left to do was to pay for the plane tickets and the Fijian cruise.

I received my assignment from Earthwatch, which will be doing artwork and designing and engineering on a thatch roof meeting house. The National Geographic was funding most of the expedition and the rest comes from the volunteers. I sent in my part, which was $1450. Little chunks of that $5000 were being put to good use. I studied the Tahitian language, which was hard to do without a teacher. I practiced my French until I had no problem to read it.

At the last minute, my reservations for the Fijian cruise came back from Fiji. They are made in the name of Mr. and Mrs. Freda Stumpf. The travel agent suggested I keep those reservations: I'll meet a guy to share the room with and marry him.

261

She didn't know, nor did I, that those words could have come true in Fiji! But of course I changed them, and then by the time the letters came back and forth to Fiji, I never did get the reservations back. Until the next chapter, may I say, "Parahi, Ua here vau ia oe." (Good bye, I love you.)

CHAPTER 22

HUAHINE EXPEDITION, FRENCH POLYNESIA

I was seventy years old when I departed for an expedition on the little island of Huahine (hoo-ah-HEE-nay) in the Tahiti islands of French Polynesia.

I left Denver on August 8, 1982 and flew to Los Angeles. In my luggage were a sleeping bag, air mattress, reference books and special clothes for the expedition. Luggage was limited to forty pounds for an overseas flight, but all this stuff exceeded that weight. The Earthwatch labels all over my luggage came in handy. I wasn't charged for the over-weight.

I boarded a 747 Air New Zealand plane. We lifted off and headed over the Pacific Ocean. We were served cocktails before dinner, and I wasn't flying first class! My first Scotch on the rocks started off my South Pacific adventure. The pilot announced that we should set our watches to Tahiti time, 6 PM. This is only a four hour difference from Denver time, but then noted that Tahiti is in the same time zone as Hawaii, but 3200 miles south of it and across the equator into the Southern hemisphere.

Freda R. Stumpf

The plane landed at the Faaa (Fah-AH-ah) airport in Papeete (Pah-pay-AYE-tay) Tahiti, at 1 AM. The customs officials were more concerned about plants and fruit than my luggage, so it was a breeze to get through. My labels might have helped again for the expedition is well known throughout Tahiti.

An Air Polynesia plane will fly me to the island of Huahine. I had a five-hour layover. I needed a rest room. All signs are in French, and I didn't see any signs for 'toilette' or 'femme' so found a French gendarme and asked for the toilette. He told me in French that it was on the second floor. With my little knowledge of French, I understood. I pointed to my luggage on a cart, with a question on my face. He motioned to leave the cart by his office. When I came back I said, "Merci." With that word he was all smiles, I was glad I knew two important French words.

At 6 AM I boarded a small plane with about 20 other passengers. No carry-on luggage was allowed except my purse. When I got on the plane I could see why. I had barely enough room for my little feet. How the man got into the seat next to me, I don't know, but he was in his seat. He was an American and we struck up a nice conversation. With this introduction to the islands I thought everyone spoke English. NOT! In about an hour we landed at the Huahine airport.

As I came down the steps, the airport receptionist, Yvonne, greeted me with a question; "You are Earthwatch?" When I acknowledged that, she led me to Martiel, who had a Volkswagon bus. "Allo, Massus Stumpf." This was the extent of Martiel's English, but Yvonne spoke English, Tahitian. French and Chinese. She made a good receptionist.

Martiel drove me to the base house. As we were riding, I tried to converse with him, but he only grunted; so I just soaked in the beauty of the island without speaking. The lush foliage and flowers were abundant. Red hibiscus lined the road and the feathery fern-like foliage of the ironwood trees bordered the road by a large lake. From the lake a beautiful lagoon flowed into the sea. Vanda orchids were growing in every yard. As we went through the town of Maeva (Mah-AYE-vah) I saw a breadfruit tree with its enormous leaf, mangoes, bananas and zillions of coconut trees. Then I spied a banyan tree with its exposed roots. As we neared our base-house frangipani (plumeria) made its debut. Bordering the road was a short-leafed grass that never needs cutting. As we neared the base house, I saw that the yard was white coral, no sand, and I soon found out that it was hard to walk on.

Muffet and Eric, who are archaeologists from the Bishop Museum in Hawaii, greeted me at the basehouse. Muffet showed me the room where I would sleep. Because I was first to arrive, I had my choice of half of the double bed or the cot. I chose the cot and slept on top of it in my gingham sleeping bag. The first volunteer I met was Shane from Michigan. From Hawaii came Betty, who chose half of the double bed in the room I occupied. Then came Nona from Washington D.C., who is a Hawiian native, and chose to sleep on our floor. From San Francisco, California, came Frank, then Bolek flew in from Pittsburgh, Pennsylvania. Dr. Yosihiko Sinoto, the Principal Investigator and leader of the group, was the final one to enter the scene. He is an archaeologist and senior anthropologist from the Bishop Museum in Honolulu, Hawaii.

After the introductions, Dr. Sinoto asked us to call him Yosi. Our group of nine includes three archaeologists and six Earthwatch volunteers.

I arrived two days before the expedition date, so had two free days to see the island. I heard that the interisland boat comes on Tuesday, and with it, a lot of activity in the town of Fare (FAH-ray). Shane was also an early arrival, so we planned to get up early the next morning to see the festivities.

The small town of Fare (FAH-ray) is five miles away. Muffet told us that La Truck, the island transportation, comes by at 6 AM. We were out by 5:45 AM ready to hail down La Truck. We barely got out by the roadside when La Truck came by and we hailed it down. We tried to talk to the driver, but he didn't understand us. We offered him money for the fare, but he wouldn't take it, then motioned for us to get in the back. We got seated, and soon discovered that we were on the morning bread delivery truck. There were natives in the back, a mother nursing her baby, a few children and some grown-ups. A tape recorder was blasting 'Jingle Bells.' The natives were enjoying the song so much that I wondered what kind of words they put to the music. I was sure that no one in that La Truck had ever dashed through the snow in a one horse open sleigh, or for that matter, had ever seen snow.

La Truck had long wooden seats on each side where people sat facing each other. I glanced down on the floor between us. It was covered with baskets of taro leaves, stems of bananas and bare feet with some in thongs. In front were boxes of freshly baked French bread, unwrapped. On the roof was more French bread, lots of it. Shane and I looked at each other; we knew we were on the wrong truck. Whoops, a sharp turn to the right and we were on a bridge over the lagoon. Now we were on a motu (MOH-too), which is a coral island. I was concerned because the bread truck missed the town of Maeva. The bread truck stopped at every house on the motu. It went by watermelon patches, which were not bearing fruit because August is wintertime in Tahiti, even though the temperature was between 70 and 80 degrees.

bread truck

We were driven by houses made of sheet metal on stilts, and grass huts. A pig roamed every yard like a dog, and chickens were strutting all over the place. The bread truck drove as far as the seashore on the other side of the motu, turned around, came back over the bridge and a right turn took us through the town of Maeva. We rode by the beautiful lake that is lined with red hibiscus and ironwood trees, and by the time we made all the bread stops in Maeva, it was almost 7 o'clock. We finally arrived in Fare. My bucket was sore from sitting on the unmerciful hard wood seat over the rough road on the motu, which was littered with large chunks of coral.

The interisland boat was docked in Fare Harbor and workers were busy loading it with bananas, coconuts, copra (dried coconuts), pigs and trucks. People were boarding with children, crying babies and chickens. They will spend the night on the boat, for the boat won't dock in Papeete until the next morning. There are no cabins so the natives must carry blankets and baskets of food besides all their luggage. Of course these people could have flown to Papeete, but to them the cost is prohibitive. The boat fare was only $6.00 U. S.

Near the boat a man was baking and selling French crepes from a small wagon, so we treated ourselves to a delicious crepe. The town WAS BUSY!

Fare has a population of 100 and is the largest town on the island. Shane and I looked for the post office, but we couldn't find it and no one spoke English. I told Shane that I had studied Tahitian a little and I knew what to ask for. I saw some boys who were standing by a Chinese store. I approached them and asked for the Fare Rata (house of letters). They gave me a funny look and went away laughing. I had mispronounced it. I didn't have the hang of the language. At the base house that night I told Muffet about the incident. She asked me how I pronounced it, then she laughed and said I didn't ask for the House of Letters, I asked for the House of Castration.

We finally found the post office on the back street. Besides stamps for our letters, Shane wanted to make a phone call to his home in America. This is the only phone on the island for public use. He asked the French Postmaster for permission to use the phone as he pointed to it. He must wait for the postmaster is sorting out some mail. He picked up his chair and placed it behind the counter, just so. Then took out his official stamp and placed it, just so. He sat down and stamped a few letters, just so. While waiting for the postmaster, Shane was looking through the many phone books lying on a long shelf. He turned away disgusted and said to me, "Can you imagine that? Not one of these phone books is from Michigan."

The Frenchman stamped a few more letters, then readjusted everything, and asked Shane about his phone call, in French. Shane said he wanted to call Grand Rapids, Michigan, U.S.A. This upset the Frenchman for he is the one who must put the calls through to America. He asked for the number. Shane didn't know it; his father moved since he left the states, and he must get information from America. The Frenchman got more upset! Then to top it all off Shane wanted to make the call collect. Then the Frenchman got REAL upset!

I asked Shane why he didn't simplify things a little bit by at least paying for the call. He replied that he never calls home any way but collect. I casually asked him what is so important that he had to call home. "My dog is sick and I must find out how she is getting along." Then I GOT UPSET!!!

The Frenchman told Shane to come back later. Then the Frenchman asked me what I wanted. I asked for 20 stamps while I pointed to my postcards and held up my fingers twice. Then he said in English, "Oh, twenty stamps." He was faking, he knew English. French Polynesia has the most beautiful stamps that I had ever seen, and they are so large that very little room is left for the address on the postcard.

On the way back Shane and I decided to hitchhike the five miles back. The Earthwatch briefing said it was easy to do. It wasn't easy, for no one knew what we were talking about and wouldn't pick us up.

After the rejection, I stepped back and turned my foot on a piece of coral. I fell down and damaged my glasses. I couldn't walk for my foot wás very painful and was starting to swell. We were near Martiel and Eneta's house, so Eneta took us back to the base house. Enete, who is Martiel's wife, could speak a little English. I offered to pay her for the trip and she kept saying, "No, not for a problem."

The foot was very swollen and the sides and bottom were very black. We all thought it was a severe sprain. I was limping and looking through a scratched lens for the rest of my stay on Huahine and throughout the rest of the journey.

During the years that followed this expedition, the foot never stopped bothering me. Nine years later an orthopedic surgeon X-rayed it and said the ankle had broken when this happened. Two years after that another orthopedic surgeon put my foot in a MRI (Magnetic Resonance Imaging) and said I had no ligaments at that spot in the foot. Unbeknownst to me, I had been walking on a broken ankle all though the South Pacific, and I still am!

At he base house that evening, we were visited by many natives who inspected my foot and gave me a sign that it was twisted. During the discussion, one of the men came over and gave me a Tahitian kiss. How beautiful and thoughtful!

Dr. Sinoto understood the Tahitian language; they told him that they will come back the next evening to pack my foot with poultices of herbs and leaves. Yosi asked me if it would be all right for them to do that and I agreed.

But the next morning, a young native died from the result of an accident. The island people are a very close knit group of natives, so of course with all this emotional confusion, my foot was forgotten.

I talked my situation over with the archaeologists. It was impossible for me to climb up to the tropical forest to help with the mapping. I told them I didn't think there was a problem, for I am the artist/draftsman on the expedition.

They did not know I was an illustrator and draftsman as I stated on my application, let alone that I was told by Earthwatch I would be doing drafting and designing on a meeting house called a 'pote'e (po-TAY-aye). I couldn't understand why Earthwatch asked me to do it and then never informed them. When I asked Yosi about it, he said the land title had not been cleared. Consequently, I made black ink drawings and several nice paintings, for I did bring my water color paints along. These drawings are being used by the Bishop Museum in Honolulu, Hawaii for publications.

As members of the expedition, we were assigned duties. You may boil water one day, cook dinner the next and do dishes on the third day. Everyone does the duty assigned him except Eric. Muffett boils his water, does his dishes, washes his clothes and sleeps with him. Full service I call it, for Eric had a wife and children in Hawaii.

There were two tables, one on the porch and one in the kitchen, with an open window between them. I dined in the kitchen, because they fed the neighbors dogs and cats by dumping their leftovers on the concrete porch floor.

I don't know why they did this, for the Tahitians were cleaner than that, and anyway to fatten the dogs and cats would only make them good stew meat because the natives eat them.

The expedition's purpose was to study the migration of the Polynesians throughout the South Pacific, based on the similarity between artifacts and fish hooks excavated from the Marquisas Islands, French Polynesia, Micronesia and Hawaii. Not only are the artifacts and fishhooks studied, but also the religious maraes (Mah-RAH-ayes), which are the ancient temples dating back to 1100 AD.

It was the maraes on Huahine Island that I was sketching and inking. I drew pencil drawings of the artifacts that the expedition members found up in the tropical forest. I painted a few watercolor paintings of Maeva by the beautiful lagoon, showing the ancient fish traps which also date back to 1100 AD, and are still in use. Dr. Sinoto has these paintings. Yosi told me that this is the favorite place of all his travels throughout the South Pacific, where he has traveled extensively. Dr. Sinoto is the foremost expert on the migrations of the Polynesians. I felt honored to be a part of his expedition.

We lived near the town of Maeva, which is on the lagoon that drains the lake into the sea. The town was originally inhabited by the ancient chiefs of Huahine Island, and they owned the fish traps. The decendents of these chiefs still own and manage them, even though it has been 800 years since they were built. The ocean tide operates the fish traps. At high tide the fish go into them and at low tide the natives remove them. They are made of the same black basalt stone that form the marae. Our modern engineers with all their expertise couldn't improve on this way to catch fish.

Across the street from the base house is a marae, thought to be owned by the last Queen of Huahine, Taapapa II. The buildings surrounding this marae are woven grass huts, which are homes of the natives.

marae Fare Miro.across from the base house

Not all houses are grass shacks or sheet metal on stilts, for the one we lived in was concrete block. The island has a municipal water plant and electric power, but the water is impure and the electric is not constant. The island is a mixture of the old and new, for it is common to see a television aerial alongside a grass hut, catching the TV beam from Papeete. The electricity goes on and off all day. These natives surely must be patient watching TV. I hope they do something about the electric power before they try to run computers.

Family life is not as we know it in America. A child can choose with whom he wants to live, relative or not, with no hard feelings. The child always knows who his/her parents are, but they consider all grown-ups on the island as their father and mother, and they are treated that way.

A young man who cleared brush for the expedition, put his wife and baby on the boat to Papeete to give the child to her mother, who asked for it before it was born. The baby was freely given, but you could see the sadness on the man's face when he put his wife and baby on the boat.

Yvonne, the airport receptionist, had three boys; each has a different father. When she wanted another baby, she went to Papeete and came back pregnant. She was choosy, for the father was a well-known man and each boy knew his father's name. For the Tahitians, this is no moral issue. It is a customary part of their culture. I heard since leaving the island she had another boy. It is also acceptable for a girl to go to Papeete to practice prostitution. She will come back to live with her mother if she is pregnant, have her baby, and then return to practice her profession again. The girl's mother cares for the baby. When you live in close proximity with these

273

people as I did, one looses touch with any moral issues and accepts it as their way of life.

Many of the teenagers have lost their front teeth. It must be something lacking in their diet. Some children have a drooping white eye. Staph infection, pink eye and tuberculosis are very prevalent on this beautiful island. A reason for some of the diseases might be traced to the living habits. The drinking water is full of algae and must be boiled. Families, who live along the lagoon, put their pig in a cage with stilts over the water, which does great for clean up, but what does it do for the water, which is full of swimming children? The families not living on the lagoon let their pig roam the yard like a dog.

If you want a chicken for dinner, you just catch one of the chickens that strut around the island. They were a nuisance, for they crow day and night. I told one of the volunteers, "Just listen to those cocks, they answer each other. One will crow 'Papeete' (pah-pay-AYE tay) and the other will answer, 'Maururu' (mah-oo-ROO-roo). Maururu is the Tahitian word for 'thank you.' The volunteer said, "Now why did you tell me that? All I hear now is the cock thanking the other for saying Papeete."

Marketable crops on the island are coconuts, tapioca, vanilla beans, taro and the red watermelon papaya, which is as large as a small watermelon. Breadfruit trees are abundant, so are mangoes.

The native mother, who lived across the street, came over one evening with her coconut grater, which is held between the knees. She showed us how to grate the coconut, and then put the coconut in a bag and squeezed it to remove the coconut cream. This cream is used for many of the native dishes including raw fish. Both taro root and the leaves are used for cooking.

The natives gave us a stem of bananas. They are not good until they are ripe, and then all the bananas ripen at once. I found out the hard way. We had a papaya tree in our front yard. I was watching the fruit, which was almost ripe. Ah, one more day and I can pick it! But the next day it was gone. Yosi just laughed at me for the natives go into any yard and pick what they want. I was rewarded the next day when some children came to visit me while I was painting on the porch, and gave me a very large papaya.

The church was celebrating the opening of a new Sunday School building, and many flowers were needed for the celebration. The natives came into our yard and picked all of the flowers.

The native men wear just a pair of shorts and the women wear a pareau (pah-RAY-oo), which is a long piece of cloth wrapped around the body, then the corners are twisted and tucked between the breasts. It is either worn over the breast or around the waist. If around the waist, they wear a tee shirt or a brassiere. They don't know that brassieres are meant for underclothing, the fancier, the better, for it seems a status symbol to wear one.

You must go to the beach if you want to see a bare breasted woman, for many French people vacation there. To me, it made the beach such a personal place. One of our volunteers spent all his free hours at the beach.

The native children loved to have their picture taken. When they see a camera in your hand, they put one hand up to their eye and say, "Click, click, click." I surprised them one day with my Polaroid Camera. I took their picture and gave it to them. They couldn't believe it. Some took the picture, but some wouldn't because they thought it was a superstition. One boy put his head down and told Yosi he was ashamed.

275

Bobby Holcomb was born in America, but spent most of his adult years in France, and then Tahiti. Bobby had a beautiful necklace tattooed around his neck and bracelets at his wrists. His English speaking voice had a definite French accent. He came over while I was doing my artwork on the porch, and we had good conversations. Bobby carried a guitar.

When I saw it, I told him that my great grandfather founded the Martin Guitar Company. He was impressed, because this is the guitar that he always wanted, but couldn't afford. Bobby is a good musician as well as an excellent artist. He was the choir director in the Methodist church.

Bobby was proud of his choir and invited me to his church on the next Sunday. I took my tape recorder along, and sat in the new Sunday school room to listen to them practice before the service. Bobby spied me and brought the choir to where I was sitting with my recorder. The native singers surrounded me and started to sing. The singing was all a cappella, and this was the first time I heard the beautiful voices of the South Pacific people. The goose bumps went up and down my arms, for it was so beautiful and in perfect harmony, and they were singng it just for me!!

The church bell sounded. It meant that the church service was about to begin. As I entered the church, the greeter said, "Where from?" I replied, "America." Then he seated me in an honor seat alongside the retired minister. I set my tape recorder on the floor and taped the songs and other parts of the sermon. There was no doubt what they were praying when they said the Lord's Prayer. I had goose bumps again when they sang 'What a Friend we have in Jesus.' I sang with them in English. A little girl standing beside me looked at me as if to say, you're singing it all wrong. The congregation does not use hymnals and they sing a cappela in perfect harmony from memory. The Methodist Missionaries taught their ancestors many of the hymns. I was touched by the hymn, 'Just as I am.' As they were singing that song, and knowing their customs, I thought how appropriate! I grew to love these people.

Tahiti church

The next Sunday I sat in the middle of the pew, which had only a slat for a back. I thought it queer that no one sat on either side of me, then I glanced down at the pew. About ten natives behind me rested their bare feet on the seat. I almost laughed out loud, for I could see them watching me for my reaction. I know these humorous Tahitians did this on purpose!

In the church no woman wore a pareau. They wore a white Mother Hubbard sort of dress. The men wore Navy blue pants and a white shirt like the missionaries taught them. Muffett told me to wear a white dress, if I had one. I wore a white blouse and a white skirt.

Missionaries founded this Methodist Church about 1820. The church is built on top of a marae, where the natives worshiped their pagan religion up until the time the missionaries came. The marae was given to them by the ancient clan, Atup'pi.

A marae is a large platform built of basalt stone. At one end is an altar called 'ahu'. (AH-hoo) The ahu is made by putting large four to seven feet high rectangular stones in an upright position. They fill this ahu with coral.

The idols of their gods were placed at the base of the ahu. Some of the early archaeologists believed that human sacrifices were made on this ahu, and that cannibalism was practiced. If this is indeed the correct assumption, it's no wonder they embraced Christianity so quickly.

MARAE RAUHURU

marae on Huahine Island

As I was doing my artwork on the porch, the native children surrounded me and bumped the table so much I couldn't do my painting. I told them, "Ohipa, Parahi." This meant 'work, goodbye.' They looked at me so funny that I thought they didn't think artwork was work, so I got a pail of water and started to mop the floor. This meant work, so they left me and I went back to my painting.

One day Bobby, the choir director, came with another man, who had a new Martin guitar. Bobby was proudly showing him the great granddaughter of the founder of the Martin Guitar Company. I didn't catch the man's name when we were introduced. I was more interested in the Martin guitar. He handed me the guitar and I told him I couldn't play it, but asked if he would play it for me. Bobby and another man, who was with him, looked at me with a shocked expression. I didn't understand why, but nevertheless, the man sat on the couch and started to play and sing.

He was so good, I went into my baggage and brought my recorder, and recorded the song he was playing and singing. He very graciously sang the song over again. After he was through, I asked him for his name again. He said, "Jimmy Buffett."

I am from an older generation and didn't know him. In fact I didn't realize to whom I was speaking until I got home and asked my granddaughter, Kathy, if she knew who he was. He said he lived in Aspen and played in the Red Rocks Theater in Denver.

My granddaughter was flabbergasted! He is a popular musician and recording artist in America. And I asked him to play for me! He was on the island composing a song, 'One Particular Harbor,' and that is the song he sang for me. The song is about Fare Harbor. He sings about the children playing in the harbor. Yes, I watched the same children. He also sings about the mountains behind the basehouse and the lake I told you about. The album is very dear to me, and in it he gives Bobby Holcum, the choir director who introduced us, credit for his help.

Fare Harbor with children playing

After I came home, I was in a store with my daughter Audrey. She picked an album by Jimmy Buffett and showed me his picture on the cover. "Is this the man you met?" Oh my gosh, it just struck me, of course it was the man I met! I put my arm around a post so I wouldn't fall down. And I was more interested in his guitar when I met him! Now I know how Audrey felt when she met John Wayne in a café in Montrose, Colorado while he was filming 'True Grit', and she didn't know who he was.

Communications between the islands in the French Society Islands is by radio. Every evening we could tune in on the conversations. I didn't understand what they were saying, but it was interesting to hear the babies cry on purpose so the party on the distant island could hear the new baby.

The yard of the base house was full of large land crabs about ten inches wide with large triangular shaped heads and big triangular shaped eyes. Breadfruit tree leaves are about two feet wide. When you saw one of them moving along in the yard, you knew a big crab was under it.

We were fortunate to have inside plumbing, but we also had an outhouse, which the neighbors used, or anyone else who happened along on the road. I wonder if the land crabs that lived around by the outhouse had anything to do with the lack of smell.

An eight-inch long orange poisonous centipede was found in the bathroom and was disposed of in a hurry. I was told the bite from one of these centipedes is worse than a rattlesnake bite. This room was full of large cockroaches as big as a man's thumb. One night two cockroaches crawled over me in my bed. I still get the shivers when I think of it. I just don't like crawling things on my body, especially cockroaches. I didn't mind the little geckos running around in the upper corners of the room for they ate flies and mosquitoes. A circular mosquito punk was kept burning all day in the house, and sometimes at night. Mosquitoes infest this island like you wouldn't believe!

Every morning the archaeologists drove me to Maeva where I did my sketching of the maraes, and as I limped back to the base house with a long pole for support, I dared not stop to rest, for mosquitoes instantly covered me. Rats liked the coconut trees and ran up and down the trees, and our metal roof, all night. I pretended they were squirrels so I could get some sleep. I don't know how one could get used to this, just for the beautiful scenery and beaches, even if the swimmers were practically naked.

I think about the mean tricks that were played on the other volunteers and me. I carried a long pole to use for a cane. Every time I wanted my pole, someone had hid it. I had to either find another pole or limp around on one foot to search for it. It was obvious I needed a cane, my foot was very swollen and still black and blue.

One day Muffett and Eric said they were driving the bus to town and would anyone like to go to the Bali Hai Hotel beach. I bit and so did Bolek and Betty. I thought it would be restful to sit on the beach. Yosi, Muffett and Eric let us off in the village of Fare, and said we could walk the shoreline to the hotel. They had other things they had to do. We didn't know how long the walk was, but soon found out that it was almost a half a mile long over rugged tree roots and a sandy beach littered with old tree stumps. When we got to the Bali Hai Hotel, we found Yosi, Eric and Muffett sitting on the veranda eating an American lunch.

I immediately went up to them and asked why they left us off in Fare when their destination was the Bali Hai Hotel. Yosi gave me a funny look and Eric and Muffett said nothing.

Muffett and Eric would tell us that they were going to town and ask who would like to ride along? When they said this you had to be ready with purse in hand sitting on the porch watching them, because they would leave without saying a word to anyone and go without you. One day they asked who would like to go along and everyone accepted.

Bolek was the last one to take a shower. For a dirty trick Muffett and Eric turned off the water supply while he was in the shower. Soon Muffett said we couldn't wait for Bolek any longer, so left without him. She was always playing dirty tricks on him because he was Polish. I asked her why she did that, and she said that she had never been around a Polack before and didn't know how to treat him. This seemed queer coming from an archaeologist, for when we signed up for this expedition, one of the queries from Earthwatch was whether we could accept the Tahitians as they were.

Seemed to me this should also apply to the archaeologists, the way they treated the volunteers.

We were told to take off our shoes before entering the house. Muffett said everyone in Hawaii does it. Well, we are in Tahiti, not Hawaii. I told her that I was never expected to take off my shoes when I visited Bill in Hawaii. She said he was not Hawaiian. I told her the only other blood he had in him was his great grandfather. Then she said, "Oh, a stupid haole." Muffet had more Japanese in her than Hawiian.

Huahine Island is actually made up of two islands connected by an isthmus. We lived on Huahine Nui, the large island. One nice thing the archaeologists did was to take us on a tour of the two islands, and then to a picnic on Motu Ara'ara, which is near the shore of Huahine Iti, the small island. A native gave us a ride out to the motu in his outrigger canoe.

The meal of canned beef stew was served on a large leaf. As we were returning to Huahine Nui we drove through the town of Fare.

Fare is located on the shore of Fare Harbor. As we passed through the town, I couldn't help but recall the song that Jimmy Buffett was composing. He sings of the children playing in this harbor. I sat on the shore of that very harbor and watched the children play. A tree extends out over the deep channel. The children get out on a large limb and dive into the harbor. I was thinking that I would rather that they swim here than in the lagoon where the pig cages are built over the water, and the feces seeps through the floor boards into the lagoon waters.

The last Sunday on the island we were given a farewell banquet at the pension that belonged to Martiel and Enete. I had painted a picture of their pension for them with the coconut trees in the background, and beyond this

283

was the sea. This was our gift to them for all their kindnesses. We were served a cocktail before dinner, so I had my second Scotch on the rocks.

Yosi seated me next to him, a reporter from the Papeete newspaper, La Nouveille, sat across from me. The banquet food consisted of raw oysters in the half shell served with lime juice, poisson cru (a delicious raw fish dish made with cocoanut cream and vegetables), lobster, Cornish hen, wine and a delicious papaya tapioca pudding.

The reporter was trying to make me pronounce 'poisson cru' correctly, and Yosi was filling my glass with wine. I could blame it on Yosi for constantly filling my glass, but I think I just didn't have the hang of speaking in French. The reporter inserted a news item in the La Nouveile paper in Papeete. He wrote, "Freda painted a picture for Enete and Martiel, then spent the rest of the evening trying to pronounce poisson cru correctly."

The next morning Yosi sent a taxi for me, and I left for the airport. At the airport, I saw many natives singing and playing guitars. Yvonne told me their minister was leaving the island for other places, and they were bidding him and his wife farewell. It was a lovely tribute. Out of respect I waited with the other passengers for them to board first. As each native put a shell lei around their necks, they gave them a Tahitian kiss. As they were leaving the minister and his wife turned around and threw tiara leis on the path. This meant that they would return some day. The ceremony was so touching, I was crying along with all the natives, and I knew no one involved with the farewell ceremony.

As I neared the plane, I saw Yvonne standing by the steps. We exchanged Tahitian Farewell kisses, and with tears in my eyes again, I boarded the plane. The plane rose into the beautiful blue sky as they circled the island. The island below us was like a jewel set in a turquoise sea. To the beautiful island of Huahine, I said "Parahi."

CHAPTER 23

TAHITI, FIJI, HAWAII

The expedition was over, so back to Papeete on the island of Tahiti. Our plane flew over Moorea (MOH-oh-ray-ah) and I saw the hourglass shape of Tahiti jutting out of the deep blue and turquoise water beyond.

The plane landed at the Faaa airport. I took a taxi to Hotel Tahiti. This is the hotel the natives stay in when they fly in from the islands, so I continued to experience their culture.

I had a lovely large room on the second floor with a balcony on the back and a private balcony on the front, overlooking the beautiful gardens and the sea. Feeling fully satisfied with my choice, I opened my bag to unpack, and there was my nightgown with a cockroach resting very nicely on top. I caught it and flushed it down the toilet. That was the last cockroach I saw in the South Pacific.

This was a restful place to be, for it was quiet and the gardens enhanced the solitude. I was coming down with diarrhea, so spent a lot of time just lying on the bed. The raw oysters I ate and the questionable water on the island of Huahine probably caused it. In a few days, Betty, an Earthwatch

Volunteer from the island of the Huahine Expedition, came to the hotel and gave me a few Lomotil pills, which did the trick and stopped the diarrhea.

When I felt like going out, Betty and I went to Papeete. I didn't manage it very well with my foot, so we stopped in a restaurant for lunch. I ordered roast duck from the menu, and it was so tough I was sure it had run around with all those chickens on the island of Huahine. The painful walk with a hurt foot was slowing down Betty's shopping tour, so I left her and boarded La Truck and went back to the hotel.

The walls of Hotel Tahiti are open to the outside, except for the bedrooms. The dining area/lounge has a thatched roof. The only exterior walls are flowered vines dripping down from the roof. Alongside the lounge is a swimming pool. Again the women wore no bras and very little in the pants area. Some of the gals should have covered up and left it to the imagination.

There were about five poodles continually running about, and a large floor-to-ceiling birdcage with many strange birds, graced the dining area. The whole setting looked like it might be a carry over from an earlier century; the way you might picture Tahiti to be.

Every evening I sat in the lounge and listened to the hotel band play Tahitian music, while I drank a Scotch on the rocks. The barman who waited on me had finally understood that I liked Scotch with lots of ice. His command of English was not good, but every evening he came by and said, "I remember, Scotch with tall ice." One evening I decided I would rather have a shot of brandy with no ice. It confused the waiter no end, and he brought me a Scotch with tall ice. I never tried to change that order again.

The hotel was stirring with activity one day. The place was being decorated with fresh greenery and party fare. I was told that a wedding reception would take place in the large building by the seashore. A roasting pig was on the spit and long tables were set up in the building.

After the affair, the best man of the wedding party (who was also the hotel band guitarist) invited a few people, including me, to have a coke and tall ice with him around the swimming pool.

The dinner hour arrived and the guitarist joined the band in the outdoor lounge. Of course I went to sit in my favorite chair for this was the night I was taping their music with my tape recorder.

Some wedding guests strolled into the lounge to listen to the band. They were beautifully dressed in typical Tahitian apparel. They weren't in the area too long before one of the women danced the hula with the band. My, she sure could swing her hips!

What happened next would make this a pornographic story, for women were trying to entice a few drunken men. I won't say how they were enticed, but the men were too drunk; it didn't work. Now I saw the other side of the Tahitians, for this was a spur of the moment dance, not professional.

I became acquainted with the woman who ran the travel desk because she could speak English. I bought a ticket for a tour around the island from her, then she asked about my canvas bag. It was La Bag that I always carried with me. I bought it in Colorado Springs. She said, "How much did you pay for it?" "About $5.00 US." "I'll give you 1000 francs for it. That was roughly $10.00, so I dumped out the old seashells and sand, and sold it to her. Then I paid 300 francs for a handmade Tahitian straw bag.

I went on the Circle tour of this island, which included lunch at the Gauguin Restaurant and a visit to the Gauguin Museum. This disappointed me for they had none of the artist's paintings in the museum, not even copies, unless you bought the postcards. But they did have a good pictorial history of his life on the islands.

The next day I rode La Truck to the market place, bought a Tahitian hat and some very nice shell carvings. I came back early, for the walking was very hard on my injured foot.

That night, I as I was sitting in the lounge by the band, I heard someone speaking English behind me. I turned around and said, "You speak English." It was a couple from Englewood, Colorado. They were on their way home from Australia where his parents live. We had cocktails together with more people from San Francisco and Tucson. We had so much fun! It was nice to be with a bunch of people who spoke English. We were enjoying ourselves so much we decided to have dinner together.

We were seated at a big round table, and while we were eating, Betty came up behind me and let out a barrage of hatred for me. I was shocked, as were the other people. I still don't know why she did this. Maybe she thought I should have hunted her down and asked her to join us, but the thought didn't cross my mind at that time. One woman in our party said she had been walking up and down behind me while we were having cocktails.

My sore foot hampered me, and as much as I wanted to just walk around Papeete, it was impossible. While I was at the hotel, Enete and Martiel came into the lobby. I greeted them with a Tahitian kiss, and as we were trying to talk, she said something to the hotel clerk and he translated it for me. He said, "She regrets that she cannot accept the invitation to dinner; but they had made other arrangements." In trouble with communications again, I didn't know I was asking them to dinner.

I stayed at this hotel eight restful days, until my flight to Fiji was due. My bill at the hotel was for 40500 francs, but a rate of exchange favored me on that day, and it cost me only $322.00. Not bad for eats, room and a daily Scotch with tall ice.

I boarded a small 707 Air New Zealand plane for Fiji at 5 AM. We stopped at the island of Rarotonga to pick up more passengers, and fuel. Because of my foot, I didn't get off the plane as the other passengers did so I listened to the pilots. They calculated that with the added weight of new passengers they would have 15 meters to spare on the runway. We lifted off with 15 meters to spare. Good Pilots! If their calculations had been in error, we would have run into the sea.

The plane flew over Tonga and small uninhabited islands that reminded me of the lonely spots pictured in those cartoons of tiny islands. The view of them from the plane was beautiful, for the white waves dashing up on the beaches from a deep blue sea, was spectacular.

A few hours later, we reached the East Coast of Fiji. I didn't realize that the island of Fiji was so big! It took an hour to fly over it before we reached the Nandi airport, which is located on the West Coast of the island.

We had crossed the International Dateline, so I adjusted my watch and put it back two hours, for now, I am into tomorrow. It's very confusing. I really set my watch ahead 22 hours. I am now 1000 miles north of New Zealand and 1000 miles east of Australia.

FIJI

I landed at the Nandi Airport in the Fijian Islands, then went directly to the money-changing window. I didn't do so well with my money in this country, for I received only 92 cents for my US dollar, and in Tahiti I received $1.25. I hired a taxi to take me the fifteen miles to the Blue

Lagoon Cruise in Lautoka. In the taxi I sat on the left side, the driver on the right. This was my first experience of driving on the left side of the road. It was harder yet when crossing the street, for the tendency is to look for oncoming traffic the wrong way.

The taxi driver was Singh, who wanted to give me a tour around the territory for $45.00. I was tired so asked him to take me directly to the Blue Lagoon Cruise office. Then he asked me if I would like him to pick me up when the boat docked after the cruise. I told him I would like that.

The Blue Lagoon Cruise will take me throughout the Yasawa Islands. I walked around town as much as my sore foot would let me, and picked up some Fijian culture. I saw a few Fijian businessmen talking together on the street. It seemed odd to me that their business suits came with a skirt instead of pants. What I didn't like were the Indians who came out on the street the minute I admired something in their window. I finally refused to window shop anymore, just to avoid having an Indian come out to entice me into the store.

At this time Fiji was 54% Indians. Their ancestors were imported from India many years ago to work in the fields. The Fijian's way of living didn't lend itself to working in the fields. The newcomers found profit in raising sugar cane and other crops. The Indians multiplied much faster than the Fijians. I didn't see any people who were part Indian. I was told that the Fijians and Indians do not intermingle. One odd thing I noticed was that our cruise ship was entirely manned by Fijians, but the office on the mainland was manned by Indians. Could it be that the Fijians were more adept at sailing? The Indians in the office were very helpful to me. They immediately reminded me that I should call Air New Zealand to confirm my reservations to Hawaii, or I would have to go stand-by. They made the call for me, then took me back into the waiting room where coffee was ready.

To step from Tahiti right into Fiji was like taking a small step into the American way of life. Even though I still see culture that was fairly primitive, the business part of it was more like home, except for the Indians with businesses on the street haggling with you.

The waiting room soon filled up with Australians and New Zealanders. I was the only American on the cruise. But thank goodness everyone spoke English. The Fijians are bilingual like the Tahitians, instead of French/Tahitian they are English/Fijian for they haven't been out of England's control for too long. So here we are, the New Zealanders and Australians with a similar accent, the Fijians with a Fijian accent and me, the only one on the ship with an American accent. I was the odd ball!

I boarded the ship Oleanda at 5:30 PM. We were served dinner on board. We are now anchored by a little island off the big island of Fiji. The night was probably spent here because of the treacherous coral reefs that surround the big island. Early in the morning the ship's motors awakened me. We were heading out into Bligh Waters.

Bligh Waters is where Captain Bligh, in a small lifeboat, sailed with a few crew members after the rest of the crew mutinied and captured his ship. Bligh couldn't land on Fiji because the Fijian cannibal warriors constantly threatened him. Bligh Waters was very rough, and as the ship cut through the mountains of sea, I was wondering how Captain Bligh could have possibly managed to fight these seas in such a small boat.

By noon, we were anchored in a delightful cove in the Yasawa Islands, and were served a delicious lunch. I was in the lovely Yasawa Islands. They are just as beautiful as they were depicted in the book, 'The Dove.'

The crew was kind to me with my sore foot. When the others went ashore to swim and snorkel, I sat on the deck atop a box of life jackets and painted pictures of the islands. Members of the crew served me coffee and cake as I painted. They were very kind to me with my sore foot predicament. They seemed to understand why I couldn't go ashore, and sympathized with me. They swabbed the deck around me, always peeking at my picture with suggestions and information about the islands. I inserted the titles on the paintings exactly as they recommended. I think I got the best of the deal without the snorkeling.

Every evening the passengers were taught the Fijian dance, which was a promenade with little short steps, which I could do with a sore foot. It was a simple shuffle with a woman between two men or a man between two women. In this way no one was left out of the promenade.

On the final day, the ship was anchored far out in the sea near a coral reef by Nacula (Nah-THOO-lah) Island. This island was home to one of the crew. The captain asked me to go with the other passengers to this island for they were making a feast, and the natives would be entertaining us later in the evening. I accompanied them to Nacula Village.

Lining the wide footpath, which is the main street in Nacula Village, are grass shacks called 'bures.' (BUR-ayes). The bures are constructed much different than the grass shacks on Huahine Island. Inside were curtain room partitions. Kerosene lanterns lit the homes, as no electricity is available. Water is hauled from a spring.

Fiji bure

As we walked by the bures, men would call out "bula" (BOO-lah), which means 'welcome' or 'hello.' We returned the greeting with a bula of our own. We heard no women, for they were down by the seashore setting up a shell market.

At the shell market I bought a nice tapa cloth, which is cloth pounded from the bark of a mulberry tree and then painted. The walk to the shell market was hard on my foot, and the ship's captain noticed it. He asked me if I'd rather go back to the ship than attend a soccer game at the school. I opted for the ship. I was transported back to the ship in an outboard motor boat.

On the ship the crew gave me a cup of coffee with a small pineapple, peeled and sliced. I swallowed a pain pill with the cup of coffee, ate the delicious pineapple, lay on the deck seat and fell fast asleep. The crew was so kind to me that you would never believe that at the turn of the century their ancestors were still cannibals.

After the soccer game, the passengers came back to the ship for afternoon tea, and in time to witness a beautiful orange sunset so common to these islands. We all dressed in our finest for the big feast called 'lovo' (LOH-voh). I wore a Hawaiian muumuu, some wore long skirts with pretty blouses and some men had acquired Fijian skirts. We were indeed a conglomeration of styles.

The motor boats took us back to the island. As we arrived back on the beach, the natives put leis around our necks.

Our cook had been working all day on the island preparing the feast. The feast was baked in the sand, and consisted of roast pig baked in leaves, breadfruit, yams, cake and pineapple. After the feast, the beach was lit up by the soft glow of four torches, for the evening was pitch black.

Out of the forest of coconut trees, which surrounded us, I heard singing. Again, the beautiful voices of the South Pacific people! They slowly came out of the black forest and into the subdued light of the torches. The forms dressed in grass skirts began dancing to the chants of natives and the beat of bamboo drums. They screamed and yelled and ran to you with raised spears, but stopped just short of the visitors they came to entertain. When they did this to me I pointed both hands at them and shouted "bang, bang." They couldn't help but put a big smile on their sober faces.

Dancing with native

After the fantastic entertainment, we were asked to dance with them. It was the dance that the crew was teaching us every evening on the ship. I was recording the music and had no idea if I was really receiving it on tape. We were about thirty feet from the orchestra where they were beating the bamboo drums and humming. I walked over to them with my recorder.

This is where I made a mistake. A Fijian came up to me and said,

"Are you married?"

"NO," I said. I had told the truth.

"I marry you."

"No. I have a man in America." This time I lied.

"You marry me."

"I'm old."

"How old you?"

"I'm very, very, very old."

This seemed to satisfy him, for who wants an old woman? Then I walked back to the other passengers. The Australians teased me and kept asking me why I didn't accept, but my thoughts now go back to the reservations on this cruise. They were made out to Mr. and Mrs. Freda Stumpf. I was kidded by the travel agent to keep those reservations because I would find someone. How true, and I refused the proposal when it came!

The next morning I awoke to the sound of the ship's motors, for we were already heading back to the mainland of Fiji. As we were leaving the beautiful Yasawa Islands, I threw my lei into the waters. This meant that someday I would return, but that dream never came true.

I brought out my tape recorder and taped the Australian's voices as they spoke to me, so I wouldn't loose the sound of their wonderful style of speaking. Then a man from New Zealand spoke in the recorder. He said, "I live in New Zealand, but was born in England and will always be English, even if George III did lose to the Americans."

Then I teased them about living 'down under,' and they came back at me for not speaking correctly. To speak correctly, they said, I must learn that 'she's apples' means that 'everything is Jake.'

My special friend the barman who served me my nightly Scotch on the rocks, sang a song for me while the other crewmembers strummed on ukuleles and guitars. The song was 'Home on the Range' because I lived in Colorado where the 'deers' and the antelopes play. I taped the song. Then I cut off the Colorado decal from my jacket and gave it to him.

As the ship was approaching the dock on the big island of Fiji, I could see Singe parked there with his taxi, waiting for me. He drove me to the Macombo Hotel in Nandi, where the New Zealander recommended that I wait for my plane. He gave me his business card to show to the desk clerk, so I would get professional treatment to care for my luggage. He stays at this hotel when on his business trips. It was a perfect place.

I went to the woman's rest room and changed into a clean dress. Then I sat in the bar reading a book that the Australians gave me just before we docked. It sure was a sexy book, and now I know why so many read the book while we cruised along.

As I was engrossed in the book a Scotch on the rocks was put before me. I was surprised because the bar was closed when I sat down with the book, I had not placed an order. I looked up and there was Ian, an Australian passenger on the cruise ship. He and I were the only single people on the cruise.

He asked me out to dinner at the fancy restaurant in the hotel. They wouldn't serve him because he was wearing the cruise tee shirt. He wanted to go to his room and change, but I said I didn't want him to, so we ate in the other restaurant below by the swimming pool.

Soon we heard entertainment by the pool. Look what we would have missed if we had gone to the fancy restaurant. Ian asked me to get my recorder, so we stood by the pool and as I was taping the music when a Fijian came up to me and started to get fresh. THESE FIJIANS! This one didn't care if I was with a man, or that I was very, very, very old. Ian thought we should get away from the man and so did I, so we went to a more populated area and finished my last tape.

It was now late and time for me to leave for my plane. Singh was outside waiting for me in his taxi. Ian helped Singe with my luggage, put me in the taxi and kissed me goodbye.

I boarded an Air New Zealand plane for the trip to Honolulu. I crossed the International Dateline and the Equator, and now I was in yesterday, for I left at 11 PM on Saturday evening and arrived in Honolulu, Hawaii at 7 AM Saturday morning. Confused? So was I.

I exchanged letters with Ian and Pio, the barman, for a year or two. Pio wrote that the ship that I was on, The Oleanda, had sunk in a typhoon as it was tied up to the harbor of Lautoka.

HAWAII

I landed on American soil in Honolulu. Undergoing customs was long and tiring. It was a good thing I had my camera, strobe light and recorder registered with the customs office in Colorado Springs. I was questioned about them extensively, until I pulled out the registration papers from the back of my passport. I was asked how much money I spent; he thought I spent too much. I told him I bought four dresses, was gone about 6 weeks and have ten grandchildren. He smiled and told me to close my bags. I guess he didn't want to go through all that stuff!

In Honolulu, I rented a small car and paid a visit to Bill's mother. She was very gracious to me and gave me some pictures that Bill had taken of me six years before. Bill was the special friend of mine that I had met in Alaska so long ago. Bill had passed away a few years before the expedition. It was he who prompted me to make this trip, for he had traveled these islands many times and inspired me with his stories of them.

I spent the rest of my time in Hawaii visiting the places that Bill and I had known so well. Memories overwhelmed me at some spots. I did some laughing and much crying, and then I was ready to come home. I'm leaving many beautiful memories in Hawaii.

I boarded an Air New Zealand plane and headed for the mainland. My son, Wolf, picked me up at the Denver airport, and I stayed with him a few days.

When I was in Honolulu I had my pictures processed, so I gave my first slide show of the 400 pictures of my trip. The pictures were all unedited, but the guests stayed until the very last one was shown.

My daughter, Audrey, came from Colorado Springs and brought me back to my home in Woodland Park. So ends the trip that took eight years of planning.

I was delightfully tired, so sat quietly alone with a Scotch and tall ice, just thinking about it all.

CHAPTER 24

MOUNTAIN LIVING

It was hard to unwind after coming home from the expedition. During the last eight years I had worked with the utmost determination to realize my South Pacific dream, and suddenly I had nothing to do!

I wandered about my Rocky Mountain yard. The soil is so rocky that I wondered how things really grew in this stuff. Walter had given me some tiger lilies, which didn't seem to like the rocky soil, but lived regardless of the conditions. The Ohio violets tolerated the soil to some degree, but the plant that didn't care a bit was the blue iris.

My thoughts of my South Pacific experience lingered with me. When I was in the South Pacific, I had entered all my daily happenings in a journal before retiring at night. I bought books and pamphlets published by Tahitian and Fijian historians, and picked up products made by the natives. I used everything I had to put my experiences on paper, and edited all my slides so I could give slide show lectures.

I was interviewed by reporters of four newspapers. Two of the articles were full page spreads. When I spoke about the expedition on the radio, someone who listened to the interview called me and said she was driving her car, and parked it to listen. I showed slides to my friends. Calls came in from clubs, churches, senior clubs and nursing homes to present my slde show.

A patient in one of the nursing homes was a woman I had met in the Woodland Park Senior Center. I asked a nurse if she was still a patient and she said she was, but was bed-ridden. I told the nurse I would visit her after the slide show. They had a better idea, they brought her down in a wheel chair and put her next to me. She was so happy to see me, and so proud to sit besides me as I lectured.

I wondered why I hadn't done this more often. I made one person extremely happy that day, even though she was completely exhausted when they wheeled her back to her room.

Summer had finally arrived, and with it came my friend, Mark, who was my boss when I worked for the engineering company in Ohio long ago. I was happy to see him, for I had been out of engineering so long that it seemed like I was only dreaming, when I thought of the magnitude of work I had done in my career. I told him how I felt and he said, "Freda, YOU REALLY DID do all those things, I remember it all."

With that comment Mark helped me more than he knew, for once I got out of engineering and moved into retirement, the old life seemed like it didn't happen. I found myself looking out of the window every morning at the cars carrying people to work, and wishing I were among them.

Mark parked his travel trailer in the RV section of our park, and we did some rock hounding. This was fun, for Mark knew more about rocks than I did. Geology was part of his studies in college, when he studied civil engineering. He stayed only a few days then went on to do more rock hounding around the state.

The next event in my life was when granddaughter, Heather, married Michael Buono, who was an Aspen musician. I wanted to record the wedding ceremony so took my tape recorder to the wedding. After I arrived in Aspen, I discovered that all the musicians in Aspen were there. I wandered amongst them and taped their congratulations to Heather and Michael.

I was standing on the porch balcony overlooking the beautiful mountains when a man came running up the stairs, shouting to me, "Are you Freda? I was looking for you. I have a message for you from Jimmy Buffett. He is sorry he would miss seeing you again, but he is in Cleveland on tour,"

Just before the ceremony was to begin, a man came up to me in a rush. He had just got there and wanted to give his congratulations to Heather and Michael. He was sorry he was late, but they just got in town from going on tour in England. I told him I had the recorder all set for the wedding ceremony, but would he please come after the ceremony? He did.

The ceremony was performed in the garden of this beautiful home, which was owned by Steve Martin's manager.

About this time, Jimmy Buffett's album 'One Particular Harbor' had come out. Audrey bought a copy and immediately brought it to me. We played the album, and it was the same song he sang to me when I was on the little island of Huahine.

As we were listening to it, I turned to Audrey and said, "Much of Bobby Holcomb, the man who introduced us, rubbed off onto Jimmy in that song." When we read the words to the song on the dust cover, we saw that Jimmy Buffett did give credit to Bobby Holcomb, who was my choir director friend on the island.

Jimmy sings of the children playing in the harbor and describes the mountains, lake and lagoon where the fish traps are located. I was overcome just listening to the song he had sung to me in Tahiti, and here it was all dressed up in an album!

Winter was closing in once more. The mobile home park was sold and the new owner didn't do any snow plowing unless the tenants complained. I shoveled more snow than I had ever done in my life. I was snowed in almost constantly with 40 inches of the stuff on the ground. It is beautiful to be sure, but the removal of it was getting me down. I was getting older.

The new owner told us we had six months to four years to move our homes out of the park, for he wants to build condominiums. Six months to four years is unstable, so I decided that if I should go through all the expense and problems in moving my home, I ought to move it to a warmer climate.

I drove to Arizona to case out the place. I found that Flagstaff has as much snow as Woodland Park, but 27 miles south, in Sedona, the climate changed drastically. I thought it would be ideal to live in Sedona. I looked more closely at the town and discovered it was an art colony and things were very expensive, similar to Aspen. On further investigation, I discovered that they do have plane service directly to Aspen and several retired movie stars live here. I was disappointed, so I started for home.

Coming back home, I drove through 97 miles of Indian country with no towns or ANYTHING! This is not for me! I felt that no one would ever come to see me if they had to drive through country like that, and neither would I like to travel through it to see them. At the edge of the Indian Territory, I went through the Four Corners area.

This is the only place in United States where four corners meet. I got out of the car and walked through Arizona, New Mexico, Colorado and Utah, and it only took one minute to do it.

I was now in Colorado. I went through Durango and came into Pagosa Springs and stopped. I was right below the notoriously high Wolf Creek Pass. There was no way to avoid it, and it was snowing and icy. I opted for a motel for the night to ponder my fear of heights. The next morning I started up Wolf Creek Pass and hugged the yellow line in the center of the road all the way.

I made another trip to Santa Fe, New Mexico. A walk through the grocery stores showed a remarkable cut in grocery prices, but a check into the cost of electricity showed it was more than the high rate in Woodland Park, and I would need air conditioning. I boarded a tour bus for a guided trip to see the city and felt DEFINITE DISCRIMINATION from the tour guide because, as she pointed out to me, I had blonde hair and blue eyes.

Santa Fe is out. I don't want to undergo all THAT! I don't know what to do about moving my home out of Woodland Park. Summer arrived and with it the feeling that to move out of this beautiful mountain area would be foolish. I had to keep reminding myself that snow does come to mountain living.

August had arrived, and one morning I looked up to Pikes Peak and it was snow covered. It brought me back to my senses that THE SNOW DOES COME TO MOUNTAIN LIVING!

I went on the road again and found a mobile home park in Canon City, but when it came time for me to sign the lease, my hand stiffened around the pen and I couldn't move it. Something told me not to. I told the manager that I would be down the next week. I went down the next week, and found they had moved in manufactured homes that didn't come up to the standards they had set for me. I went back home.

I went to Penrose to visit friends, who were my neighbors in Woodland Park. They had already moved their home down to Penrose. In Penrose I found a real estate agent who told me to look into Salida. In Salida I couldn't find a park that suited me. I knew more parks were in the area, but I didn't have a clue as to their location. No one would discuss it with me. I went back home thoroughly disgusted and dismayed. I probably asked the wrong people for the information.

One day I was going over some literature I had picked up in Salida and in it was an ad for a manufactured home mover. I called him and he told me about a very nice park I had over looked. I called the manager of the park; he had some vacant lots for seniors. One was next to an open field. I told him to save that one until I could come down to look at it.

In September, I went down to Salida with my friend Sue Webb and her daughter Stacy. The manager was not in, but one of the tenants showed me the two lots. We stopped at the lot next to the field. Stacy ran out into the middle of the lot and looked at the field with cows in it, and beyond, the high mountains. She jumped up and down saying, "Freda, take it, take it, take it."

I phoned the manager the next day, and said I would move my home onto the lot with the field next to it. I told him I would be down in a few days with the money.

By this time October had come, and with it, the snow. It snowed and snowed. I was snowed in for the last time in Woodland Park. I put a yardstick in the snow and the yardstick disappeared. The snow came up higher than my wrist. I called the manager of the park in Salida and told

305

him that I had to dig out of 40 inches of snow.I would be down when I could get out of the park.

It took me three days to dig a walk way to my car and then I had to dig my car out of the snow. The next morning I took off for Salida with two feet of snow still on the roof of my car. I stopped on top of Wilkerson Pass as I always did, to take in the tremendous view.

Two men parked their Jeep alongside me and asked me why I had so much snow on my car. I told them of all the snow in Woodland Park and how it took me three days to dig out, and I was too tired to get it off the roof of my car. They opened up their Jeep and got out some brooms and removed the snow. After expressing my gratitude, we parted in opposite directions. They probably knew what I meant when they went through Woodland Park.

In Salida I couldn't believe what I saw. Salida was barren of snow.

I called the mover to move my outfit, but he didn't have a flatbed truck to move the studio. He asked me to locate one. Another mover owned the only one I could find, so I hired him to do the whole job.

Because of the heavy snowfall, he was back-ordered and I had to wait my turn. On top of this problem, he must have safe wind conditions to move my home across South Park, which has an altitude of 10,000 feet, and often has terrible ground-blizzards.

My neighbor, Willie, disconnected the studio and made my home ready to move. This took about three days. As Willie was doing his job, I was digging up the tiger lily, violets and the blue iris.

CHAPTER 25

SALIDA

Before leaving Woodland Park the mover and I made a bet. He said that a glass of water on the table would not move or lose any water when he transported the house. I disagreed, but filled the glass with water and put it in the sink. I followed the mover until we came to Wilkerson Pass. The slow 4-MPH movement of the house got to me, so I passed it.

I stopped in a small restaurant for lunch and then on to Salida. The mover showed up an hour after I got to my lot. We went inside to look at the glass of water. It hadn't lost any water in the move, but I lost the bet because I put it in the sink instead of on the table. After that the whole move was fun and teasing. The mover said he never moved a house that was so much fun! But then the REAL fun began.

A swarm of men took over on their particular job: telephone, electric, and gas and local inspectors. I took a room in a motel for the night. The men were still doing their thing the next day. The electric company had to bring in 100 watts of power. The gas company had to put in new gas jets on the furnace, range and hot water heater' because I was changing from

Propane to natural gas. The phone, sewer and water connections had to be installed; busy, busy, and busy.

The mover said he tries to get the owner to go on a vacation when he moves the home. I stayed, but it.got to the point where it was hard to take, so I went shopping for groceries. I don't know why they call them mobile homes; they aren't very mobile.

HUD in Washington changed the name in 1980 from 'mobile' to 'manufactured' homes. It irritates me when some people go back fifty years and call them 'trailers.'

Salida is a beautiful place to live, surrounded by high mountains in the Upper Arkansas River valley. Not more than twenty miles to the west is the Continental Divide.

Many times I would go for a jaunt to the 11,313-foot high Monarch Pass to view the high peaks, and of course, people. People watching I call it. Very few license plates on the parked cars are from Colorado. Kansas and Utah people are just passing through. Very few walk around like myself to view the peaks, and when they do, they have a camera in hand. Some rush into the souvenir shop.

I resumed my painting and made many trips to Twin Lakes. Of all the places I painted, this is my favorite. It is not a place that you can view from only one place. One can drive around and paint mountains, or if you didn't have your paint box, a camera did just fine. One of my favorite photos is Mt. Hope framed with orange aspen leaves.

From my home I had a full view of Mount Shavano, Mt. Antero and Mount Princeton, all over 14,000 feet high. It made me feel so tiny.

My son and his family came from his home in Denver to visit, and I put him to work planting the blue iris.

It was in 1985 that I moved to Salida, Colorado. Equal Rights for Women slipped back at least 20 years in this town. I soon found out that the town is full of chauvinistic men in the older generation, who battered my personhood around again. It was hard to be a forerunner in the women's movement, for men in my age bracket in this town haven't kept up with the times or refused to do it. My personhood was taken away from so many times I couldn't count them.

I was not alone with these feelings, for a school principal, who was a friend of mine, experienced the same thing. The men in high positions in the schools worked until they got rid of her. In Texas, she had a higher position than principal. I told her that the town was 20 years behind times, but she disagreed; it was more like 30 or 40 years behind times.

I was interviewed on the radio about my South Pacific expedition and given a plug for my slide show, to be given at the Senior Center. I was pleasantly surprised when 75 people showed up. I displayed many things I acquired in Tahiti and Fiji. One woman picked up a Tahitian shell necklace and begged and begged me to sell it to her. Finally I said, "OK. I'll sell it to you. She said, "How much?" I said, "As much as it would cost me to go back to Tahiti to replace it." She didn't buy it.

Because of the expensive move to Salida, I was low on funds. I needed a job of some kind. I went to the Women's Resource Center for help. I inquired at the first desk I came to, but it was the wrong one. Colorado Mountain College had a desk in the same building and it was to this desk that I made my inquiry about a job.

"I could enter you in a college course to train for a secretarial job," said the gal behind the desk.

"I'm the world's worst typist. I've been a draftsman for forty years."

"Have you ever taught in a vocational school?"

"I did a few years ago when I lived in Northglenn, but the certificate is probably expired by now."

"We've been looking for a drafting instructor for several years. Bring in your old certificate and I'll try to renew it."

My certificate was renewed and I taught a drafting workshop. I was scheduled to teach a two-credit-drafting course for the spring term 1986. In this class I had one of the local chauvinists as a pupil. He was a carpenter and refused to buy the required drafting board. He said he could make one. I gave him a few pointers on how to do it. He came to the next class with his drafting board. He had made it out of a bright red piece of Formica. You couldn't possibly use it with drafting instruments, but he insisted on using it.

Another pupil asked me about a drafting term he thought I knew nothing about. I told him if he would open his drafting book, he would find it on page 68. Luck was with me this time, I wouldn't have known the page number if I hadn't been studying that very page on that day.

One thing led to another and Workman's Compensation hired me to teach drafting to men who were handicapped, on a one-on-one basis. I didn't have any problem with these men.

I worked all summer on a three dimensional map of mountainous Chaffee County. It was a project more difficult and tedious than I thought it would be. I used my knowledge of civil drafting, carpentry, math and art ability to build it. I took several months to cut intricate shapes on a jigsaw to form the mountains and valleys. I covered my work with a plastic material and finally painted it. By using the United States Geological maps, it was exactly to scale. It now hangs in the Buena Vista Airport.

The next one I did was a ski slope. I had no problem selling it. Then I made a map of the Aspen ski areas. I displayed it in Aspen for a few weeks, an architect wanted it; but you can't sell something without an exchange of money.

My friend, Sue Webb, had been trying for several years to get tickets for a Jimmy Buffett Concert in the Red Rocks Amphitheater in Denver. She finally connected, then called me and said that she had the tickets. I was wracked with arthritis pain, especially in the foot that had been injured. I told her that I couldn't get to my seat.

My daughter Audrey told me that I hadn't tried. I should call the manager of Red Rocks. I made the phone call and was given the facility manager of Red Rocks. He was trying to get me some help, when I told him I had another request. I was acquainted with Jimmy Buffett and would like to go back stage and see him. He said he would have to get permission from Jimmy Buffett. I told him I didn't think it would be a problem, and it wasn't. Jimmy granted the request and I ended up with a better seat and VIP treatment.

I arrived at Red rocks with Sue Webb, who was driving her car. I had been told that we were to talk to a man in a yellow vest at the entrance. He was expecting us and parked us nearby and told us to wait. When he was ready, he directed us up a narrow winding road.

Along this road, guards at 6 stations stopped us for identification. At one station near the top, the guard said, "Wait right there." He pulled out his walkie -talkie. I didn't catch what he was saying until there was a long pause, then I heard him say, "Yes, she did say her name was Freda, but this is an old woman!" Another long pause, then he turned around, and with a red face, and told us to proceed. I had no idea where we were going on this

311

long narrow drive until we were parked near a big limo. Then I realized that we were next to Jimmy Buffett's limo at the stage entrance.

I was given a VIP sticker to wear, and then we were taken through the stage door and up to our seats. I was very familiar with the music he was playing, for I had bought every Jimmy Buffett record that I could find.

When the band struck up the music to 'One Particular Harbor,' I was overcome. When Jimmy sang this song to me in Tahiti, it was in an unfinished state, but here it was with a full orchestra. I was overwhelmed. I couldn't help but think of the first time that I heard the tune as Jimmy sat on the sofa in the base house on the island of Huahine. Jimmy had been told that I was the great granddaughter of the founder of the Martin Guitar Company, and he came to meet me. Then he showed me his new Martin Guitar. I asked him to play it for me, not knowing to whom I was speaking.

I left the show a little early, so I wouldn't have to buck the crowd with a hurt foot. Two men came to my rescue and helped me down and through the stage door. The manager met me just inside of the door and escorted me down to the stage entrance by the parking lot. He asked someone to get a glass of lemonade for Sue and me. We sat talking about Jimmy and how we met. The manager said I shouldn't get my hopes up too high of seeing Jimmy, for he dashes to his limo. I told him I would take my chances.

The concert was over and I stood by the entrance to the stage door. When Jimmy came through on the run, I held my hand out for a shake, and said, "Hi, Jimmy, I'm Freda." He stopped and grabbed my hand, then gave me a hug. "Hi, Freda, how did you like the concert?" We walked arm in arm towards the limo as we talked, and then he was off. He stopped just before he got in the limo and turned around and asked how I was feeling. I told him I was better, now. After nine years, we finally met again. Out of the 7,000 people attending that concert, I was the one who got personal attention from Jimmy.

After I got home, my school principal friend told me that her son was at the concert and sat about a row behind me. He told her everyone around him knew I was someone special. They saw me come out of the stage door, and go back that way.

After the concert I was thoroughly disgusted with the condition of my feet. With the help of my doctor I rid myself of some pain, but the pain in the right foot persisted. With the help of my son's diagnostician, I went to a foot doctor who X-rayed it and found that I had an old break in my ankle.

I told him I never broke my ankle. He said, "Now think back." "Oh yes, when I was in Tahiti I turned it on a piece of coral and thought I had a bad sprain." The bone fragments had to be cleaned out of the foot. I had high hopes that I would be put back in one piece again, but it never happened.

I met Jimmy Buffett the day after I injured my foot, and we met again just before the injury was diagnosed as a broken ankle.

I was in my eighties, and I thought that I was living in a nice mobile home park. In a few years I began to have very little water pressure or no water at all. I tried to cope with it, but lack of water is very frustrating. I tried to work things out with the manager and the owner for several years, with no cooperation. They finally told me that if I wasn't happy, I should move. I decided to move.

My friend Lois and I searched the town for manufactured home lots. We found a lot overgrown with weeds, and piled high with rubbish, but it had potential.

My daughter had told me that the Farmer's Home Administration had government grants for older citizens. I must move my home on my own lot

313

and on an engineered foundation. They would help with utility installation. I was assured by the real estate company that my house qualified for the lot, but first I must get building and zoning permits. I put $500 down with the stipulation that if I didn't get the permits, it would be returned.

I went to the zoning department and the Zoning Administrator helped me make out the forms and signed them. The Building Inspector scanned my drawings, made a few changes and signed and issued his permit. I closed on the lot. The foundation was put in and I settled with the contractor.

Thirty minutes later I got a call from the Zoning Administrator who helped me make out the zoning forms. He said he got 5 phone calls that afternoon saying that the zoning was wrong for my home. I couldn't move onto my foundation. I asked him who made the calls, and he said he didn't get the names. I hired an attorney.

The Salida City Manager phoned me. I asked her who the five persons were who did the complaining. She would not reveal the information, but made an appointment to come to my home.

My brother was visiting me at the time. He wanted to leave, but I told him I needed a witness. Then he told me to use The Freedom of Information Act with the phone calls.

The first thing I asked the city manager when she came was the names of the five persons who did the complaining. I sited the Freedom of Information Act. She said the phone calls came from one person and gave me his name, Andy Granzella, who works for his uncle, the owner of the Ford Garage and Sales.

He lived down the street and his uncle lived up the street from my lot. This area has low cost homes and manufactured homes. The house abutting my lot is a manufactured home. I went to the Zoning Administrator and insisted on examining the zoning book. While I waited, he went through cabinets and the vault. Then tackled a couple of stacks of books that were on the floor. He finally found a black 3-hole binder in the stacks. After seeing this, I went to the library and requested that they ask for a copy of the zoning book. It was done.

I attended the Salida City Council meetings. They admitted the Zoning Administrator made a mistake, but said, "To err is human." They offered to put a foundation on a lot in zone 4. The lots in zone 4 are too small for legal setbacks on all sides, but that legality didn't bother the officials.

The lot I bought had been on the market for at least ten years. I spent all my life's savings on the cost of the lot, foundation, rubbish removal, weeding and planting the garden and trees.

My architect friend, Arnold Vollmers, thoroughly inspected my home and wrote out an affidavit that it met all requirements for a manufactured home. After all these problems, the City of Salida passed an amendment excluding me from moving my house onto my lot.

My son called my attorney to find out why the case was taking so long. My attorney told him he was having a hard time to do anything on the case because it was pro bono, and that my son had no interest in the case, neither did my daughter, nor the architect. He didn't want any of them to bother him at his office any more.

I am 81 years old; of course my family has interest in the case, and so did the architect who did a professional examination. He told my son he would withdraw from the case as soon as he filed a brief.

I wanted to see the brief before he filed it. I went into the attorney's office to see him the next day. He said the brief was finished and that the architect's affidavit couldn't be used. Then he told me he couldn't win a case against a city.

After much prodding from him when I asked for an explanation, he said he couldn't seem to be able to talk with me so I would understand. I told him I was trying to comprehend him, but he was giving me no reasons. I asked him if it was because he was on the school board and had a conflict of interest. He jumped up and said, "That's it!" and made out a new withdrawal. He pushed the pen in front of me until I signed it. When I picked up the brief at 4 o'clock, he shook my hand and said, "We are still friends, aren't we?"

I hired a Denver attorney who worked 'pro bono'.

I was front-page news in the local newspaper on a regular basis. A reporter from a Denver Television station came, and took pictures. While they were taking pictures of me and the lot, a neighbor, who didn't like me to move near his home, came over to tell his side of the story. As he walked back to his home, the camera followed him to his back door and taped the trashy backyard of his home. It did get on Denver television.

While all this was going on, the manager of the mobile home park discovered the waterline was broken under my home. He wanted permission to move my home 10 feet so they could fix it. That meant disconnecting the sewer, the waterline, the gas line, the electric line and the phone line by utilities servicemen; then disconnecting both sections of the house and putting them back together again.

I asked him if he was going to pay for it, and he said, "Of course not." Finally, a backhoe was brought in to dig up the whole yard so they could get to the waterline. A man was in a hole six foot deep under my house, fixing the pipe. He told me he was scared to death, and he had reason to be, for no safety precautions were used.

I wasn't feeling good one day and called my doctor. I told him I could feel my heart was doing all kinds of irregular beats. He said to go right to the hospital. I was on an EKG when the doctor came into the room. (I wish more doctors were like this.) I was in atrial fibrillation. Everything was too much for me. Now I was put on medication for a heart problem.

The city held a hearing in the fire station. Time of the hearing was for 7:30 AM and, surprisingly enough, the place was overcrowded in spite of the early morning hour. Some manufactured home salesmen came from Canon City, 60 miles away.

The room that the hearing should have used was up a long flight of stairs, but the doctor wouldn't let me go up the stairs because of my heart. My attorney and my architect friend were there and so was the Salida City attorney.

The city attorney said he couldn't understand why there was so much fuss about moving my 'trailer' because all one has to do is to hook it up to a pick-up truck and away you go. A big roar of protest came from the audience, especially the salesmen who came from Canon City.

I tried and tried to find a place to move my house to, in Salida, but to no avail. The Salida City fathers offered to buy my lot from me for exactly what I paid for it and no more. Nothing for cleaning it up, nothing for the expensive foundation, nothing for the trees, nothing for hauling water for the trees and garden, and nothing for all it cost me to fight them. I received seven phone calls from people who offered to buy the lot.

I called the first one on the list. He bought the lot, and paid me almost twice as much as I paid for the lot. This enabled me to go to Canon City to find a spot for my house. I found a beautiful lot, but it was full of rubbish. WHY DO PEOPLE DO THIS TO A VACANT LOT?

My daughter, Audrey, came to help me clean the lot, but we soon found out that the clean-up job was beyond us. I hired a man to do it, and he removed seven dump-truck loads of rubbish. We found a twenty by forty-foot concrete pad that was in excellent shape. This is a perfect place to put storage sheds. Audrey and I each bought a storage shed, and friends helped us place and erect them.

I hired contractors to install a septic tank, put in a waterline, gas line and electric. Everything was in proper order to move my home onto the foundation.

I went to the Fremont County Courthouse for the permits. The Building Inspector said to move onto the lot as soon as possible, because the zoning was changing very soon.

I later discovered that my half-acre lot would have been too small for the new septic tank zoning. What a difference from the way I was treated in Salida!

Back in Salida we were preparing to move the studio section. The person who was contracted to move the studio, didn't brace it before he moved it away from the main house, and it collapsed.

I decided right then that it was time to use my engineering knowledge that came along with my career. I took over, and the mover let me. I engineered the job of putting the section back in the upright position, then instructed the men when, where, and how to brace it. It looked like a bunch of junk with a broken window and all the bracing, but I knew it wasn't. It went down to Canon City first, and then the main house was moved.

Just before the move my daughter, Marlene, came from Ohio for a visit. She filled a pail with the blue iris roots. I put the pail of irises in my car and I was ready to go.

I followed the main house, but before I left town I went into a small restaurant, 'Uncle Scruffy's.' It was down the street from my lot and I had gone into the place now and then when I worked on my lot. I enjoyed his good sandwiches. He gave me my last sub sandwich as a going away gift. That was the last time I was in the town of Salida, Colorado.

I got in my car and proceeded down the highway to Canon City. I met the mover with my house, parked on the side of the road about 20 miles out of Salida. They had a flat tire, but were taking care of it, so I continued on to Canon City. I had just about enough time to eat my good sandwich when I spied the mover coming with my house.

CHAPTER 26

CANON CITY, COLORADO

In August 1994, my manufactured home was moved to Canon City, Colorado. I watched as the house was set on its foundation and leveled. Then because no utilities, water and sewer were connected yet, I stayed in a motel for the night.

The next day I was at the lot bright and early and a swarm of men came about 7:30 AM. Each one did his own thing and all the utilities were connected except the telephone and gas. Two men from the gas company came in the morning, looked at their project and disappeared. They had not returned by 3 PM, and time was running out.

I called the gas company on my cell phone. The men came back after the phone call, and I gave them a piece of my mind. One of the men said in a voice loud enough for me to hear him, "I hate working with women." The gas company got another phone call and their supervisor came out. He gave me back my personhood that I almost lost, again. I bet the guy REALLY hates women now.

Sometimes things happen when you move these homes. I went into the linen cabinet, under the bathroom sink, and found all the linens soaking wet.

I called a plumber. I washed all the linens and threw things away like Q-tips. The plumber tightened up the screw underneath the faucet. It worked for a few hours and then began to leak again.

A man came to look over the house for a new swamp cooler. I told him about the screw and he tightened it up. It worked a little better this time, but leaked enough so that I couldn't dry the place out with a hairdryer. While I was waiting for the plumber to come back, the linen cabinet started to mildew.

The electrician left a big hole alongside a pole he had set in. He came for his money. I told him I wouldn't pay him until the hole was filled in.

The mover came and connected the studio to the house.

A lady came to paint the exterior of the studio.

I went to bed that night, but was worried about the cupboard. I couldn't sleep. At 3 AM I looked into the linen cabinet and saw yucky mold. I washed both sides of the shelves, then used my hair dryer again, because of the slight leak I was getting nowhere, and the carpeting was getting wet. I barely had a few hours sleep.

At 7 AM the electrician came and filled the hole.

At 7:30 AM the plumber came and worked on the leak.

I tested the furnace, something's wrong. I called a heating company to inspect the furnace. A man came to work on the electrical system for the furnace.

The lady painter came again to paint the studio.

The swamp cooler man came to install the swamp cooler.

A man on the roof was.installing the flashing at the studio connection. A man with a hose was washing the footing to clean it for concrete block work.

A man was installing posts under the studio.

A man was removing the window that had broken in the move.

I walked around the outside of my house and to my horror, I saw the lady painter standing on a folding chair to paint. I got her my stepladder. Then I noticed that her boss gave a male employee a new aluminum ladder for his work.

I had been up since 3 AM and I was tired, so I laid down in my big chair for a nap. I told the plumber I was 82 years old and earned the right to a little nap now and then.

Man on the roof installing my cooler was hammering on the roof.

Man was hammering on the roof installing flashing. ·

Man was squirting foundation.

Plumber was plumbing pipes.

Furnace man was running back and forth from furnace to thermostat.

The lady painter was quietly painting.

Plumber came by my chair, "Did you get any sleep?"

"No."

At 4:30 PM everyone disappeared. Then I glanced at the sky in the west. Dark clouds were forming and the weather looked ominous, so I nailed black plastic rubbish bags in the opening of the window that was getting repaired. I was standing in an inch of mud created by the man who washed the foundation, who was also the man who neglected to cover the window. It started to rain and hail before I was through.

Even though I ordered my phone four months before the move, I had no phone service for lack of a line to the lot. I had to get a cell phone for emergencies.

At 7 PM a lady called on the cell phone and asked for "Dru." Two minutes later the same lady called and asked for "Dru."

The paperboy rang the bell and apologized for being late with the paper delivery, because he had football practice.

Early the next morning, the man who was installing the skirting around the base of the house was upset, because the government inspector is inspecting the skirting on Tuesday and he can't possibly get it done. The skirting hadn't been delivered to the supply company either so it got him off the hook.

I was telling the man, who was setting the concrete block, how I wanted it done, and he got mad and threw the block under the house. He didn't like a woman telling him what to do. He probably had in mind to throw the block at me, but it went the other way and saved my skin.

He said he would come the next day and grade the front. I told him I could do that. He said it took a man who knew what he was doing. I said, "If I can design parking lots for companies, I could do that little job." He got mad again and left in a huff. This was also the lady painter's boss who gave her a folding chair to stand on. I never recovered my personhood from this man, and I often wondered if the lady painter ever recovered hers.

The next morning:

Man came to install repaired window.

Lady painter finished her painting.

Man finished installing cooler.

I went to town to pay for the cooler and do some shopping. I couldn't do shopping because I forgot grocery list.

I came home and tackled a stack of dirty dishes. The water wouldn't get hot.

I thought, "Oh, no! Not a new water heater?"

I inspected the water heater and the flue was warm. I glanced at the dial and saw that someone had turned it to PILOT. I turned it to ON and had hot water.

At 7 PM the cell phone rang. The lady called again and asked for "Dru." I yelled, "You called yesterday, now cut it out." I hung up. One minute later, the cell phone rang again. I didn't answer it, it's probably the lady asking for "Dru."

It was Friday night and the stuff from the linen cabinet was scattered around my bedroom. But what the heck, I was deliciously tired, so left the whole mess and said to myself, "Goodnight."

I can't help but recall what the City of Salida Attorney said at the hearing in Salida before the move, "It's no big deal to move one of those homes, you just hook it behind a pick-up truck and go."

Summer was nearly over, and I cast about 35 little mountain panoramas from the molds I made when I lived in Salida. This was done in preparation for my winter work, when I would do the final assembly and paint them in mountain colors.

I spite of the fact that the move was full of problems, it was good to move to Canon City, but my problems weren't ended.

DOCTORS, DOCTORS, DOCTORS

I needed a doctor to prescribe a heart medication, and learned Canon City was going through a severe shortage of doctors.

I went to the only family practitioner in Canon City. I'll call him Doctor #1. He wouldn't prescribe heart medication without records from Salida. He asked me to send for them, but I found that he was wrong, I must sign a release from him so he could get them. Nearly three months had passed since my visit to him, and every time I asked if the records had arrived, I was told that they had not received them. It was necessary to have the prescription, so I made an appointment with a cardiac doctor.

Cardiologist, Doctor #2, wanted to put me on a treadmill. I told him about my unstable ankle, and I wondered if I should be on a treadmill. It seemed to me that I was not making myself clear about my ankle, so I told him I had a handicap license plate on my car which was parked right outside of the window. He said he would put me on the treadmill for only one phase, so I agreed to the test. He said he needed my medical records from my Salida doctor. I signed a release form.

When I came back for the treadmill test on December 27, 1994, he said he didn't get the records from the Salida doctor. He called the Salida doctor and the girl said that they had sent them to Doctor #1 several months ago and he should use them. Why didn't the doctor make sure he had the records before he made the 50-mile trip to Canon City from Colorado Springs to put me on the treadmill? Without trying to get the records from Doctor #1, whose office was only a block or two away, he went ahead with the treadmill test.

Instead of stopping the treadmill after one phase as he told me he would do, he speeded it up. He had his back turned towards me during the whole test and never asked me if I was doing OK.

The doctor told the nurse to take my blood pressure. She asked me to take my right hand off the front handrail and put it on her shoulder. I was working hard trying to keep up with the fast speed and attempting to tell her at the same time that I couldn't do that because I needed both hands on the

325

rail to keep from falling. I knew my foot must be forward at all times, and she was at my side, not in front of me.

During my frantic protests, the doctor screamed in an excited voice, "TAKE HER BLOOD PRESSURE!" I turned and put my hand on her shoulder and my ankle failed. My foot turned under me and I fell, while still holding onto the handrail with my left arm. She was trying to hold me up with the doctor still screaming. She screamed back at him, he screamed, she screamed. I don't know what she said, but he turned around and saw the problem and shut down the machine.

While the doctor/nurse screaming match was going on, I was the one in trouble. After this happened, the doctor told me to take an aspirin every day and walk a lot, then quickly left the room. He had never listened to me when I told him about my ankle!

The nurse took off the wires that were connecting me to the treadmill and asked me if I was OK. I was sitting on a chair and hadn't had a chance to stand, but I told her I thought I was all right. Then the nurse hurried out of the room without offering me a drink of water, and I was extremely thirsty.

The office was very quiet and I knew they had left the building to go back to Colorado Springs. After they left me alone in the room, I put on my coat and started to walk into the reception room.

I had problems walking. I barely got out of the doctor's office. I asked the receptionist of another doctor where I could get a drink of water and she pointed to a drinking fountain. I had a difficult time getting to the fountain, but did get a drink and walked towards the door. I hung on the door for a minute and noticed the receptionist was watching me with a frown on her face. I hung onto one porch pillar and the next until I got to my car. I was in shock!

The next day my whole body was racked with pain. I thought the pain was from using muscles I hadn't used for years. Day by day and little by little the pain subsided, except the left shoulder, neck and arm. I waited weeks for that to go away, but it persisted, so I made an appointment with Doctor #1. I told him about the treadmill fall and asked him if he had the medical records from Salida. He said he didn't have them. I told him that I knew the Salida doctor sent them to him, so he called his assistant. She came back with the records. He glanced through them and said the records don't say much, a lot of blood work and an injured ankle. He missed all the EKG heart tests, but did find the injured ankle, which was the very problem that caused the fall. Doctor #1 wrote out a prescription for neck and muscle pain therapy, and told me to go to the rehabilitation center for treatment.

I wrote a letter to cardiac Doctor #3 who headed the Cardiac Association where Doctor #2 was a member. I told him about the fall in the treadmill. He called me and said he fired Doctor #2 and asked me to come into his office. I thought he wanted to discuss the treadmill fall, but he put me through a sonar test.

I told his secretary that no one over 80 years old should be put on a treadmill. She replied, "Last week we had a 92 year old man on the treadmill." I said, "Shame on you."

The doctor assigned me to another test in his 'Colorado Springs office. This test had a medication cost of $150 and if I refused the test, I would have to cover the cost of the medication. I was all hooked up and almost ready for the test, when they discovered that I couldn't go through with it because I had to raise my left arm over my head for 20 minutes. I couldn't raise the arm high enough to even touch my ear, so it was impossible to go through with the test. This is the arm and shoulder that was injured in the treadmill.

The next week the doctor called me into his Canon City office. The doctor came into the room. He immediately said, "You refused to take the test in Colorado Springs," and then said in a whiney sing-song voice, "because you said YOUR arm hurt."

It made me angry and I told him, "You said that because you want me to pay $150 for the medication. I didn't know I had to raise my arm over my head, but you knew that it was necessary for the test. You also knew that I couldn't do it, because I wrote you a letter about the fall in the treadmill." He wrote out a prescription for heart medication and didn't charge me the $150.

I went to Social Services for help with my problem. They said that I needed an attorney. I hired Attorney #1 who contacted the doctor's insurance company.

In the rehab center, where Doctor #1 sent me for therapy, Therapist #1 gave me stressful exercises. I complained the exercises were too much for an 83-year-old person. He said he didn't care how old I was, it's the same for an 80-year-old as it is for a 30-year-old.

In one exercise he held my arm and pulled it out of the socket and walked up and down with it. I tried to stop him when he struck a pain, so he would know what was going on with my arm. He ignored me because he was conversing with his assistant about a personal matter, not business.

I yelled at him and said, "I'm talking to you." He said he knew what I said. I replied, "Then why didn't you stop and recognize me? I'm your patient, I'm paying for your treatments not your assistant." I had been in his care for over 4 months, and was not improving. I seemed to be going downhill. The therapist said it was because I wasn't exercising at home.

Then he decided to turn me over to Therapist #2 who had his assistant, Therapist #3, give me myofacial treatments. I went back to the doctor who prescribed the treatments and told him I liked the myofacial treatments. He felt my shoulder muscles and wrote a new prescription. Now I was getting myofacial therapy.

Therapist #1 and Therapist #2 came into the room, excused the myofacial Therapist #3, and proceeded to have a conference with me. I got upset, angry and started to cry about my treatment.

I told them that I wish I had a doctor like my Salida doctor, he would have done something else about my shoulder long ago. I was so angry with them that I told them that both of them needed a course in geriatrics.

The therapists wrote a letter to the doctor #1, and told me that I should go back to him and give him the letter. They forgot to give it to me and the next time I came they handed it to me. I told them that the best way to deliver letters is through the mail and I didn't understand why they wanted to save the postage. Later I found out what they had written in the letter. They wrote what I had said about my Salida doctor, and that I was well enough to continue therapy at home, not myofacial work. Why did they want me to deliver THAT letter?

That was childish of both of them to ask me to hand-deliver such a letter. Now I know I was right when I told both of them that they needed a course in geriatrics.

When the doctor got the letter, he phoned me. He said to go back to my Salida doctor if I liked him so much, he didn't want me for a patient. I was 83 years old and 60 miles of winding mountain road to Salida was too much for me. There was no other family doctor in Canon City.

I went back to the attorney. When he heard the problem I had with Doctor #1 he dismissed himself, because he was a close friend of the doctor.

The pain and inability to move my arm high enough to comb my hair and other movements was getting to me. Because there were no other family doctors in town, I went to an internist, Doctor #4. He gave me a thorough examination, blood tests, pap test, urinalysis and the whole bit. Then he opened the door and said I should make an appointment in three weeks. I reminded him that I came in for pain in my shoulder, neck and arm, which was caused by a fall in a treadmill. He came back in the room and felt my shoulder and arm. He said my muscles were hard and tight, then quickly left the room.

I went to a chiropractor, Doctor #5, who had a myofacial therapist. The chiropractor's myofacial Therapist #4 was excellent, and gave me relief from pain, but she left the chiropractor, so I had to look for another.

I knew that my shoulder needed more than therapy. I didn't know where to turn so I went to an attorney in Colorado Springs.

Attorney #2 wouldn't take me as a client unless I went to an orthopaedic surgeon, and was surprised that I was not sent to one. I had no idea I needed one. He said it looked as though I had a problem like one he had from a skiing accident. I didn't know an orthopaedic surgeon, so he recommended the doctor who operated on his shoulder.

Orthopaedic surgeon, Doctor #6, said I had a tear in the tendons around the rotator cuff in my shoulder. Then he looked at my ankle and said, "It is swollen, something is wrong." He sent me for X-rays.and gave me a prescription for a therapist.

Therapist #5 had his own business in Canon City. He relieved the pain, softened up the muscles and would not let me exercise. He used a computer to monitor my progress.

I went back to internist, Doctor #4 for the follow-up visit. I told him that I wished it had been he who recommended an orthopaedic surgeon, not an attorney. His face turned as red as a beet, then sent me to an orthopaedic surgeon in Canon City for a second opinion.

Orthopaedic surgeon, Doctor #7, was a nice guy. He thought that the exercises did more harm than good.

I am old and very tired and its been 9 months since the accident, and I have had 7 months of therapy, 3 times a week, and many doctor visits. The trip to Colorado Springs is a 45-mile trip and so tiring I must stay with my daughter over night before returning home. I made the wrong decision to stay with a local doctor only because I was old and exhausted.

On the second visit to Doctor #7, his attitude turned 180 degrees. Things he told me made me think he was favoring the insurance company. I asked him if he thought an MRI (Magnetic Resonance Imagery) would help. He said it might for the shoulder, but not for the foot. He didn't think the ankle had anything to do with the accident. He got up and walked to the door, and said I might have an ear problem that caused me to loose my balance, then walked out. If it was my ear, then it had been overlooked for ten years. I was angry with him.

I was extremely despondent, mixed up, confused and the pain and loss of movement in the left arm was too much to bear. I went back to an orthopeadic surgeon in Denver for a third opinion. He had helped me in 1987 after an automobile accident.

I gave his receptionist all the X-rays on my shoulder and foot that I could get. Orthopaedic surgeon, Doctor #8, was extremely upset because I had too many doctors and accused me of wandering from one to another just to find one who would agree with me. His supposition was wrong, I was looking for answers.

In my confused state I was unable to communicate, especially when he became emotional and excited about my visit. I couldn't speak anymore. I closed my eyes and was trying to find a way out of this mess. He was not the doctor I knew 8 years ago. He started to walk out of the room without any explanation, then turned and came back in. He picked up my foot and looked it over and said he would not operate on it. I didn't ask him to.

His Medicare request for payment of the visit said only that I had a flat foot. Medicare saw it didn't agree with the report from orthopedic surgeon Doctor #6, which told of the shoulder problem, which was caused by a broken ankle. The Denver doctor was investigated for fraud, and I had nothing to do with it.

It had been over a year since the accident and I went back to the orthopaedic surgeon, Doctor #6, who had operated on the attorney. It is very tiring for me to drive to Colorado Springs, especially with an injured shoulder, but I must do it. He wrote out a prescription for an MRI, one for my shoulder and one for my foot. The MRI showed a complete tear of the tendons on the rotator cuff and ligaments are missing in the ankle. He will do open surgery on the shoulder, but after I heard what was entailed for an operation of the foot, I opted to leave it alone.

Doctor #6 gave me a high five just before the anesthetic took over on the shoulder operation, and that was the end of my doctor problems.

I was sent to a nursing home for post-operative care, and to be nearer to the doctor until I was well enough to travel the 50 miles to my home.

Because I am growing older, the story in this book is changing. "Equal Rights for the Aged" has been added to "Equal Rights for Women."

THE NURSING HOME

After the operation, I was taken by ambulance to a nursing home. The cardiac doctor's insurance company chose the nursing home because they pay the bill.

In the ambulance on the ride to the nursing home, I was joking with the guys and asking lots of questions about the equipment.

When I arrived, I was put in a room with a dying patient. The bed I was put in was messed up like someone else had just occupied it. The men had sad expressions on their faces as they laid me down.

I was given an examination of all female parts, body parts, skin and an examination for lice. What did they expect, coming from a hospital after an operation? They said they had no orders what to do with me and no one told them I was coming. I told them I was to go to their post-operation section for post-operative care. They said I was mistaken, there was no such section in their nursing home. I was treated like "That's what they all say" even though my shoulder was bandaged and a sling strapped my arm to my body.

The sides of the bed were put up and I was a prisoner. I couldn't use the bathroom. No call button existed so I had to holler for help to get to the bathroom. I was finally let out of the bed to go to the bathroom and put in another room across the hall.

This room had two beds and I was told that I would have a private room. The nursing home attendant thought I was lying. I was not. Finally she told me that this was a 'Medicaid Room' and she was following government regulations. She said that I was mistaken that I was on private insurance.

The room was depressing. All three doors and all drawer fronts were painted black, inside and outside. The toilet door had not been washed or scrubbed for years by the looks of the greasy finger marks and the toilet stank. Every time I used the sink the water drained on the floor instead of in the drain. A nurse came in and saw the pool of water, so she shut off the water below the sink. She mopped the water with a towel and left it on the floor. She gave me some hygia washcloths to clean myself, when I protested that I couldn't wash my hands. The cleaning personnel folded the towel and put it with the clean linen on my chair.

I had no drinking water and no drinking fountain existed. I was making sure to drink several glasses of water at my meals. I complained about it and was given a pitcher of water. It was not a hospital pitcher, it was a two-quart household type with no cover. What in the world do the bed-ridden patients in this hospital do for water? The next day after I was given the pitcher of water, I asked the attendant for some fresh water. She looked in my pitcher and said, "You still have some left, drink that."

(I am pausing here to tell you that what I am writing about this nursing home is true! I've visited in nursing homes that looked like palaces when compared to this place. The insurance company probably put me in the cheapest one they could find.)

I had no water on my body, until I bitterly complained that I had been a patient for five days and had not had a bath or a shower. The sink problem was never repaired, even though the maintenance room was just a few doors down the hall. I made a personal complaint to the man in this room to no avail.

I could talk to very few patients for most were silent or crying. I wasn't in a good physical shape either, for besides being handicapped with the arm strapped to my body, I had to use a cane for my ankle. I had no access to news or what was going on outside of this depressing place.

After I complained, they brought in a television, but it was broken and I got nothing. They left it in my room probably show the doctor and visitors that I did have TV. No television, radio, newspaper or magazine to read was in the assembly room, and a sign stated that no papers, books or food was allowed in the room. I felt like I was a prisoner confined in a locked jail.

In the dining room, I was put at a table with a woman who continually counted everyone in the room and a man, whose nose discharged down the front of his shirt.

An attendant with compassion finally put me at a table with two lovely women and a man who wouldn't talk. He finally conversed with me when I asked him about the beautiful western hat that he wore into the dining room. He always hung it up before sitting down at the table. He told me he was a rancher. I believed him and was sure he owned the ranch because his good manners told me so.

A lovely woman at the next table had reverted back to childhood and cried like a baby instead of eating. I told her she was a lovely person, and then she would eat. A black woman at my table told me not to complain about anything. I told her that Martin Luther King wouldn't have done that and she nodded her head.

I talked to a patient whose daughter had not visited her in two years, even though she lived in the same city. I wondered why she was there she had all her senses and walked around very well. Why do so many families forsake them? These patients are famished for love or just a visit from family or friends. When I entered this home and was put in the messed up bed, the woman in the other bed said, "Oh, someone is coming to be in my room, that's so nice." That night she died. Where was her family? Or didn't she have any?

335

The offices have a beautiful view of the mountains. The assembly room is next to them, but a storage room had been added to each side of the main entrance door, blocking the windows and eliminating the mountain view for the patients. Patients always occupied the benches outside by this door, and the entrance hall was lined up on each side with patients looking outside. This all seems odd to me now, because I remember playing an organ in this very room about twenty-five years ago. Patients were clapping their hands to the music and some were dancing.

I was ready to go home, but to leave wasn't so simple. One of the top personnel came in my room to give me a mentality test before the discharge. The first question was "What day of the week, month and year is it?" I was able to answer it by counting the days since the operation. Without a radio, TV, or newspaper how could anyone in this nursing home answer that question? I asked the gal who was posing the questions, "If I fail to answer these questions, would you make me stay in the nursing home?" Her answer was, "Yes."

I was questioned in the main office several times, with at least five top personnel conducting the inquiry. I didn't think I came in because I was a mental patient, but was treated as one in order to be released. I lost my personhood, and a patient in that place has also lost his or her personhood. They are nobodies.

I was happy to get out of that nursing home, but it was hard to leave those patients, especially when the woman who cried instead of eating said to me when I said my goodbye, "Now I'm alone." No one can tell me that these patients don't have the ability to think. I cried for them when I left. If reading this makes you cry, you're not alone, for I still cry for those patients.

THE INSURANCE COMPANY

The insurance company did not finish paying for all the costs of the treadmill accident. They still owe me several thousand dollars for things they told me they would pay, because as the attorney for the insurance company said, "It's partially your fault." He wouldn't elaborate when I asked him to describe my faults. The only fault I can think of is the trust I put in the doctor who put me on the treadmill, the trust I put in the doctor who sent me to the rehab, and the trust I put in the two rehab therapists. I was paid nothing for the pain and suffering I endured.

I was never able to finish the mountain panoramas. I lost over $800 of my investment in them, not counting about 600 hours of labor. The injured shoulder caused my left arm to be two inches shorter than it was.

If the chief cardiac doctor had taken my shoulder problem seriously and sent me to an orthopaedic surgeon immediately, they would have saved themselves thousands of dollars and my costs, plus the pain I endured for several years. I think they thought I was just another old woman who is passive and accepts things as they happen. One may think that when you fall with no fault of your own, in any professional's office, his insurance would just take over. Wrong!

It doesn't happen that way, you must hire an attorney and SUE!

THE ATTORNEY

The attorney I hired, when the cardiac doctor's insurance company refused to pay for the injury, was very considerate of me at first. In a few months his attitude changed drastically. I think his attitude changed when I told him that I did all the technical work on the exterior of the judicial building he used. After I told him this, he continually called me a liar, berated me, and didn't give me instructions before I went in for a deposition. He treated me like I was stupid.

He accused my daughter, Audrey, of not taking care of me properly. In my presence, he told her that I should be declared incompetent. I thought it was his job to stand up for me, and not berate me behind closed doors.

If this attorney had succeeded when he told my daughter I should be declared incompetent, he would have been in charge of all my possessions and me. Is this what he wanted? He legally could have sold my home and put me in a nursing home. Unbeknownst to me, I had hired a woman hater and lost my personhood.

I sat in on all the depositions of six doctors, two therapists and one assistant. They all raised their hand and swore to tell the truth and nothing but the truth, but only one doctor and one therapist honored their declaration.

My attorney believed them and not me, and wouldn't let me tell him what the errors were. He just berated me again. One odd thing comes to my mind as I look back on those depositions. The questions asked by the insurance attorney pertained to the problems I had with the therapists and doctors. How did he know about them? The nature of the problems were something the therapists and doctors wouldn't tell the insurance attorney, but I had told my attorney about them.

Doctor #1 said in his deposition that my first visit to him was for pain in my shoulder. This threw the court case into turmoil, because that date was three months before the accident. I went to him for a heart medication prescription on that day. My attorney wouldn't let me tell him it was a lie. He shut me up and said, "After a postmortem, we don't talk." This time it was the insurance attorney who saw the error when I told him I cast over thirty mountain panoramas and hosted a tea for thirty people, after the first visit to this doctor.

My son and daughter thought that if we had a four-way phone conversation with my attorney, we could clear things up. My son arranged the call, then the attorney yelled at my son, daughter and me. He said, "I don't give a damn what you want," then took over the whole conversation by yelling so no one could talk. He said something about being threatened and hung up.

The attorney withdrew from the case just thirty days before the trial. I had signed that I would be responsible for costs. He provided me with a cost sheet that was full of errors. I didn't have the money, so he filed a judgement against my personal property and a lien against my file. I was informed of the judgement court date by courier. The date written on the form was actually the day after the hearing.

My personal property meant that he could take all the things I have in my house. Some of them are antiques I've owned for 50 years, and paintings. I was distraught. He wrote that the county sheriff would come to my house and take my personal belongings.

I went to the sheriff, gave him a copy of the attorney's letter, and asked him when he was going to do it. The sheriff never heard of the man, nor had he received any letters or court papers from him. Now the county sheriff was involved and he answered that letter. Because of the threats in the attorney's letters, my heart went into atrial fibrillation.

I had to get the attorney off my back and stop his threatening letters. My bank helped me open an account that I could pay into every month. The attorney could get his money only after he sent me proof that he paid the accounts he said he did. The attorney's last letter responded to the bank account when he wrote," I'm not going to jump through your hoops." With that remark I regained my personhood because he DID jump through my hoops to get his money.

This is not the end of my problems. I was trying to get the insurance company to finish paying for all my medical expenses. In one of their letters they quoted a law from the Colorado Revised Statutes. (so they said) I wanted to look it up in the statutes book and discovered that the statutes books were no longer in the county building, because the judicial department was now in a new Judicial building. I inquired about the law library, and was told the books that were in the old library were donated to some people and that a law library no longer existed. I would have to go to Pueblo or Colorado Springs to use theirs.

Then I was told by the man in charge that I could use them on the internet. I asked him how I could get them on the internet and he didn't know. I went to the local public library and they knew they were on the internet, but they didn't know how to get them either. Then I discovered that they did have a law library in the new Judicial building, but it was closed to the public.

I knew it was illegal to refuse the public use of a public financed library, so I went to the new building and asked to use the Colorado Revised Statutes, and was refused entrance. By this time I had a newspaper reporter working with me. The newspapers in Canon City and Pueblo gave the problem front page coverage in color.

There are at least ten prisons in this area, and I knew that by law they must have the Colorado Revised Statutes. I called the new Federal Prison. Yes they did have a set and I could use them, but I would have to use them with prisoners in the room without protection. My last effort was with the

Fremont County Jail. I paid them a visit. Yes, they did have a set, and I could use them without prisoners in the room. They copied what I wanted, which at this time was changed to include the Library Law pages.

Through an inquiry to the Colorado State head law librarian in Denver, I found out how to get the Colorado Revised Statutes on the internet. Now I had two sources. In researching the two, I discovered that they were not alike. The Library Law itself was the same where it states that the public cannot be refused use of a public funded library, but the definitions on the internet were drastically changed, and used a reference to the American Indians to do it.

I would like to get on the internet again to see if the definitons are changed back to what it says in the book, but I cannot do it. A new plan affecting the public is being used. You must pay a yearly fee to use the internet set of the Colorado Revised Statutes. (Which are funded by the public.)

Before the yearly fee was introduced, I had taken the issue to the Fremont County Commissioners. They did realize that the public needs the Colorado Revised Statutes, and did put in a new set for the public to use in the local public library. The public still needs a set of the Federal Laws available to them.

I am an old woman now, and I am sitting by my window and looking at a new bloom on the blue iris. I've gone through a lot of personal fights for Equal Rights for Women, and Equal Rights for the General Public. At the present time I am fighting for Equal Rights for the Aged. The errors in the internet version of the Colorado Revised Statutes, and the unavailability of the Federal laws still bother me. I'm too old to tackle it but:

SOMEBODY HAS TO DO IT!

REFERENCES

The Lincoln Library, 1957. The Frontier Press Company, Buffalo 3, New York.

Bulletin de la Societe des Etudes Oceaniennes, Chesnaux et Marcantoni, 1926. Papeete, Tahiti.

Stone Remains in the Society Islands, Kenneth Pike Emory, 1933. Bishop Museum Bulletin #116, Honolulu, Hawaii.

Tahiti aux temps anciens, Publication de la Societe des Oceanistes #1, Paris, France.

Settlement Pattern Survey of Matairea Hill, Huahine, Society Islands, Session I, 1979. Yosihiko H. Sinoto and Elaine Rogers-Jourdane. Bishop Museum, Honolulu, Hawaii.

History and Culture in the Society Islands, 1923. E. S. Craighill, Handy.

343

Huahine, Jean-Francois Bare. Nouvelles Editions Latines, 1979. Paris, France.

Earthwatch Briefing, Who lived on Matairea Hill? 1982. Yosihiko Sinoto, Principal Investigator. Earthwatch, 10 Juniper Road, Belmont, Massachusettes 02178.

History of Fiji, Kim Gravelle. 1981. Fiji Times and Herald Limited, 20 Gordon Street, Suva, Fiji.

Blue Horizones, National Geographic Society, Washington, D.C.

Columbia Encyclopedia, Columbia University Press, 1956. Morningside Press, New York.

National Geographic Magazine, December 1974. Washington, D. C.

Colorado Revised Statutes, Colorado Library Law: 24-90-102. Legislative declaration, and 24-90-103. Definitions.

ABOUT THE AUTHOR

Freda Ruetenik Stumpf was born in Brooklyn Heights near Cleveland, Ohio on April 2, 1912, one of eight children, and a twin. Freda worked in the building industry for many years, first designing her own home while studying architecture, later working for contractors, and then did drafting for a valve engineer. Freda drafted for a civil engineer before taking a position with a precast company where she was a precast job captain, and finally Freda was known as an expert on the 'skin' of commercial buildings. She now lives in Canon City, Colorado, painting with oils and designing relief maps of the Colorado mountains.

Printed in the United States
1516400004B/211-216